INTO THE RED

For Zelda, Sylvia, Steve, Sheila, Cath, Chris and Paul, and for Thomas and Violet Williams, 'bunners' and Liverpool fans. For Roy Hammond: friendliest and nicest critic. I miss him.

MAINSTREAM SPORT

INTO THE RED

LIVERPOOL FC AND THE CHANGING FACE OF ENGLISH FOOTBALL

JOHN WILLIAMS

MAINSTREAM
PUBLISHING
EDINBURGH AND LONDON

First published in Great Britain in 2001 by
MAINSTREAM PUBLISHING COMPANY (EDINBURGH) LTD
7 Albany Street
Edinburgh EH1 3UG

ISBN 1 84018 673 9

This edition, 2002

A catalogue record for this book is available from the British Library

All illustrations courtesy of the *Liverpool Echo*

Typeset in Univers and Book Antiqua
Printed and bound in Great Britain by
Cox & Wyman Ltd, Reading, Berkshire

CONTENTS

1. SEASON'S GREETINGS?

REDS AND BLUES

Welcome to the madhouse. We are on the brink of another new football season in Liverpool, 2000–01, and already the rival Bluenose midfield is in a glorious mess. Everton's John Collins has taken his skinny six-pack waistline to join up with French mate Jean Tigana at Fulham and Don Hutchison, ex-Reds stripper of course, has got the hump with Walter Smith and has gone to join Peter Reid, Niall Quinn and the other scallywags at Sunderland. In steps Walter's prodigal 'son', the life-worn, bulging Gazza, and surely this is a blissful prospect for the whole of the city of Liverpool. But, best of all, England man Nick Barmby has walked across Stanley Park from Everton – to Anfield. Gérard Houllier, cool as you like, allowed himself a sly little smile at the press conference called to confirm Barmby's six-million-pound move to Liverpool. A local scribe, to sniggers in the audience, had asked the top table whether Barmby expected any problems in the city because of his move. 'What is this?' asked Houllier coyly. 'Is Nick changing his religion, or politics, or what?'

Any *problems*? Houllier knew well, of course, that local howling mobs lay in Barmby's path this season. Bill Kenwright, Chief Executive at Goodison, knew it too: 'The worst six words in the world,' he accuses Barmby of uttering: 'I want to play for Liverpool.' In fact, virtually everyone on Merseyside is already gleefully anticipating the first derby match, lining up fat-boy Gascoigne puffing around for Everton and Barmby, boyishly dodging half-eaten pies and burgers, for the Reds. A gritty treat surely lies in store: roll on October 28 at Anfield, Liverpool 4.

It's not for nothing that Barmby is the first player to move directly from Everton to Liverpool since centre-forward Dave Hickson more than 40 years ago. A few have moved the other way since. The Reds have generally been lording it over their neighbours for most of the time, so players moving from Anfield to Goodison have seemed, for Kopites at least, mostly like making a patronising act of benevolence aimed at sickly, poorer neighbours who you can't really stand. The transfers of Beardsley and Sheedy to Goodison, to name just two, have shown just how dangerous this kind of condescension can prove to be. These Liverpool 'rejects' haunted us for years afterwards, and especially in derby games.

Houllier's serious point, of course, was that in the age of the 'new professionalism' in football, players will move around increasingly regularly and indiscriminately: that these old attachments, enmities and divisions no longer have the force of old. After all, (deep breath here) Liverpool may yet want to import new blood from, say, Manchester United. Of course he underestimates local football rivalries in England, which is one of the ways, after all, that football supporters still make sense of the current pick-and-mix global football transfer chaos. At the heart of this sort of talk is (inevitably) the free market, and the hidden text is that, in the age of the 35-player squads, it would be advisable if supporters did not get *too* attached to their heroes. They could leave at almost any moment.

Michael Owen's clinical assessment, at 19, that he's happy at Liverpool – 'as long as the club win trophies' – is a recent marker. But the 'lifelong Liverpool fan' claims by baby-faced Barmby really stung Evertonians. This is a painful and familiar theme of late in this city for those of the Blue persuasion. Fowler, Owen, Rush, McManaman and Carragher, even out of the very recent Liverpool crops, are all, famously, young Evertonians, converted to Red. It's hard to think of major cases in the opposite direction, though Gladwys Street regulars will undoubtedly have a short list which will include Peter Reid.

The Heysel disaster involving Liverpool in 1985 meant, of course, that Reid's Everton champions of 1985 and 1987 – the club's best team for more than 20 years – never got the chance to run up against the top outfits in Europe. Since then, the Blues have rather struggled. The Reds of Anfield have not done much since 1990 either. Some Evertonians have never forgiven their near neighbours for this derailment of the outstanding Howard Kendall team. At the derby game at Goodison Park in 2000 some home supporters were still wildly abusing Reds fans about Heysel even as we filed out of the Bullens Road, their barely welcomed guests from across the park.

It is true that families in the city of Liverpool do harbour fans of both clubs and that there is no real geographical or important religious distinction between the clubs' fans these days, which all contributes to slightly more harmonious derby meetings than in, say, Sheffield, Manchester or North London. But the 'friendly derby' moniker is also a myth here. There is a proper unease about these meetings, which sometimes spills over later into violence. Evertonians also like to forcefully tell Reds fans to 'Fuck off back up the M62' after these affairs, mindful as they are of the *national* draw of Liverpool now, set against the stronger active localism at Everton. Local surveys show that visitors and money flood into the city at weekends, especially when Liverpool FC are at home. Unsurprisingly, football is now central to the city's post-industrial promotional work and tourist trade. Even in these lean times, football still helps the city breathe and eat.

These relatively new tensions, between national and local ties, have been deepened, of course, by Everton's recent financial trials and Liverpool's desperate and costly attempts to modernise on and off the pitch – including their move for new top man, Houllier. For the Blues, the annual lashings dished out by Everton to Roy Evans's fragile Liverpool team of the 1990s have been a confirming reminder of the sweetness of local pride assuaged. Houllier's new mixture of local lads and the foreign legion is expected by Reds' supporters to conquer Europe and also routinely to beat the Bluenoses – quite different projects, believe me.

While talk of the importance of local football dominance remains loud on Merseyside, supporters of both clubs also know well that these satisfying old tribalisms are now played out in the deep shadow of a more distant neighbour up the motorway, whose mansion really does have many rooms. We sometimes maliciously accuse the Park End at Goodison of 'Loving Man U'. But no one in Liverpool really does that. The preferred Evertonian result in a match between United and Liverpool now is for both to lose.

But for Liverpool FC out-of-towners, especially, the footballing battle lines have long been redrawn. For many of them, the Nick Barmby move to Anfield is no great shakes; it's just another big-money transfer. Also, everyone living in the city, Blue or Red, is well aware that winning the struggle for Merseyside is no longer a measure of national stature. The real front line has now, depressingly, moved 20-odd miles east. That's why when the 2000–01 season started for Liverpool it was all about trying to catch Manchester United, the all-conquering new football corporation.

When I was growing up as a kid, football mad, in the 1960s on Merseyside, things seemed very different from the football rivalries and the sporting timetable we have today. For the seasonal footballing last rites, for example, we used to end up, late at night, on BBC TV (always on the Beeb) with innocent and flush-faced young men in the FA Cup winners post-banquet booze up. Most of this was excruciating stuff. We got more and more out of the managers too, some of them noticeably freezing in the media headlights as the years wore on. In 1974, Liverpool's Bill Shankly and the clearly shaking Newcastle United manager, Joe Harvey, were interviewed on a split screen on the morning of the final tie between these keen northern rivals. At the end of the exchange and thinking himself off camera (perhaps!) Shanks made the telling aside that Cup final rookie, Harvey, was clearly 'a bag o' nerves'. On the field, Liverpool crushed the jittery Geordies. The early power of the football media?

On national TV at night, after the annual big match and the feast which followed it, these impossibly young football heroes were shown now quite spent, nerves and trauma far behind them – and they were also gently, but transgressively, pissed. Strangely, on these occasions drink and glory seemed to make otherwise monosyllabic young men, with brains in their feet but less up top, more, rather than less, articulate. Certainly, more interesting. Nothing, it should be noted, seemed to have this effect on the BBC's Jimmy Hill. All this was, above everything else, the signal for footy obsessives that it had all ended, the beautiful game, for another year.

The FA Cup final was still pretty much the only live football anybody saw on TV in the '60s; certainly the only *club* football of this type. Then there was the famous Wembley turf itself, proudly unblemished, and depthlessly green compared to the mud heaps or the dust bowls of the semi-finals played on only weeks before. But the turf (good cliché this) was also notoriously cruel, lying in wait to cramp up those for whom the nervous tension proved simply too much. And, of course, there was the inevitable sunshine, the north London summer heat, which was surely made for foreigners – for the languid but explosive Brazilians – rather than the doughty, honest, British journeymen of the English game, now fully exposed in this last crucial act of an over-long season.

On Merseyside, as elsewhere in those days, local finalists brought a new intensity to Cup final day. Special souvenir editions of the local newspapers emerged; *The Road to Wembley* plus pull-out team photos for display in the front window. People 'dressed' their houses then to advertise Cup final footballing allegiances, though my mum would never allow my brother's Evertonian blue to go up in case neighbours or passers-by mistakenly took us for Catholics. Some people in Liverpool still do this now, put up their football pictures, though the gusto and some of the collective spirit has inevitably gone out of Cup final fever. In triumphs in 1965 (Liverpool, gloriously, for the first time) and in '66 (Trebilcock's Everton) the city of Liverpool boasted back-to-back FA Cup winners. We had no sense then, I think, that people from outside the city – unless they were actually from Merseyside, doing missionary work elsewhere – might also be closely following our own football cause.

In the '60s, after all the FA Cup hype and the TV drama was over there was – nothing. Unless, of course, as incredibly happened in Liverpool in 1966, the World Cup finals came to town. Or, of course, your club had actually *won* the thing, in which case it was a few days more, decking out lampposts and hanging bunting on the Town Hall for the obligatory double-decker parade with the trophy in the city centre. Even following a Cup final triumph, and Bill Shankly's mad and inspired speeches about how we, the fans of the 'Pool, were stronger and more passionate even than Mao's Red Army (which division were *they* in?) – fans, players and football staff, well, they soon just melted away, disappeared for the summer.

Then it was cricket: Ken Barrington, Colin Cowdrey and John Edrich (no cricketers ever had Liverpudlian roots or accents), at least until late August. One or two footballers even *played* professional cricket. No top football player left his club in the closed season unless the club actually wanted rid of him. No one *could* leave. Few new players, if any, arrived. Managers were generally more secure and in charge. Largely anonymous chairmen wrote gnomish match programme notes and made sure the pies were hot. We *expected* the same guys to return, reassuringly, to do battle again in the following campaign. This was 1960's football, ritualised and vaguely comforting.

These days things are very different from these sepia memories. In 2000–01, for example, and for the first time in many years, the FA Cup final was not even the last event of the domestic campaign: FA Premier League matches were scheduled for the week *after* the final, to allow for more fixture space and to satisfy the new football god, television. We are also probably in a post-FA Cup era of the game's development, as the FA itself fumbled its own blue riband event, and as European club football grew ever stronger, more commercially attractive and more important to players and managers.

The 2001 final was even scheduled to take place for the first time outside England, in provincial Cardiff, while the game's administrators squabbled, without success, over the future of the crumbling Wembley Stadium. Cricket and football matches freely overlap these days, testimony to the ever-spreading domains of the global sporting calendars and signalling the demise, probably for good, of the footballing cricketer.

On our television screens, football never disappears now. As the FA Premier League goes into uneasy summer hibernation, so the satellite channels fill with live games from Asia and South America and even Australia. The TV stations also compete these days for coverage of the pre-season friendlies involving English clubs, so June is barely out before the prospects of sun-drenched strolls between international rivals becomes compulsive viewing. Why? Because far from returning with the same staff as last year, as happened in the '60s, the new credo in the post-Bosman version of the sport is that you have to buy – and buy big – even to stand still. The increasing power of players and the huge sums pumped into the sport by television today means that 'good professionals' these days are defined less by their own loyalty to clubs than by the number of lucrative moves a player and his agents can squeeze out of a short career.

So the sign of a good football *manager* these days is one who can claim access to the top tournaments for his club and then go directly to the board with a bloated shopping list. Fans also seem to crave this sort of fetishistic collecting of players, no matter what the previous season's achievements. Pre-season friendlies are, thus, vital and lucrative forums for assessing the prospective new talent. Supporters can also spend many satisfying and inconclusive hours trying to work out exactly how their own managerial guru plans to fit 20 or even 30 full international stars into just 11 starting places. But, hey, haven't you heard? Football these days is a 14-man game: it's rotation, stupid. Liverpool manager, Gérard Houllier, would soon turn this into a new football mantra on the Red side of Merseyside. Top players, especially forwards, were increasingly expected to be satisfied with a crucial and strategic 15 minutes' playing action. For some, it was now a short sprint, no longer a playing marathon.

What is also different about football in England today, it seems to me, is the way in which, in a general sense, the season normatively opens now with the sport in some sort of identifiable crisis. This is apparently required these days in order to get the competitive juices properly circulating at all. At the start of the 2000–01 league football campaign in England, for example, the central football crisis was about the quality of coaching in England – or rather about the dubious qualities of English footballers and their coaches. Euro 2000 had proved little more than an embarrassing farce for the English game, if not for the English Premier League, which boasted the backbone of the winning French team. We were shamed in Holland and Belgium, not only by some of our spectators (no surprise there) but also by our players and the England management team. Sent abroad on a wave of the usual mixture of media-orchestrated boasting and foreboding,

England had lost a 2–0 lead to the talented Portuguese, beaten old rivals Germany in a match which was generally agreed to be the worst encounter in the entire tournament, and then haplessly succumbed in the first phase, via a late penalty, to an ageing Romania.

English footballers, it was widely said by the broadsheet media back in England, were technically limited and tactically naive. Ex-Liverpool forward Kevin Keegan also seemed hopelessly out of his depth as the England football manager. Calls were made to recruit a foreign coach for England – and to reduce the number of foreign players now playing in the Premiership. It wasn't just that the players and their English leaders were allegedly inept, but something was said to be wrong with the very culture of the English game, indeed with the English themselves. The *Guardian* sports journalist, Richard Williams, was one of many who argued that young English footballers' cultural experience was depressingly and narrowly limited to 'what they see or hear or read in the overheated and hyper-sexualised mass media, in the tabloid exposés and prying docu-soaps'. Players with limited horizons like these could hardly be expected, it was reasoned, to compete with their more worldly and cerebral counterparts abroad, who now also seemed fitter, more athletic than the English.

Similarly, John Cartwright, director of Crystal Palace's academy for young players, and one-time technical director at the FA's coaching school at Lilleshall, was positively scathing in his assessment of the dully masculinist values of many young English footballers, arguing that the game had helped produce a 'thug culture'. He went on:

> We've played thug football and we've produced a thug relationship between the player and the spectator . . . There have been gradual improvements. Coaches and players have come in from abroad and they've shown a different attitude to preparation. But we still go out there with a gung-ho attitude. If you can't think it out, fight it out.

'Fighting it out' had long-since failed the English off, as well as on, the field. New strategies were urgently needed.

Much of this myopic and outmoded reading of the game seemed mirrored in Kevin Keegan's own approach to the sport as he urged the England team to 'revert to more traditional qualities, like getting into them . . . I want intensity and aggression to become trademarks of my England side'. Keegan went on to describe the limits of continental play – and his own team – before Euro 2000: 'The foreigners don't play at a Premiership pace for 90 minutes; they play slow, slow, quick, quick, slow. If we get sucked into that, we don't look so good.' The England national team manager, someone with considerable experience of playing abroad, in Germany, seemed to insist that the 'tempo' and the 'intensity' of the English game could still bring success, even in the rarefied air of top international football competition. It seemed a faintly ridiculous claim.

But Keegan's ideas – defensive strength, fast pace, counter-attack where and when the opposing defence is weakest – also had some supporters in the summer of 2000 in the low countries, including from those among the very ranks of the new international modernisers of the English game. Gérard Houllier's passion for elements of traditional English football in general, and for Liverpool FC in particular, not to mention his more generalised affection for the English and English traditions, made him a keen student and supporter of the England team in Euro 2000. The Frenchman not only defended some of the qualities of the English game (while commentators in England were ridiculing it), but identified himself as an England *supporter*, experiencing the real pain of their defeats against Portugal and Romania, and the short-lived high after the weak Germans were dismissed in Charleroi.

Houllier, especially, was convinced that some of the traditional qualities of the English game, if better channelled and allied with a more 'continental' approach to tactics and strategy, and also coupled with a much more professional attention to the conditioning and preparation of players, could indeed succeed at the highest levels of the international and club game. At Liverpool Football Club in 1999–2000, Houllier had begun to put some of his ideas to the test, first by ridding the club of influential older players who still favoured a strongly 'laddish' (and, for Houllier, distinctively unprofessional) approach to the game, and then secondly by building his new squad around younger players from home and abroad, who could not only be schooled into the new professional ethos, but who also had the pace, athleticism and the physical attributes which Houllier identified as being so central to the modern game.

Under the new player freedoms offered by Bosman, Houllier was also convinced that modern players had to be strongly connected to a 'project', to an adventure, at their clubs: they had to see themselves almost as Blairite stakeholders, because top clubs now lacked the authoritarian tools which had guaranteed player loyalty in earlier periods. This translated into offering players a real belief in their clubs and coaches – *and* delivering trophies. Money is important, sure – but footballing success is also what keeps top players motivated and interested, reasoned Houllier.

As some of Liverpool's barrack-room lawyers left the club in the summer of 1999, so Houllier started to bring in his replacements. He concentrated, initially, on defensive stengthening, and on bringing in players who could best withstand the intense physical trials of the English game. He built the new Liverpool defence around Dutch goalkeeper Sander Westerveld, the giant Finn, Sami Hyypia, and the dogged Swiss central defender, Stephane Henchoz. The midfield he shaped around the simplicity and defensive solidity of the German international, Didi Hamann. The African Titi Camara brought hard running, strength and pace to the Liverpool attack, while the Czech, Vladimir Smicer, promised to offer invention and guile from the flanks. Houllier also knew he had some young aces up his sleeve at Anfield. Robbie Fowler and Michael Owen were already exceptional talents and Jamie Carragher an emerging and determined young defender. But the Liverpool coaching staff talked of little else other than a young midfielder from the city who they thought just might make a player; his name was Steven Gerrard.

In Houllier's first full season in 1999–2000, robbed by injury of Robbie Fowler for virtually the whole campaign, and of Smicer, Liverpool looked defensively secure but sometimes lacking in strength and variety in midfield and attack. Michael Owen seemed plagued by injury doubts. To the despair of Liverpool supporters everywhere, Manchester United were, once again, crowned Premiership title winners. Liverpool were consigned to the minor UEFA Cup.

This meant that to satisfy Anfield ambitions, Houllier's Liverpool had to do much better in the new season. The signs seemed promising: Fowler was slowly approaching fitness again, and so was the mercurial Smicer. Owen seemed more at ease. Markus Babbel and Gary McAllister, tough and experienced professionals, had both signed on free transfers and had given up international football in order to concentrate on their new Liverpool careers. The pacy Barmby had arrived from Everton and Christian Ziege had been lined up from Middlesbrough. Houllier had spent – so the press reported – in excess of fifty million pounds on his project to produce a new Liverpool, one which both competed and created, and which had the mental strength and consistency to challenge United's stranglehold at the very top of the English game and beyond.

Houllier cautioned patience on the part of Liverpool's staunchest followers. He saw his strategy as a five-year project aimed firstly only at securing Champions League status, the new Grail. Most Liverpool supporters saw his point, but unseating the rampant United *now* was also in their minds. Neither Houllier, nor the club's keenest followers, could have quite expected the sort of trip they were about to embark upon together. Not in the '60s, nor even in the '80s when Liverpool teams had dominated at home and in Europe, had anyone in the city –

or anywhere in England – seen anything quite like the ten months they were about to experience, from August 2000 to May 2001. This is a fans'-eye view of Houllier's Liverpool adventure during this seminal season, set against some of the wider developments which were occurring at the time in the English and the world game. It was quite a ride.

2. AUTUMN HOPES

19 AUGUST 2000: LIVERPOOL 1, BRADFORD 0

A new season. Opening accounts at home always invites a scouring of the 'Flattie' (the Flat Iron pub, Liverpool 4) for new faces and those lost from the last campaign. Pre-match talk at this stage in a new season is like a bout of macho non-dependence therapy: 'I hardly missed it at all', 'I can't remember the last time I looked forward to a season less than this', and so on. Of course, they've all been to the pre-season friendlies, including a 5–0 Liverpool home battering of stone-cold Italians, Parma. This kind of talk is now a ritual, part of the usual anti-Sky TV, anti-commerce, anti-'new' football venom which has been kept nicely simmering over the summer, but for us it is also partly a hangover from last season. Looking like a Champions League shoe-in, Liverpool failed to score in the last five matches, home and away; we even lost 1–0 to Bradford City in the last game, for God's sake, a gutless capitulation of Roy Evans proportions. We'll no doubt be visiting, in the impossibly difficult UEFA Cup, some unpronounceable club in Eastern Europe that used to be someone else. We could easily lose, early on.

Another reason for gloom is that for all the talk of it being the *club* not the players you support, there is a strange and cold unfamiliarity about the Liverpool team these days, which makes loving them rather harder. We're stacked with foreign players now and some – Hyypia, Camara – have really stirred the crowd, while others – Smicer, Hamann – have found it much more difficult to make their mark. And to be honest, we haven't had too much of the technical spin-off which a foreign squad is supposed to bring: Berger and Rigobert Song can mis-control with the best of the British and Henchoz sometimes passes like a dyslexic Phil Babb. Houllier, well aware of the physical test in the

English game, has tended to go for power and work-rate rather than poetry in his signings. We've tightened up at the back, sure, but we struggle to really excite – and to engage. We are haunted by 'the nightmare scenario', as our mate and football guru Rogan Taylor calls it, as we ponder this new era on the Kop: 'Just a bunch of anonymous fellahs on a meal ticket.'

So a sort of dark anticipation, tinged with uncertainty, is the general tone among the Liverpool faithful assembled today in the Flattie before this new season begins. These are 'ordinary' fans, but in some cases with extraordinary memories: 25 years or more recall of unmatched Liverpool playing success, the heavy monkey now on our collective backs. Sheila Spiers even remembers the great Billy Liddell; Paul Hyland every Reds' signing and departure, every promising Melwood youngster since the early 1970s. There is serious knowledge here.

The anticipation comes, as it always does at this stage, from our new summer outfield signings: Bernard Diomède, Gary McAllister and German international Markus Babbel, the last two on Bosmans, and the deliciously provocative addition of Nick Barmby from across the park. If Robbie Fowler can get fit we will look a little more dangerous going forward. With no goals in five games last time out it would take a true genius to move us the other way. It is sad to see local lads, David Thompson and Dominic Matteo, going before the season's start, each just failing to make the grade here. No doubt Leeds will now make some left-sided genius out of Matteo but, with almost eight million pounds banked in transfer fees for these two, the leftovers also ought to help keep the Liverpool Youth Academy running for a few years. It's good business by GH, really, and we hope the Liverpool lads do well elsewhere.

The uncertainty today comes with having no clear idea who might play in this opener, a product of Houllier's new rotation strategy. Could both Barmby and Smicer play? Who would get the nod in central midfield? Will Berger recover from a knock for the left side? Would controversial transfer target Ziege yet jet in to play at left-back, Boro's Bryan Robson trailing and whingeing in his wake? And what about current Houllier favourite, Carragher, or Kop hero, Titi Camara? Robbie's pre-season bad luck – a large Irish keeper fell on him, springing his ankle – means that we know who will play up front: Heskey and Owen: *Of Mice and Men*. But crucially, could the fêted Boy Wonder, Michael, find his old pre-hamstring form at last?

We watch home matches on the Kop these days, block 207, about a third of the way up and just to the right of the Kop-end goal. There are four of us: Steve, Cath, Rogan Taylor and me. Of course, we have our own little reference group around us, our sounding boards. Behind, it is a couple of the obligatory moaning woollybacks, panickers and complainers, but nothing too disastrous. The Fellahs in Front are more like it: a group of eight, mainly middle-aged Liverpool working men, who give us some stick sometimes for the crap we shout and the stuff we talk about. They like to roll in from the pub on kick-off. There are a couple of fellahs our age in front that we get on with really well, and there's an older guy with them I like to talk to about the great Liverpool sides of the '60s. A younger, aggressive fellah in this group sometimes gives us more grief. As Fergie said of Paul Ince, he could pick an argument in an empty house, this fellah. We have seen him carted out at away games. Fair enough.

Cath and Rogan are low-key at the match, but my mate, Steve, is usually a source of amusement or anguish for all around us. He has a compulsion, like thousands of others around the land, to stand up, arbitrarily, and make loud, uncharitable speeches about the match officials. He does this about two or three times a game. This can grate. Maybe he was dropped on his head as a child? Or perhaps he has been secretly hypnotised to respond in Pavlovian fashion to the whistle? Some guys in front wonder why nobody has ever filled him in (next season, perhaps?). We think Steve might well have a heart attack at the match one day; he'd like nothing better, of course, than to drift away, a foaming critique of an errant referee's assistant still lingering on his quivering lips.

The Kop is not what it was. Discuss. We all have great memories of the standing Kop in full flow, of course. The writer, Arthur Hopcraft, described the Kop memorably in its pomp in the late '60s as being:

> Hideously uncomfortable. The steps are as greasy as a school playground lavatory in the rain. The air is rancid with beer and onions and belching and worse. The language is a gross purple of obscenity. When the crowd surges at a shot or a collision near a corner flag a man or a boy, and sometimes a girl, can be lifted off the ground in the crush, as if by some massive, soft-sided crane, and dangled about for minutes on end, perhaps never getting back to within four or five steps of the spot from which the monster made its bite.

Ah, happy days. The Kop today is quieter, nothing like Hopcraft's image. It is certainly safer, too. The Kop *is* less collective and less spontaneous today than its old standing version; it misses its ribald and fluid young core, from where most of the early songs sprouted. We miss the flags and the swaying and these days attempts at songs often roll forlornly around small banks of seats all over the Kop, most of them not taken up by the whole. We do stand up for European games – but it's not the same. Like most football ends – and public culture itself – the Kop is also much cruder today than it was in its prime. Hardly the march of progress, then – or a winning argument for those who claim for a creeping football gentrification, by seats.

Inside Anfield today, the Kop faithful gather for what promises to be another spluttering seasonal journey. George Sephton, our familiar master of musical ceremonies at LFC, works from a glass box elevated to our right. George has gotten all hip lately, by playing Cast and Pete Wiley, but inexplicably today he also plays the most unfamiliar Frankie's 'Two Tribes' – very loudly – as the teams come out. This is well out of order, as he knows: our song at this very special moment is 'You'll Never Walk Alone', which George now plays later, just as the players line up to kick off – a right royal bollocks. Already the Kop is confused and annoyed, even before the first home booking.

Houllier was right when he said that Bradford would be sharp, having played competitively for a month already in the crass Intertoto Cup. Vladdy Smicer starts – and even finishes – for Liverpool, a nice change and a good beginning. Young Frenchman, Traore, plays at left-back, warming the place for Ziege, and he looks solid if not exactly Maldini material. Barmby is busy and lively, a new Craig Johnston perhaps, and McAllister eventually comes on, a proper footballer, one right in the Anfield mould. Babbel shows some good things, too, but he'll need time to get used to the pace of this. Camara, ominously for him, doesn't even make the bench.

In a patchy first half, Westerveld keeps us intact as Bradford make chances on the break. The second half is more like it, as the Reds begin to get on top. But the 'best fans in the world' are just beginning to jump on Heskey's vast back when the big man turns and bursts away on the right, swatting defenders, before planting it in the opposite top corner. Compared to the rest of this opener, these five or six seconds have been a startling blur. Cue 'Em-ile Hesk-ey' chants from around the ground, naturally. The words 'shamelessly two-faced' come immediately to mind. The manager says Emile scores like this in training all the time, but he 'lacks confidence' in match situations. Sounds like the Anfield crowd whine might already be having its terrible effect.

Noticeably, Michael's continued form trough produces nothing like the same narky reaction from the Liverpool crowd, but his real performance dip must be worrying the coaching staff. It worries me. He's substituted, another passive home display in a season when we have to score more goals. Heskey will probably get 15 or so, if he stays fit, but someone else will need to come up with 25. Robbie could do it standing on his head – if he was right. Michael still looks like he has a severe bout of self-doubt about both body and mind. Let's hope it somehow dissolves. Let's hope he *smiles*.

But this is a reasonable start, three hard-won points at home. We move to Arsenal on Monday night. Arsenal have so outplayed Sunderland today – with Vieira sent off – and *lost*, that you have to feel they will be really up for it on Monday. There is a kind of hidden football DNA here which connects all clubs: the chemistry of the season and its mini-contests. Exactly *when* you play teams, what mood they are in, whether it is best that they have previously won or lost, etc., is a mysterious formula fans spend many wasted hours trying to unravel. But this is the worst combination you can face, really: they've played well and lost. Arsenal won't be complacent, they'll be the opposite; they'll want a win against us to get their own season started.

YOUR MONEY, OUR PRIORITY

Liverpool have introduced a new Official Supporters Club. For £22 you get a video and a CD, plus free access to reserve games. For £32 you are offered the above and priority access to tickets for four home games. Effectively, it is an extra charge simply to be eligible for match tickets at home, tickets you are not even guaranteed to get for the matches you choose. If you don't pay up, your chances for home tickets look poor. Great scheme, obviously.

21 AUGUST: ARSENAL 2, LIVERPOOL 0

I love going to the Arsenal: the pubs; the location; the great modernist tube sign; the historic stands close to the pitch; the price. My God, the price. A decent seat at £19.50 puts their London neighbours (all close to £30) to shame. When Arsenal move from here – plans are afoot – I'll really miss it. There are black and brown faces and plenty of father-and-kid couples in the Liverpool section tonight, a typical *London* away end for the Reds, in fact. A drunken scouser behind us spends almost all the first half chanting 'tatty head' at unidentified Arsenal players. It could be at the newly pony-tailed Seaman, or else their new man, Lauren, from the Cameroon, who has natty little locks. Our own new Frenchman, Diomède, has his own fly-away stuff of the 'I can't do anything with it' variety. Anyway, this fellah moves in front of us for the second half, still chanting, still pissed.

There have been no Liverpool defeats in the last 12 against Arsenal, so cometh the hour, cometh the man: take a bow, referee Graham Poll. Last season the comic Rob Harris was the refereeing dunce in the Premier League and he eventually got sent down to the Nationwide as a result. Poll may soon have to join him if this is anything to go by. Hugh Dallas's abject performance in Euro 2000 is also a sign that the Scots have it no better than us. We have fallen behind Europe in this area, refereeing, just as we have in most other things football-wise.

Houllier's tactics at places like Arsenal are always ultra-defensive now, so they are also high risk – we think unnecessarily so. So it proves here: with Owen left out, we never look like scoring. Tony Adams baulks Westerveld at an early corner (really?) but in the end it has to go down as a goalkeeper's mistake. 'Sandra' drops the ball at Lauren's feet, all girls together, who must think this English football is easy. On other occasions, Wester does well tonight, but this was a crucial lapse at a place were mental strength in the first half-hour is vital. We haven't shown it.

We could still come back, of course, plenty of time, but with the willing but pedestrian Carragher in a defensive and crowded midfield, the ideas and movement we needed have to come from out wide, from Smicer and Barmby, and both do far too little tonight. It isn't pretty, but McAllister's first-half clumsy challenge on Vieira deserves only yellow. The red which Poll delivers instead means we just have to battle on and hope for a break. And there's more. Arsenal's Vieira is talented and looks at home in international football, but he's not in love with the physical buffeting and the (racist) baiting which goes on in the FA Premier League, on the field and off it. He loses his head here in the last 20 minutes and Poll despatches him, too, soon followed by Hamann – for shirt-pulling.

It takes a special refereeing performance to unite a *whole* crowd in collective free-flowing abuse, as happens here in the last 15 minutes, after they get a late second. It gives us all something enjoyable to do at least, in the Liverpool section, as this misery winds down. Let's hope the FA sees sense (fat chance) and doesn't hide for once behind its 'referees, right or wrong' stance. We don't deserve points *or* suspensions from this, but it's been a lousy start on the road.

WORLDWIDE ATTENTION

McAllister's global profile will certainly suffer with suspension because the FA Premier League, warts and all, is now watched every week by an international TV audience of 440 million, up 12 per cent on last season. No wonder sponsors queue here to offer investment for attention. Thirty-seven per cent of these armchair fans live in the Asian Pacific region, one-quarter in North America – juicy markets. Rumour already has it that new global brands – McDonalds, Coke, Budweiser, Sanyo – are lining up with bulging wallets to sponsor the Premier League. Manchester United's new shirt sponsorship deal with Vodafone alone clocks in at thirty million pounds over five years. It's crazy money. It's the FA Premier League.

26 AUGUST: SOUTHAMPTON 3, LIVERPOOL 3

This is a scrawny ground, tight, difficult to play in, usually difficult to see from. This is the last LFC visit to the Dell, another new ground coming, and Southampton make loads of fruitless early chances to mark the occasion. We make a bundle of chances, too, and score *three*. With Smicer at the controls, and Michael alone up front because of an injury to Heskey, the little fellah even scores two with his *left* foot. The message here is if you can get Owen isolated against lumbering defenders like Lundekwam and Richards he will score: even at half pace and low on confidence, he will score. With Hyypia heading in from a corner, and only 17 minutes left, we are a massive 3–0 ahead – home and hosed.

Except they keep coming. A far-post cross to Pahars, and dopey Westerveld actually *steps* out of goal, expecting it to be headed across the area, and the little striker scores, easily. *Embarrassingly*. This is the goal that lets them see light when there has only been gloom. It's like any Sunday football match: you are strolling and then the opposition get a pawky goal, and suddenly it all looks different, panic takes over. Hoddle, the pass master, is not so proud as a manager, so now Southampton bomb us and torment young 'Jimmy' Traore down the left. This is all new to the inexperienced Frenchman, and even to the tested Babbel on the right.

'What kind of crazy football is this?' our new men must ask themselves. Firstly, this Southampton team should be dead, it *should* lie down. Secondly, this is not football at all – this is an assault. We look flustered and can't keep hold of the ball in midfield. When the second Southampton goal comes from El Khalej you know there is more. Finally, in injury time, they pump it in again, high to Jimmy's side once more. He stretches to try to get to a ball he can't possibly deal with and heads it directly into Pahars' path on the penalty spot. The Latvian can't miss – and he doesn't: 3–3.

Afterwards, Houllier is apoplectic with rage. You can see him positively fizz with it. 'A time for throwing teacups,' he jokes between gritted teeth. But he also expects more than these players can yet deliver. He expects them to close down games like the old Liverpool could. But his team is young; it is full of young foreigners, players not yet used to dealing with this sort of peculiar British way, this kind of abuse. This Liverpool team cannot keep the ball yet, not even like Roy Evans's fragile team could.

OWNERSHIP MATTERS

The new owner at Notts County is an American Pulitzer Prize winner who ominously likens football clubs in England to a *television* show.

Talking of which, Granada reportedly buy a 5 per cent share in Arsenal for forty-seven million pounds. A 10 per cent share in us recently cost the same company only twenty-two million. Admittedly, my mathematics are not brilliant but . . . Liverpool FC also reveal multi-million pound plans to update their Melwood training ground, to make it a 'state of the art' location for players to train and to be treated for injury. 'Our players deserve the very best,' says Houllier, surprising no one. Call me cynical, but with these sort of comforting improvements on the way it makes you wonder if we will ever get Redknapp, Berger, Robbie and the rest back on the pitch where they, supposedly, belong.

6 SEPTEMBER: LIVERPOOL 3, ASTON VILLA 1

The talk in the now famous Flattie – as glamorously featured in tonight's impressive new-style Liverpool matchday magazine – is already of our apparent lack of progress from last season. Babbel still looks slow, Jimmy Traore is inexperienced and why sell Matteo so quickly with no real replacement available? (Ziege has yet to materialise.) The goalkeeping isn't right. There are glum faces and much finger-pointing at Westerveld for the collapse at the Dell.

On the way to the ground today the prospective local touts get ever younger; kids who look about ten are asking for 'spares'. The heritage police horses, not needed now for bruising supporters into line outside the Kop turnstiles, are stationed instead at the corner of the Kop and the Kemlyn Road. One of the police mounties is a black woman. West Midlands Asian Reds are regular sights on the Kop these days, turbans and all, and they will turn up tonight to see us beat the Villa. But I bet this is the only black woman anywhere on these embargoed premises.

The Kemlyn Road lower tier, where I'm temporarily based tonight, is a less grizzly crowd than on the Kop: more women, a wider range of accents, macs, and the occasional soup flask – you know the sort of thing. There's no singing here either, the punters lost instead in the new matchday mag. You can also really see the extreme pace of the English game from this lower pitchside spot and you can *feel* the tackles thudding in. Hyypia puts in a huge first-half block tackle on Villa's Nilis, for example – and comes up limping, but unbowed. He stays on, but the injury he receives in this moment will keep him out of the next few games. From here you can see why.

Villa have turned up in a truly gothic shiny all-black number, which makes them look like a bunch of Chicago pimps; our pukey new orange away kit seems positively traditional by comparison. The Kop gives ex-Red keeper David James a great welcome, a sign of affection and maybe a hint that we might need Jameo's multiple weaknesses to help us win here. Last season Villa came for a snore-inducing point – and got it – so an early goal for LFC would be a blessing.

Liverpool line up very 'narrow' as we coaching gurus say. Smicer seems to be playing between a middle three and a front two, with Hamann, strangely, on the left. Villa opt for a Roy Q-style five across the middle, with the impressive Barry and little Alan Wright getting chalk on their boots and Merson adopting the Macca free role. This means they see a lot of the ball and play some pretty football but without too much end product (Roy Evans, again, circa 1995–96).

After five minutes, Heskey, impressively, bursts down the right and slides a great ball early into the Kop six-yard box and, lo, the Boy Wonder scores. Soon after, our transferred goalkeeping hero comes and misses a corner and Michael outjumps a defender to head in. After barely half an hour, and under George's very nose, we score a third: 'Nicky Barmby!' according to our eagle-eyed man in the PA box. Of course it is Owen again (how could we doubt him?), stealing the ball from James for his hat-trick. Villa miss their chances in an open first half and then we shut up shop in the second – at least until Stone scores a clever late consolation. Ginola comes on for them and looks – well, fat. The appearance of the hapless, hardworking Dutch forward, Erik Meijer, on as a sub for us, is tantamount to Houllier putting up a big red sign saying: 'We have now officially stopped trying to score goals'. It ends 3–1, and they're three welcome points.

Later, in the pub when we watch the highlights, a drunk stands up and yells at the TV: 'Michael, you are the best fellah around. No one is better than you, Michael.' Playing like this, he may be right. Elsewhere, there is more keen football controversy. 'David Ginola no longer has a sexy backside' – Sheila Spiers (retired).

THE LANGUAGE OF DEFENCE
(FROM *FOUR-FOUR-TWO* MAGAZINE)
In the Liverpool FC English language laboratory, Terry, a 'specialist', is working with new Liverpool defenders on communicating in match situations.

> Rigobert Song pipes up in his Cameroonian accent: 'When I give the ball, I want to speak to him that there is another player.'
> 'You know this, Rigo,' says Terry.
> And Song does know: 'Man on,' he announces confidently, and leans back in his seat.
> Corners are a bit more tricky. 'What is it called when you stand next to opponents?' asks Terry.

'Marking,' says Traore, which has Terry scurrying back to the screen.

'But what is he doing?' asks Terry, pointing at a player who's not doing very much at all.

'Looking ze ball?' suggests Song.

He's nearly there.

'Ballwatching,' Terry corrects. 'Ballwatching. So what do you tell him?'

'When they get a corner, you have to mark your man,' says Song.

Another stage of the Liverpool defensive rehabilitation is successfully completed.

1 OCTOBER: CHELSEA 3, LIVERPOOL 0

A scrambled 3–2 home win against Manchester City, Hamann weighing in with two goals, is no real preparation for this trip. A real Colombian on the station platform, wearing a Colombia football shirt and drinking Colombian beer. Groups of young Japanese in replica shirts, mixing with the locals. The gargling laughter of large Thatcherised baseball-hatted white boys. Haughty women with some style. This is Chelsea, where else? The Sunday underground in London is the usual nightmare, and the Mancs are playing Arsenal at Highbury at the same time as we meet Chelsea. Presumably someone is marking the Euston Road down for later wide-boy stuff.

The original outer wall of the old Shed is still standing here and is now marked, outside the new Stamford Bridge consumption palaces and Chelsea Village paraphernalia, with one of Ken Bates's own dodgy blue plaques, like some noted archaeological exhibit from the time when man ran wild. They should excavate here for the bones of missing visiting fans from the 1970s.

We get all the usual crap from the locals, loads of: 'In your Liverpool slums', 'Same old scousers', etc. We respond, quite reasonably, with: 'You've never won fuck all' and 'Where were you when you were shite?', so no marks all round for originality. All this, plus the routine casual flying obscenities, and the later loud stand-offs outside the ground – 'Do you fackin' wan' it, scousers? Cam' on, then!' – means that although we are forking out about £32 a piece for this, and you really do end up afterwards alongside punters who are talking about restaurants and art as you walk to the station, a visit to Chelsea is still no obvious matinée alternative to the opera.

We have scraped along since the Man City win, sneaking past Dynamo Bucharest in the UEFA Cup, getting a decent point at West Ham and then really struggling at home, even with new man Ziege, against a suffocating Sunderland, another 1–1, so we need to get back on track. With home manager Vialli recently sacked by chopper Ken, after leading Chelsea in their most successful period for 45 years, the big ask is: can the new Chelsea manager, the Italian Ranieri, get something out of these London posers? Chelsea normally cream us here, no matter how they are playing. Last season we were two down here in 14 minutes, game over.

The idiot Chelsea pre-match announcer adds his own little spin to the day's events, so when Le Saux's name is called he is: 'Certainly the best left-back in England' and when Chelsea score their first goal – because, readers, news of a truly awful defeat is approaching – which is punched quite unaided into the net by our own expensive, arrogant goalkeeper, the announcer loses his way because what he should have said is: 'Chelsea's first goal, scored by that bloated clown, Sander Westerveld .' But he doesn't.

Of course, Dennis Wise is fouling Sander. It is, after all, a home corner, and opponents have started to mess with Sander's head now by blocking him. But our man also needs to *grow up* and do his job. Our new gloves man, Arphexad, must wonder what sort of calamity has to befall the Dutchman before he gets a shout. I would, if I were him, and so would you. The second Chelsea goal comes (down the bemused Ziege's flank, since you ask) while we are still narking about the first. Henchoz also might have done better, and he is at fault (with Gerrard) for the third. For Chelsea fans, with our Fatherland contingent, we *are* Germany, prompting 'Dambusters' renditions. We are, certainly, whatever the German is for 'shite'.

Later, on the tube after this 3–0 crushing has mercifully ended, some chaps from the barbarian north-west start hunting out locals who are accused of unnecessarily 'bringing up Heysel' in some, clearly, lively post-match discussion on the wider state of the European game. Meanwhile, the Liverpool club website and the radio phone-ins are already openly hostile to Houllier. Someone moans, ridiculously, that Leicester City are top of the Premiership when it *should* (obviously) be us. We actually do look like Leicester – but without the lunatic and effective Gerry Taggart locking up shop. We urgently need to take stock. This is my message.

PAOLO, THE TALENTED DIRECTOR

Paolo di Canio's autobiography has just been published, to general public approval, for its insights and 'honesty'. Paolo was recently hauled off and away from a brawl in a *testimonial* game for gentle Julian Dicks. But he's a foreigner, right, so he is also likely to be hiding some deeply embedded understanding of the symbiotic links between football, art and culture? Wrong. I like di Canio, the footballer, but he also swims with some strange and dangerous fish. I'll summarise his unusual story: talented poor boy, son of a brickie, Lazio ultra and born fighter, rises against the odds to defeat bad coaches and incompetent referees. No wonder they like him down in Stepney.

Benito Mussolini, *Il Duce*, thoughtfully sent a three-word telegram to the Italian team on the eve of the 1938 World Cup final. It read: 'Win or die'. Fortunately, they won. Di Canio, unsurprisingly, is a keen student and supporter of Mussolini, who we learn here is 'a deeply understood individual', Both Paolo and Benito are 'nationalists' – but not racists, mind – though di Canio also warns us that, due to recent immigration, 'If we're not careful, in ten years' time, Italy could be a Muslim country.' Yeah, right, Paolo. Decent player, weird guy.

7 OCTOBER, WORLD CUP QUALIFIER: ENGLAND 0, GERMANY 1

A Premiership-free weekend and England versus Germany is on TV, in my parents' house in Bootle, the last football match at Wembley. In the hail of media hype about the twin towers before the game, little has been said, of course, about Liverpool's near residence there in the late-'70s and most of the '80s. Instead, it's all been 1966 and Kenneth Wolstenhome thinking 'It's all over'. Like many people in this wilfully independent and strongly Irish city of ours, my own interest in today's clash between *The Sun* and the Hun is only lukewarm.

But there is *some* interest. Michael Owen will play for England, after all. Will his recent good form last? Will he score? Will he (more darkly and more importantly) get injured? Liverpool's Hamann and Ziege are both likely to be in the German team. Truly speaking, club loyalties properly to the fore, I should now be supporting the Germans, not England. Evertonians, inevitably, have no such agonies to consider.

Early on, Germany are well in charge. England's 4–4–2 is hopelessly narrow, and Keegan's wild and fatal selection of Southgate in midfield seems as blindingly optimistic as Houllier's favouring of the willing Carragher in the same spot has been at Liverpool. Hamann, meanwhile, looking not at all like the peripheral figure he can often be at Anfield, is running the game. The Germans are enjoying themselves. St Michael, looking volcanic, is not getting a kick.

An early free kick for Germany outside England's penalty area, and Hamann, full of self-belief, takes the strike quickly, and somehow it Exocets its wobbly path between red and white legs and arms, and squirms off the sodden green through Seaman's desperate late dive. One nil to the Germans; Liverpool's Hamann the scorer. Seaman's silly mid-life-crisis pony-tail droops sadly.

I can't help it. I automatically and loudly cheer this (Liverpool) breakthrough. 'Yeeess!' My elderly mum, thus far distracted and only half-watching, is now all attention.

'What are you doing?' she asks. 'That's not Liverpool who've scored. Liverpool are in the red.'

'No, England are in the red,' I tell her, with exaggerated patience. 'Germany in the white. Liverpool aren't playing.'

She digests this obviously surprising information and then comes back: 'So why are you cheering the *Germans*?' She can barely believe this.

'I'm not cheering the Germans,' I say, 'I'm cheering Hamann. He plays for Liverpool.' I'm now tilling the difficult and contradictory soil of club and country affiliations.

Now she is truly on her guard. And indignant. 'What, a German playing for Liverpool? Go 'way!'

I'm starting now to enjoy this exchange – much more than the match. You see I know what's coming next.

'We don't just have one German at Liverpool,' I tell her slowly, closely watching her face. 'We've now got *three*!' Her big eyes widen.

I begin to think what might be more shocking to my mum than this stunning revelation. Martians playing for Liverpool? Cilla Black orchestrating *Blind Date* contestants in the Anfield back four? Or convicted child molesters being given a second chance by Houllier, up front? Are any of these *truly* stranger than a trio of Germans playing for Liverpool, I wonder?

I await her response to my clearly terrible news. She watches the screen for a while and considers her family football duties against this recent unwanted invasion. 'Well,' she says sucking in the air sharply, her loyalties clearly stretched, 'I didn't know that!' No more is said until Michael Owen mis-controls a defence-splitting pass in the second half, and with it England's last chance is gone. 'Tom,' she asks of my dad, disbelievingly, 'is that the England Liverpool fellah?' He nods, glumly. It finishes England 0, *Liverpool* 1.

Another ex-Liverpudlian, Kevin Keegan, resigns as England manager soon after this is over. My mum says she is really not interested in the job.

8 OCTOBER: EVERTON 5, LIVERPOOL LADIES 0

The first derby game of the season is always an important marker, with local pride at stake. This result then, a rout, is a catastrophe for Reds fans everywhere but it won't have many Liverpudlians calling off sick on Monday. That the female teams here still, primly, call themselves 'Ladies' is probably an indicator of just how seriously they – and we – still take the women's game in England. And yet Merseyside has three teams in the women's National League: Tranmere Rovers and the Blues are also up there. Are you watching, Manchester?

This National Premier League clash attracts about 100 to Marine's modest little ground in affluent Crosby, north of the city, so you can see that the women's game on Merseyside is still a closely guarded secret. And this is just a couple of years before ambitious FA plans to professionalise the sport for women in England will roll into view. Fulham and Arsenal already employ their own female players, and to good effect. Although the Liverpool Ladies train at Melwood, and wear the official club kit, this is just about where the real support for the women's team stops dead at Anfield. Personally, I'd be made up if we had a decent women's team, but it is hard to get the locals, or the club, excited by the prospect.

Here at Marine, a neat goal-end stand ('Take yer feet off the seats, gerls,' insists a local steward) and the famous Marine FC 'Scouse House', serving tea and chip barms on a Sunday morning, at least offers hangover comfort. The 'crowd' today is mainly family, and young female players from around the region: tracksuits, baseball caps and pony-tails are *de rigueur*. The female accents here are more St Helens and North Wales than pure scouse. In short, and despite the real vigour of local enthusiasts, support for the women's game in England's soccer hotbed – from fans, from clubs, from local sponsors, from the media – is pathetic.

Liverpool Ladies are officially in a 'transitional period'. So transitional, in fact, that Arsenal recently thrashed them 10–0. No doubt some distant Reds fan picked up this disturbing result on the wires somewhere and cursed Houllier's continued reliance on wobbly defenders. Even the official England scout who is here today to run the rule over international hopefuls can confirm names only for the Everton team. For Liverpool, he offers two likely youngsters: the athletic and lively centre-forward, Sarah Dyson, and classy new centre-half, Lisa Sandys. Apart from long-serving midfielder, Maz Catterall, a Sammy Lee-style battler, Liverpool are otherwise made up of unknown young wannabes, so we have a lot of ground to make up.

At half-time, it's 2–0 to Everton, Shimmin and Britton the emphatic scorers. Liverpool have missed chances, but Everton are already beginning to overpower the Reds' midfield. Young Welsh prospect, Jade Bell, is brought on by Liverpool to play wide-left in the second half but she gets little change out of the powerful Hill. Dyson is forced off with a knee injury and Liverpool soon begin to look ragged, as Shimmin starts to pick holes on the right side of the visitors' rearguard. Sandys is overworked now and Shimmin scores again. Two more goals follow, one painfully from ex-Liverpool player, Jody Handley, as the visitors, briefly, look in danger of shipping another ten-goal haul. The final whistle is a relief.

Liverpool assistant manager Steven Cavanagh says later: 'This was probably our worst performance of the season and heads dropped when Everton scored three second-half goals in ten minutes. This is the first time we have given the players a rollicking this season.' Which means he spared them at Arsenal. The Liverpool parents mutter darkly about 'managerial mistakes' and 'poor selection', but they are actually incredibly positive about the state of the Liverpool Ladies team. This is a young side they point out. Our time will come again. I believe them. Keep your heads up, the Liverpool women – it could be a long season.

15 OCTOBER: DERBY COUNTY 0, LIVERPOOL 4

Luck is still very much a totem in English football. Houllier, despite himself, got lucky here. The truth is, Derby's performance is so awful – definite relegation stuff – that it is hard to judge what this result, or performance, really means for the Reds' season. We shall see. Derby's functional new ground now means pre-match visits to the Railway pub are sadly sacrificed for joyless parking at Toys-R-Us and a couple of pints under the concrete oppression of Pride Park's away end. The stadium bars here announce, uncomplicatedly, 'BEER' – a message some young scousers tuned into hours ago, judging by their repeated renditions of the delightful 'Gary Neville shags his ma, up the shitter'. More work for hard-pressed civil servants currently musing on the distracted state of English male adolescence.

The luck? Firstly, Henchoz and Hamann are already injured, which means Babbel is at his preferred and best centre-back position and McAllister is back in midfield. Secondly, right-back Heggem is clattered after five minutes and Murphy substitutes in midfield, which means Carragher moving from midfield to right-back. Thirdly, Michael is injured after 20 minutes as Heskey scores our first, from a McAllister corner. What all this means is that Murphy and the still sprightly McAllister become the central midfield two, ridding us of the painful constipation previously offered by Carragher and the ponderous Hamann. Secondly, Babbel is composed and happy to have the ball in the middle of a footballing back four, and so, gone are the panic-inducing aimless hacks away of Henchoz. Thirdly, Robbie gets 70 real minutes up front with Heskey. Fourthly, Derby are truly terrible: no pressure on our ball-playing midfield and no shots on our goal in 90 minutes.

The transformation is extraordinary. With Berger also fit and reinstated on the left with Ziege, we now have three authentic left-footers in the team, which looks confident and balanced for the first time as a result. The ball comes smoothly and quickly through the midfield for once, and Heskey has also got his East Midlands derby head on, offering power, skill and determination. He scores three, Robbie having a big hand in two of them, and generally Robbie looks sharp and hungry. Berger ends the rout with a thunderous and classic fourth, after a Liverpool passing movement which seems to go on for a couple of weeks. A convincing victory on the road at last.

RADIO WAVES

Are we really *this* good? It seems unlikely. Let's see how we cope with Leicester's Savage and Lennon snapping at the midfield at Anfield next week. At listless Derby, Jim Smith will struggle to last out the season at this rate, as Radio 5 callers quickly inform the flatulent Alan Green. Smith comments later that Liverpool, impressively, continued to work hard, even when three goals up. He's right. One *606* caller rings to have his say in the 'next England manager' debate and puts forward the case for Roy Evans as a possible coach. No bad shout this. Another caller wonders why Brian Little (now at Hull City) hasn't yet had a mention for the England manager's job. Not even the spluttering Green can make this guy sound sane.

21 OCTOBER: LIVERPOOL 1, LEICESTER CITY 0

The start of four home games on the bounce and first up is Leicester City, a real Reds bogey team. Under Martin O'Neill our troubles with Leicester went from the 'merely difficult' to the 'impossible-to-get-a-result' pile. O'Neill cleverly carried on football management at Filbert Street, with his shambolic Forest mate John Robertson in tow, as if all this fancy continental talk about changing players' diets and a more 'scientific' preparation and focused training was all, well, phooey. Martin wouldn't know a coaching video digest or the *Opta Index* if it slapped him on his ruddy chops.

His midfield terrier, Neil Lennon, once said that even when he's calm O'Neill is a difficult man to look in the eye. His players would run through walls for him, because they all owed him. Under Roy Evans and Barnsey, of course, we never managed to get even close to matching their ugly and necessary motivation. If truth be told, the new City manager, Peter Taylor, has not done too much to deserve being in the England coaching frame. Sure, Leicester have been riding high, but they have managed only seven goals in nine games. His new strikers have not been firing. Leicester's defence – *O'Neill's* defence – has been awesome.

Today, a heretic in O'Neill's former kingdom, Taylor opts for his own favoured 4-4-2, instead of Leicester's trusted three at the back and five in midfield. So, instead of strangling us as usual, we swamp *them*. With Gerrard solid at full-back and McAllister in the side, getting into the box, we pepper Tim Flowers – who saves *everything*. Owen is out but Heskey is a non-stop threat, messing up his old mate Elliott, but we can't score. Emile has been pointing to Houllier's encouragement and confidence-building and to shooting drills after training as the reason why he is scoring more goals for the Reds: 'Everyone thinks their game has stepped up 20 to 30 per cent more than before Houllier came.' He looks sharp, and the Main Stand loudly applauds a 0–0 with Leicester at half-time. Even these inveterate moaners know what this match means to us.

After the break, Leicester briefly threaten, but soon it's back to Flowers versus Heskey. And then, just when we might have started dumping it aimlessly forward, the elegant Babbel dumps it aimlessly forward, fully 40 yards from centre-back, and Elliott and Flowers play 'After you, Claude' while Emile nips in to score. It's mainly relief, the crowd reaction; ecstatic relief. Taylor's been too cautious. We hang on, as if defending against a combined Real Madrid/Barcelona select eleven. But we do hang on. Houllier is *thrilled*; he has that little twinkle in his eye later, when Sky TV corners him. He knows it's been hard, but he's delighted. Later, in our own post-match beer fest in the Flattie, 'Bring on those real [Everton] dogs of war' is what everyone in the pub is carelessly thinking. Everton, ominously, have won away at fancied Newcastle.

THE CONDITION OF ENGLAND

The debate about English football and on the nature of Englishness itself is now pretty much in full swing again. Is there an English coach of sufficient quality to take over from the departed and unlamented Keegan? What is the real *quality* of the English game? Houllier is impressed with the ability of the young players in England, the 18–25 generation, arguing that World Cup 2006 is a 'realistic' target for the English. This actually seems wildly optimistic to me. When Howard Wilkinson, guilelessly, seemed to suggest the same thing recently – that we should aim for 2006 – the tabloids rounded on him with accusations that he was ready to 'surrender' the 2002 World Cup after just two rounds of qualifying matches. It's all mad, of course, quite mad.

29 OCTOBER: LIVERPOOL 3, EVERTON 1

Okay, *this* is the real thing. A poor home show by us against tiny Slovan Liberec in the UEFA Cup, leavened only by a late Heskey winner, added to more team messing about by Houllier, is scant preparation for this shuddering clash. John Barnes once told me, as we lost to Everton time and again in the '90s, that Liverpool fans should take comfort from the fact that at least we were usually the better side in derby games. Cold comfort. And as a consequence of our, admittedly stylish, derby defeats in the '90s, most Reds here tonight would now settle for waving goodbye to the ball until we score a freakish last-minute winner off Michael's arse or Robbie's nose plaster – anything.

But when the rain begins lashing down as we walk up to the Kop, old forebodings begin to raise their ugly heads once more. It's 'dogs of war' weather for sure. With so many overseas players in both Blue and Red ranks these days it must also be chilling for the players to hear the Kop baying as it does before the derby. Can they *really* know what it still means, winning this ancient local spat, to most of the people here? And let me say now, don't you believe for a minute all this 'friendly derby' shit. There is real bile here; as there should be.

The Bluenoses begin well and our midfield is bypassed as Gascoigne cheekily runs it for the first 25 minutes. But we manage to get in front early, for once, Barmby benefiting from Robbie's little nudge on Ball to head in at the far post. Serves the visitors right for howling at our new man: 'Die, Nicky, die.' For Godsake, you'd think this match was really important. Could we hold on? From here? Get a life, will you. Barely five minutes on and Sander and company watch a regulation corner float gently to beanpole Weir at the far post and Campbell can't miss the second header: 1–1.

Slowly now, Gary Mac begins to start challenging for us in the over-33 midfield category, and even Berger, perpetual passenger in derby games when it starts to get rough, actually starts sticking his foot in. Steven Gerrard, at right-back, looks as if *he* wants to catapult the fragile young Israeli, Tal, into the Centenary upper tier. Level at half-time and, unlike most recent derbies, it's a real football match.

The Fellahs in Front agree: we're fortunate, really, because *they* have come to play and have missed good chances. They're impressed by Gazza: 'Fuckin' class.' But in the second half Liverpool start to take over. Heskey now looks a positive steal at just eleven million pounds. He works, he holds up, he goes past people, and he scores goals. Glorious goals. This one, whipped passed *their* Gerrard in goal, is a long-range stunner, and it turns the game. Now Everton are hanging on. Smicer comes on for Robbie, strolling around at first, but he soon starts causing problems for their lumpens at the back. It's a clear penalty on him after a 50-yard dash from halfway: Graveson off, Berger scores from the spot – emphatically.

The Kop is now in rapture, the Fellahs in Front positively glowing, no doubt thinking about the local goading possibilities which now lie deliciously ahead. Against just ten, we play it really cleverly and they never look like getting back in. In the end it's been comfortable and we hug this thought on the way back to the delirious Flattie where the new pub manager, daft get, had earlier hung up his Everton scarf. It's gone now.

OPENING GAMBITS

The opening league and cup exhanges for Liverpool are now complete and, let's be honest, we have made a muddled start. We have suffered real setbacks on the road, especially when playing south of the Watford Gap, but we have also done well in matches at home that we have struggled to win in the past few seasons. Michael still looks unsure, but Heskey has done well, surprising his doubters and possibly himself. Robbie is a 'maybe' so far. Barmby and Babbel look promising additions, but Ziege still has plenty to prove. Steven Gerrard already looks like a frightening, if fragile, talent. Our defence needs to settle. Liverpool's solid home form is the real comfort, but winning well in L4 is no title promise on its own. We end this opening phase with a hard-won League Cup success at home to Chelsea, Robbie scoring the winner. Eleven league games played and we are a respectable third, three points behind Arsenal and United, the usual suspects. But around the corner is our old Nemesis, black November, which begins at fancy Leeds. We will need to work much harder than we have so far to keep it all on track.

3. INTO THE TUNNEL

4 NOVEMBER: MARK VIDUKA 4, LIVERPOOL 3

A couple of times in the Roy Evans years, poor league results in November had given us much too much to do later, so we need to be on our guard now. And this is not a good start. Apparently, the new-look *Financial Times* broke ground this weekend by using the 'F' word, unexpurgated, on its front page – and above the crease at that. The reference was to George W. Bush's Republican presidential election 'strategy' of DFIU – 'Don't Fuck It Up'. We could do with a bit of that now at Liverpool.

Elland Road these days is a strange mix of the old-style malevolence and the newer consumer football mentality. Howling at any half-baked refereeing decision seems to be a requirement of local season-ticket purchase here, ever since Leeds were denied the title in 1971 because of some admittedly dodgy whistle work. The words 'siege mentality' come easily to mind. Plans to build a new ice-hockey rink and sports arena nearby – a Leeds Sporting Club – now seem to be on hold as recent PLC profits have dipped. Manager O'Leary has spent, but wants to do more (who doesn't?). A result in Milan for Leeds next week and it's a second phase Champions League windfall in West Yorkshire. In the long run, success for other English clubs on the continent, with only a few exceptions, is bad for your own club. It raises their profile, and thus the image, the finances and the morale of direct rivals. In a harsh global marketplace, you don't need it, believe me. So, next week we want Milan to hammer Leeds. And today *we* need to win this.

Actually, our fan visits to Elland Road are usually fairly benign affairs, mainly because of the shared Manchester United antipathy. On the important matter of hating football rivals, the Argentinian writer,

Osvaldo Soriano, recalled a Boca Juniors fan asking to be wrapped in a rival River Plate flag on his deathbed so he could celebrate, with his final breath, the death of 'one of them'. Leeds fans in a similar spot would probably seek out a red shirt marked 'Cantona' or 'Beckham'.

The consumer mentality at Leeds comes mainly from the huge new East Stand, part spectator container, part exotic family shopping centre. But it is confirmed best by the guy who does the on-pitch 'entertainment' here. Imploring home supporters to 'Sing your hearts out for the lads' seems like an oxymoron; a major contradiction in terms. If we ever get this sort of sub-human US marketing guff at Anfield it surely will be time to call the whole thing off. Rick Parry and George S., please take note.

We have arrived here in good heart, with five straight wins, with Robbie at last getting a goal, the League Cup winner against Chelsea. Perversely, Houllier now decides that Robbie needs more bench-time, and so Smicer is in. Murphy keeps his place after impressing against Chelsea and so does Carragher. McAllister starts. Michael is still nursing his sore head from Derby away, so our bench reads: Fowler, Barmby, Gerrard, Henchoz. Which is nice. Leeds also have injuries (what, in football?) so O'Leary and the papers have been bleating, as usual, about the woes of it all. Their team still looks strong, though, with Bowyer, Bakke, Dacourt, Viduka and Alan Smith making up a very tasty front end.

We start by threatening to stroll it and two headed early goals from free kicks, Hyypia and Ziege, set up an easy win. Ex-Red Matteo is at centre-back for them, so this reversal from our Evans days of conceding in the air from free kicks seems perfectly understandable. If we get to half-time at 2–0 this is all over, no danger. Then, the Ziege moment occurs. Apparently, his name means 'goat' in German. (Really?) We have wondered already at his too-casual approach to defending: he strolls back from attacks and he gives opponents space to cross. Now, he fatally delays a routine clearance and that talented little monster, Alan Smith, charges it down. The ball could go anywhere, but it *does* go, of course, straight to Mark Viduka's feet, just inside our box. It was the great Real Madrid forward, Alfred Di Stefano, who said an open football net was an 'unforgivable crime' meriting immediate punishment. Viduka scores: 1–2.

Houllier and Phil Thompson, like us, will have said at half-time (add expletives for Thommo): 'Look, give nothing away at the start of this half. Quieten the crowd and we can get more goals here. Simple.' Patrik Berger must have been in the bogs during this little speech, because immediately after the break he lets Kelly dance past him on our left and Viduka, unmarked by goat or man, heads in the cross at the near post.

We still come back. Ziege and Berger down the left, a cut-back to Smicer on the penalty spot who cleverly threads in the finish. But our problem is that Leeds are now playing hard into the gaping black hole between Ziege and Hyypia. We can't hang on. While the goat is briefly off for treatment, Viduka twists in the box and takes out four defenders and Westerveld, and scores his hat-trick goal. Three shots, three goals. Now we are in trouble, and Viduka – who else – soon scrambles an (offside) winner from the same area: 4–3. In all of this, Sander has made only one save.

Losing away, especially like this, is even worse than losing at home – much worse. Walking through these chattering, smiling faces is like turning up alone at the wrong party, or being abroad and stupidly not understanding any of the local language. And if you now want a drink here you have to 'congratulate' the locals or at least accept their mealy-mouthed commiserations. If they give a shit, that is. Me, 0–2 down and 4–3 winners? I wouldn't care. Now we must go to little Liberec, in the Czech Republic, for the UEFA Cup, feeling down and needing a decent performance.

RICH MAN AND PRAWN SANDWICH FIASCO

Juventus and Barca are out, Manchester United successfully into the second phase of the Champions League. And are they happy, the men from Manchester? Far from it. The Old Trafford cognoscenti gave the home boys some stick for looking less than convincing in a 1–0 win against Dynamo Kiev. Captain Roy Keane, on £50,000 a week, responds by suggesting that some of the corporate 'prawn sandwich' set at OT 'can't even spell football, never mind understand it'. Wise words, Roy. Andy Walsh, from United's independent fan group, IMUSA, calls for a noise detector on every seat at OT. 'Quiet' fans should be chucked out, he argues. At Anfield, virtually all of the Centenary upper tier would have to go. By the way, United still haven't conceded a goal this season to a *British* player. Scary.

MICHAEL'S RETURN

Labouring, we beat tiny Liberec 3–2 away in the UEFA Cup. Ex-Red Ray Houghton, back in the Channel 5 studio, clearly cannot believe it is Liverpool he's watching here. The Reds' passing is slack, and there's no urgency or bite. Robbie isn't in it, Hamann is sleep-walking. At least a *Flat Iron* flag is spotted in the 'home' corner. Good lads. When the Boy Wonder emerges from the bench he nets after being on for just 21 seconds. Channel 5 commentator, the mad patriot Jonathon Pearce, almost wets himself with England dreams as a result. At 3–1 to us

(Barmby, Heskey, Michael) the tie is truly dead, but conceding a second in the dying minutes, to Breda from the edge of the box, is no decent way to end this. In truth, it has been a thoroughly unprofessional night, and the Champions League effluent joins us now in the next UEFA round. Some garbage: Barcelona, among others, are dropping down. Europe starts here.

19 NOVEMBER: TOTTENHAM HOTSPUR 2, LIVERPOOL 1

We beat Coventry City at home, 4–1, which sounds easy but it still had its little tremors. Davy Thompson scores a cracker for them, and Heskey two for us, to wrap up the points. Now it is Tottenham, N17, the back of beyond.

Spurs, like a lot of city clubs in England – like *us* – are probably almost completely divorced now from the area where the club is based. Poor, declining neighbourhoods, black and Asian, now host the pretty exclusive entertainment palace which is White Hart Lane. Well-padded white supporters come in for games in their 4x4s down the M10 – or, otherwise, miserably, on the tube from nicer parts of London. Certainly, the young black and white kids who used to stalk the Shelf in the 1970s, and then came mirthlessly looking for trouble after matches here, are no longer part of the furniture. The Spurs crowd these days looks like a painting – and often sounds like one. But the lights, the screens, the green and the warmth of the stands at least make you forget the gloomy abyss outside.

The terraced residential areas here are that usual mix of part-gentrified, part-petrified London-edge housing stock. This is home to Mark Perryman, new-left football activist and entrepreneur, Chair of the England Members Club; and Ann Coddington, writer of *One of the Lads*, a recent tome about women and football. We are here for our pre-match briefing. They are Spurs season-ticket holders, six-hundred quid's worth, and six rows behind the Tottenham dug-out. Mark, another string to his bow, runs the *Philosophy Football* T-shirt business. We suggest a new Bob Paisley shirt, 'Don't drink the tea', to recall uncle's legendary suspicions of European football travel. Mark, strangely, is vaguely encouraging.

The talk here, and in the press, is of 'Spurs in crisis', but we don't fall for that. Spurs are strong at home, often poor away; a bit like the current Liverpool. Of course, George Graham is not much loved here, and there is moaning about Wenger's Arsenal playing like Spurs, and about Graham now peddling his sell-by-date Highbury ideas down the Lane. What is really gnawing away here is the idea that Spurs – one of the '80s 'Big Five' – now lack allure and ambition, cannot catch up with the new order, and that Chairman Sugar has deep pockets but short arms. A home-fan protest is even promised today. Let's hope we give them good reason.

The walk along the gloomy High Road in the November rain for a 4 p.m. Sunday TV kick-off at Spurs is about as apocalyptic as it gets at the top level in England. Perhaps only Manchester's Moss Side in the winter has a residential match. Here, it is mainly sprawling off-licences and monumental nightclubs, along with dilapidated small 'businesses' and grimly lit bars and shops. The sorry trudge of football punters has a truly Orwellian feel about it. So, too, does the unexpectedly thorough body-search outside the away end.

We boldly play Smicer and Traore on the left, with Henchoz at the back, and start with Fowler and Owen up front for the suspended Heskey. Barmby ran himself soft for England on Wednesday in Italy (the dope) so he's on the bench with the ever-fragile Steven Gerrard. Berger has gone to the US for surgery after getting injured at Leeds – 'Hopefully for a heart transplant,' according, cruelly, to my mate Steve. Ziege has a knee problem (and much more, if you ask me). Spurs have some local young kids in their team, including Ledley King, a strapping centre-back, playing in midfield.

At the start we are in charge in a poor game and we score early, Fowler passing into the net Murphy's cleverly hooked deflection. We miss a few more, naturally. Tactically, we still look odd: we have no real full-backs to talk of, but we are resolutely 4–4–2 against their wider 3–5–2, with the lightweight Smicer and the inexperienced Traore trying to deal with Rebrov and Spurs' best man, Carr, on our left. But we are pretty comfortable until real problems start to come down the Liverpool right, where Rebrov has suddenly appeared. 'Keep it fuckin' tight, Reds,' comes from behind me, but it's too late. Henchoz gives it away on the touch-line on the half-hour and Ray Clemence's lad Stephen (the traitorous bastard) is put away wide. His low cross beats a diving Westerveld for pace and Ferdinand bundles it in from inside the six-yard box, in front of the watching Traore.

It's that weird away sound to a home goal we have now become so used to this season: silence all around us, a split-second, and then distant but loud humming, like the angry sea in a shell. I look at my shoes, depressed; this is how I deal with it. They have had no shots before now, and it's 1–1. Been here before? It gets worse. Clemence, put away again from a back-heel from Rebrov – possibly offside – and a precise high cross this time finds Sherwood in the box between Henchoz and Traore. Everyone can see this is coming, this cross. There's no danger of Sander coming out to claim it, or to batter Sherwood senseless, of course, no danger at all. Failing this, Jimmy should bundle into the Spurs man, push him, do *anything*, but instead he allows Sherwood a free jump and Sander, stuck on his line, has no chance. We go in 2–1 down, the crowd now well into the game, and the Tottenham protest (ha ha) terminally on hold. George Graham? A genius, obviously.

Smicer has now started to stink, drawing out all the 'shithouse' taunts from those travelling Reds who think he doesn't fancy it, won't stick his foot in. Carr, on the other hand, is now playing like Roberto fucking Carlos and after an arcing run he chips one exquisitely onto the far post, Westerveld beaten. Carr's on four grand here: they're joking, ain't they? A week after this he will finally sign an extension which multiplies his money by five. Smicer, for one, ought to have a cut.

It tails off, this scruffy affair, the same old story. People in front of us can barely watch now: they quiver with frustration, or rage. We all do. Fifteen goals conceded already away. We're *soft* away from home, is the truth. No heart. No steel. That's the kindest thing which is said around here. 'Fucking disgraceful.' 'Fucking fainthearted shits.' 'Cheats.' People can't help it. It *feels* so bad. After the whistle, Hyypia gives his stupid double-thumb downward loser signal – the prat. And then they slink off.

Later, on TV, Houllier is really mad with Henchoz, you can see it. A row Z job and instead he tries to *pass* his way out, and gives the ball away. An international making a juvenile's mistake, which has invited Spurs back in. Houllier calls our defending 'childish'; it is a headmaster talking, slipper at the ready. In the Victoria pub on Scotland Green afterwards the Tottenham lot are beaming, of course. Protest, what protest? 'We only had kids out there.' And now we have to go to play Olympiakos in Greece, in the UEFA, with our arses well and truly hanging out.

MAC – THE SPANISH KNIFE

Macca is back with Real Madrid, at Leeds, Champions League second phase. Does he make a mess of the Peacocks, whose fans stupidly start by booing him? It's embarrassing, I tell you. A 2–0 *thrashing* by Real. Leeds don't know who to mark, can't find their men, as the ball pings around them. They also boo Figo, these Yorkshire football connoisseurs. Radebe, a man among narks at Leeds, has just won the FIFA fair-play award for his work with poor South African kids and for his campaign against racism. Top man. He must have some interesting dressing-room conversations at Elland Road with the you-know-whos.

SANDERS SPEAKS

Westerveld's personal website says we should be hoofing the ball clear more when we have to. Future coaching material, clearly. Apparently, he has made *no* mistakes yet this season. Official.

23 NOVEMBER, UEFA CUP: OLYMPIAKOS 2, LIVERPOOL 2

We are still sore from the Spurs loss, and the Greeks are supposed to be hot stuff, controversially knocked out of the Champions League, and 15 matches unbeaten at home in Europe. We fear the worst, but somehow they just don't get going. Instead, they look slow and uninterested, not in love with their manager. For us, Henchoz has been relegated after the Spurs fiasco, and Babbel is moved to centre-back. Houllier has made some not-too-subtle pre-match references to the need for strong refereeing here. We get it, too, from a friendly Dutch giant with a beer-belly. We also gradually begin to see that this is actually no footballing hotspot tonight – and Barmby scores just before half-time after Heskey heads on Carragher's long throw. All right, it's not pretty, but it's a vital goal, and Barmby now has three in three away legs in Europe. A few minutes later, Michael, with clear space to run into behind their lumbering centre-backs, ominously finds absolutely *nothing* in the accelerator. But it's 1–0 to us at half-time.

In the second half we come on stronger, Heskey brilliantly and bravely leading the line: Barmby hits the bar; Staunton, on for the naive Traore, the post. Then, out of nothing for them, a stunning scissors-kick equaliser for Alexandris. No matter: Gerrard scores with a header from our next corner. Now, their arse really goes. Smicer, on for Michael, has a one-on-one in the clear – and hits the post. The locals give the home lot real grief now, and they visibly give up, they really do. They are disgusted with themselves, probably a Mediterranean thing. But you know what happens next: this is Liverpool in 2000, after all, everybody's home banker. Two minutes of injury time, and a high ball into the box is nodded on and squeezed in from the far post, across Carragher and Westerveld, by Alexandris again. It could have been 6–1. Instead, we have murdered them: 2–2.

WHEN OPPOSITES COLLIDE

The Yin and Yang of football: black, white; attack, defence; home, away; foreign, domestic.

THE RACE GAME

Last week at Spurs some Reds near us started the old hissing business, mimicking the sound of gas escaping. A few even started singing the 'Auschwitz' song, before being booed down or swamped by other Liverpool singing. On this score, I saw a letter last year – sent to me by the *Kick it Out* people – from a Jewish Spurs season-ticket holder describing the horrible abuse he and his family had received from some Liverpool fans at Tottenham. This kind of stuff is never really far below the surface, not far. Songey, Emile and Titi have made it more difficult, recently, for open racists at Liverpool, and we have even attracted to the Kop some Asian supporters from outside the city. But the club does the minimum here: get out the 'Kick Racism Out' Liverpool team poster, a page in the match programme, and there's racism solved for another season. John Barnes in his autobiography recognised how little football really does to oppose racism and change attitudes in Liverpool – or anywhere.

When Stan Collymore, at Aston Villa, faced what he claimed was racist abuse from one of his old Liverpool buddies at Villa Park a couple of seasons ago, the PFA told the two of them, later, to just kiss and make up. By this time the accused, Steve Harkness, was laid up with an injury delivered, of course, by Stan. Darcus Howe points out how grotesque it is that the game and the British press actually congratulate players such as the brave Heskey who, unlike Stan or the volatile Vieira, stoically gets on with the job under this sort of abuse; the 'Negro' turning the other cheek, you see. He recommends, instead, that black players should walk off the field and invite their white colleagues to follow. Start a Stephen Lawrence-like movement in football. Deduct points. Suspend clubs from the league. *Rumble.* 'Black players should not allow their silence to be bought,' he argues. He has a point. But who, exactly, I fear, would follow their proud example and their just walk to the touch-line?

26 NOVEMBER: NEWCASTLE UNITED 2, LIVERPOOL 1

Getting the right balance between attack and defence; it's crucial in top-level football. Last season Liverpool played some real garbage away from home, we really did. But we *won* games. We won at Arsenal, for example, by stealing a goal through Camara and then just whacking the ball anywhere in the second half. It was embarrassing: but we *won*. In the mid-'70s Liverpool hardly scored at all away from home in some seasons, but we kept on winning titles. Just 15 away goals in 1976–77. Grinding out results, locking up shop. Championships piled up. 'An efficient machine', they called us, a defensive machine, and no one really loved us. It's much harder to do this sort of thing now. Home forwards are much cuter, for one thing. For another, in the age of the fan consumer and endless live TV coverage, you can't hide behind a 'win means everything' mentality any more. You have to 'entertain' now in the Super Sunday glare of Sky's FA Premier League. Bob Paisley would have hated it, of course. Rightly so.

Houllier is blaming our 'little problem' (five away defeats already, count them, and three on the bounce) on not getting the balance right between attack and defence. 'The team is in a phase of progress, of improvement. The problem is there is a fine line between good attacking and efficient defending and at the moment we do not have the balance right,' he says after our latest defeat at Newcastle. 'It won't change the way I want us to play. We just need to work a little harder to get it right.' So this is his defence: we are more attacking this season, so we are losing it at the back. The chemistry needs a bit more tinkering, more alkaline, less acid.

We don't fully buy this. We have often played lousy away, and we are just making costly mistakes; the goalkeeper is making no saves. Carragher, now at left-back, evidently touring all positions, drops a clanger here after three minutes to let in Solano, who scores, naturally. After this, it is all uphill: concede a goal early anywhere in the Premiership and it is hard to get back. We just couldn't today. And note this date, 26 November 2000, just over a third of the way through the league programme: today Houllier and Arsène Wenger publicly conceded the league title to United. It could be sixth-form psychology, of course, but it is more likely the new football rationality. It stinks, naturally, and we shouldn't accept it.

FOREIGN AFFAIRS

Chelsea, like us, lose away again, this time at Everton. They *hate* it away. They are disappearing without trace, and the Radio 5 airwaves are hot to David Mellor, every Chelsea fan's mate, obviously. Fingers point at their foreign players (only the spiky Wise is British), their perplexed non-English speaking new manager, Ranieri, and at their gutless struggles away from Stamford Bridge. Away from home in the FA Premier League, fans close at hand, is not like some of the stuff you see on TV from Italy, and especially from Spain. The lowly home teams there don't dig in and scrap like they tend to do here, supporters and players breathing down your neck, abusing you, messing with your body and your head. Pires at Arsenal and Rebrov of Spurs have also both remarked on the 'frightening' nature of the physical side to the English game. David O'Leary blew a wicked kiss this weekend to Arsenal's Pires from the Leeds bench and then told him to 'fuck off'. Later, the Frenchman completely lost it in this battle with the sly coach. Arsenal lost the war, too, 1–0. Welcome to England.

29 NOVEMBER, WORTHINGTON CUP: STOKE CITY 0, LIVERPOOL 8

How do you read the League Cup these days? In the '80s, I'll be honest, we were very happy to win it, very happy. Back then you aimed to win every competition you entered; that was the accepted professional mantra. We enjoyed it, too: another London day out, more silver for the shelves. Rotation back in the '80s was something for crops or helicopters. Today, with the Champions League and squad systems to the fore, the Worthington is strictly B-list for the top clubs. Man United use it to field their kids and itchy fringe players, Arsenal the same. Even Fulham field weaker sides, a sign of Jean Tigana's continental disregard for any cup football. *We*, however, do not have that luxury. So whisper it: we are favourites for the also-rans cup and the final is in Cardiff.

This visit to Stoke is laced with all the signals outlined above: we rest Hamann, Gerrard, Barmby, Heskey and Westerveld, and Ritchie Partridge – a tiny Irish right-winger, a Davy Thompson double without the psychosis – makes his début. But we also look suspiciously strong at the back and in midfield – and Robbie needs goals. Stoke are a decent club fallen behind, League Cup winners back in 1971. Today they are an Icelandic Division Two franchise sited in a gossamer and chilly new ground. This new English footballing colonisation means that this match is also being beamed live to Reykjavic, where Liverpool – and perhaps now Stoke, themselves – do battle with Iceland for national team status.

This is a stark story of the haves and have-nots. A few years ago we would have come here, full-strength, and worried about coming away intact. Now, with the sort of loot clubs like Liverpool have to spend, this really should be a stroll. And it is: Robbie gets three, makes three more. Everyone else who really wants to also notches, after a shaky start in which Arphexad shows us exactly why the unconvincing Sander is still our first choice in goal. Ziege makes some great passes – and *no* tackles, as usual. But we are faster, stronger, better – and the home side gallantly refuses to kick us. Long before the finish Stoke are demoralised. Even before Robbie takes a penalty to finish the job, the scoreboard here shouts 'Goal!' – and then, asking for it, 9–0. By the end, three sides of the ground are empty.

My mate Alec, a Stokie, suggests later that in earlier times good professionals would have stopped at, say, five in a game like this: a sort of collective code of honour to limit the humiliation of other pros who they are likely to meet again on the way down. The new individualism means, instead, a real tanking. Cath says, football-speak firmly in charge, that actually, 'The most pleasing thing about this win is the "nil" part.' Since we have managed *eight* – a record Reds away win – we all agree that this risks taking defensive priorities to extremes.

In the (not so) Jolly Potters pub in Hartshill, a spit from the old Victoria Ground, the locals take it all in good heart, pointing to the early chances for Stoke and the fact that the cost of one Barmby easily makes up two or three teams for a proud club like Stoke these days. There are also acid comments here about the Icelandic links. On the walls are pictures of a local League Cup win against a full-strength Man United in the early-'90s. They hint, silently, at a harsher new age. 'We have a chance, mebee, to get close to the Coventrys or the Derbys,' says a glum Stokie on the bus later. 'But we have no chance now of getting near these buggers.' Too true, I'm afraid, unless you have cash to burn: we next play Al Fayed's Fulham at Anfield, Houllier versus Tigana. *Allez les Rouges*, as they say in Huyton. The Millennium Stadium beckons.

STRIKERS

Titi Camara is something of a hero here, a bundle of tricks and flicks, a fans' favourite who got our season going last year with a fine goal in a great early win at Leeds. He also played heroically against West Ham at home – and scored – immediately after the death of his father. We often ignore the real problems players have when they cross the white line. We assume their minds and bodies are clear, so respect is due here. But this season he has annoyed Houllier and he has now been cast into the outer darkness as a result. He is a rotation victim. We are hardly so spilling with creative inspiration in this squad that we can afford to let a Camara leave lightly – but it looks like he's heading away anyway, possibly to Celtic or to follow Songey, who has just joined West Ham. Houllier is talking already about a replacement.

7 DECEMBER, UEFA CUP: LIVERPOOL 2, OLYMPIAKOS 0 (AGG. 4–2)

The highlight of the 3–0 league win against Charlton at Anfield is a dust-up between Heskey and Rufus, our 'baby' attacker showing Houllier just how tough he can be. Charlton deserve better, after Ziege forced an early own-goal for Liverpool, but Smicer changes the game when he comes on late for a sluggish (again) Fowler and he chips in a lovely cross from the right for Heskey to head home into his favourite Kop goal. Smicer and Gerrard then combine to produce a late close-in gimme for Babbel.

Now it's back to Europe. Best European nights at Anfield? *May 1965*: Liverpool 3, Inter Milan 1, European Cup semi-final first leg. Shankly sends out Inter to the Kop end, where they are blown back inside by the noise. *October 1973*: Liverpool 1, Red Star Belgrade 2, European Cup second round. A sublime footballing lesson from the East, which we learned and put to good effect in Europe later. *March 1977*: Liverpool 3, St Etienne 1, European Cup quarter-final, second leg. Supersub Fairclough's night, an 84th-minute clincher against fantastic opponents. There are others, of course: we are going through them in the Flattie on a filthy night – which is what fans are supposed to do on occasions like this. It is 16 long years since we last won a European trophy.

Cheap tickets and live BBC coverage means that the Reds in Europe is much more of a local Merseyside event: passionate, committed, the

Kop in standing mode. Nobody complains. These feelings are clear in the way that 'You'll Never Walk Alone' is positively bawled out by the Kop before the game. The Greeks have a good contingent here and they are loud and orchestrated in their support, adding to the atmosphere. But this is too comfortable a win to be a really great European night. Heskey, with Smicer, Barmby and Murphy playing behind in a new 4–2–3–1 formation, scores halfway through the first half, meaning the visitors must get at least two goals to survive. Instead, with Smicer to the fore, Barmby is put through by Murphy and scores early in the second half, and it's over.

Players such as Vladdy Smicer still divide fans in England. In this city, if you take strategic action to avoid a full-blooded tackle with any opponent who may be twice your size, you are still a shithouse, a gobshite, no doubt. You can still get respect here simply by fronting up, spilling blood, you don't need to do very much more. Smicer has talked about the 'flying tackles' and the 'hundred miles an hour' style of the English game and he has tried to adapt. Houllier has seen this: 'He is unfairly criticised because he is not physical. Maybe people don't like Vladimir because he does not kick people,' he says. 'He just kicks the ball.' Smicer has real pace and talent, and he does get in sly little kicks and shoves when he wants to, but he also sensibly refuses reckless bravery and to worthlessly run his guts out – or to milk the crowd. Ziege reluctantly comes on as a late sub tonight and then, very publicly, gives his shirt to a wheelchair case at the end of the match, inevitably to general acclaim. *We* are suspicious of Ziege. He doesn't work and is too flash by half; someone who arrived as a 'world-class' left-back and is now being kept out of the side by Carragher, a limited right-sided foot soldier. And he thinks, this new German, that he is doing okay.

EUROPEAN PARLIAMENT HEARINGS ON FOOTBALL HOOLIGANISM

Labour MEP Glyn Ford has called these London hearings on hooliganism in order to assess where we are today, and to look forward to Japan and Korea in 2002, who have representatives at today's event. I'm gently hungover from the travel and ale from Olympiakos last night at Anfield. The event turns out, thankfully, to be a glorified press conference: a small room in Queen Anne's Gate, with empty seats and a small audience, but the debate is good. Someone says this will not be a talking shop but it *feels* . . . well, like a talking shop.

My session is about the future, and Northumbria Chief Constable Ron Hogg first makes the reasonable, if hardly original, point that we must get a grip of the media, which starts stoking things up well before tournaments begin. Why, Fox TV were even pumping him before Euro 2000 with nonsense about the English hooligan 'generals' and the military precision of England's travelling naughty support. Of course much of this sort of thing had actually emanated in the first place *from* the British police themselves, but no matter.

We end by agreeing that a lot of progress has actually been made in England – but that there were obvious costs: pricing, loss of atmosphere, the occasional over-management of fans, and the 'revival' of lower-league tribalisms. In fact, given the high general level of public violence in this country, the relative calm at football in England can only tell you about the 'success' the game has had recently here in separating itself, American style, from some of the strife on the streets.

In suggesting that, perhaps, we need to look at how we can better manage stadia in ways which allow people to express themselves – at least short of using racist abuse and hooliganism as tools – I am soon accused by the press here, and by FA representatives, of seeking 'fuck-off' areas in stadia. They seem to think that football people now don't use this sort of talk (and much worse). Or that journalists or footballers or virtually anyone in the game doesn't use this sort of talk (and much worse). Their answer here, of course, is that man-to-man swearing, well, that's okay. But swearing in front of women and kids – it's not on. I tell them that an ejection policy which is *really* based on chucking out fans for swearing would soon clear all grounds of a good proportion of decent male fans – and some women, too. We leave it there.

10 DECEMBER: LIVERPOOL 0, IPSWICH TOWN 1

We learn some important things here in the rain: that Houllier really does value the League Cup over any possible Liverpool title hopes; that Ipswich are a battling side which plays good, intelligent football and with whom you take no liberties; that our second-string forward combination is now named Fowler and Owen; and that the Liverpool manager sometimes gets things badly wrong. Gerrard and Heskey are rested, rotation-style, and Michael and Robbie, still both far from match fit and never proven as a partnership, play together up front. The result is a disjointed display and missed chances. Michael messes up an open goal in the first half and Houllier will return to this theme, these missed chances, in his own defence later. We are 0–1 down at half-time after Marcus Stewart coolly rounds Henchoz and a hapless Westerveld just before the whistle.

Rogan Taylor, just back from a football trip to Brazil, cheers us on the Kop at the break with news that the stadiums there are falling down, the top Brazilian clubs are corrupt and deep in debt, but that club football in Brazil could also be the next big thing. It is unlikely, on this showing, that *we* will be. During the interval, too, the debates really rage on the Kop: little clusters gather to both abuse and defend Robbie, Michael, Houllier and 'that fuckin' rotation shit'. People are feverish, deep in proper, passionate football talk, just as it should be.

Smicer replaces the injured Barmby, and Heskey finally comes on for the last half-hour, for Michael – and, of course, he immediately misses a sitter. Only our new £5.5 million Croatian midfielder Igor Biscan's impressive first 20 minutes for the Reds as a sub gives any cause for real optimism. In fact, this has been like any of Roy Evans's home defeats to lesser rivals – except we have played little decent football today. Magilton, an ex-Red who is still in love with Liverpool a decade after he left us, is absolutely outstanding for Ipswich. They have, deservedly, done us and we are now sixth to their third.

What is clear is that Houllier does not really *know* anymore who his best eleven are. In fact, the whole concept of the 'best eleven' makes no sense to him. The secret, according to Houllier, is to choose the most appropriate team, given fitness, fixtures and forthcoming matches; even if it gives your opponents hope. The second thing is that Ipswich were actually *happy* today that they were facing Fowler and Owen. This is the extent of the crisis. The fearsome twins, the urchin poacher and your daughter's ideal boyfriend, together scare no one at the moment. Why should they? *This* is the extent of the current Liverpool crisis.

CUP PROSPECTS

In the Flattie later, we glumly watch the FA Cup draw. The FA's 'big idea' is to have the draw made by two *rowers*, Redgrave and Pinsent. Does anyone know why these oarsmen should make the draw for the world's most famous and oldest knock-out *football* competition? I thought as much. With a win today, we would have been looking forward to this daft draw, confident, expectant of a good run, ready to take on all-comers. Instead, we now look for comfort and hope: to be at home against a Morecambe or a Scunthorpe, a Leyton Orient or even the surviving Northwich Vics. Of course it's pathetic. We miss all of these, and draw Rotherham at Anfield, to relieved cheers. We now expect to be in the fourth round, rotation permitting.

Our midweek League Cup tie with Fulham turns out to be a muddy tease, with the Anfield green by now looking more like brown Aintree sludge (will it ever stop raining?). Owen finally scores in extra time from Smicer's cross, and then we get two comfort goals, Vladdy himself and Barmby, another late sub. Three-nil is flattering, but we have been solid, and Smicer and Gerrard have done well. But Tigana, more than Liverpool, is trying to play a cerebral passing game. We look a little crude in comparison. Stevie G. later does a great TV interview, all nervous scouse guttural and looking at his feet. On Radio 5 Alan Green rubbishes us as usual. But how *tired* will we now be on Sunday, at OT?

VALERY'S FREEDOM ROAD

The Russian international, Valery Karpin, has won his labour court case on discrimination in Madrid against the Spanish football federation. Karpin argued that because Russia has a special relations agreement with the EU, the Spanish authorities had no right to limit non-EU places at Spanish clubs to five. This constitutes discrimination. It will not end here, of course, but this ruling potentially opens the way to free movement for all players in Europe. Maybe the troubled smaller clubs in England will now pick up a few more value-for-money Latvians and Serbs. Meanwhile, we have other things to consider: the UEFA draw has teamed us up in February with Serie A leaders, Roma.

17 DECEMBER: MANCHESTER UNITED 0, LIVERPOOL 1

Welcome to the £1 billion football Corporation. But on Sir Matt Busby Way, where Lou Macari's chip shop and the United off-licence is doing a roaring trade at 11 a.m. for this midday kick-off, you won't find too much trace of the new United terracotta army, the OT merchandise ground troops. Here it's the great unshaved, cans of lager in the fists and baseball caps, but the talk is still about Europe: grounds, future trips, problems with the police. United is now a global business and a fully European club, and also a convincing England alternative to many, even despite Beckham's recent promotion to national team captain. A Liverpool fans' coach passes this grizzly crew and catches a half-full can and multiple 'fuck offs, while local touts try to buy and sell: £120 will secure entry to a match we haven't won for ten long years. It may be worth that much to leave before the end today.

Salford Quays, not long ago little more than a depressing brownfield *homage* to Lowry and Engels, now does a passable Seattle impersonation, all smoked glass and steel, and the new tubular redevelopment of OT is also mind-boggling. Stripped of most of its surrounding neighbours, OT now stands proudly alone, a football stadium absent-mindedly tacked on to a gigantic new megastore, which now relentlessly sucks in customers at the back of the old United scoreboard end. The statue of Sir Matt Busby still stands aloft here, now calling in the faithful who have travelled from all points today and are anxious to purchase a United 'Monopoly' game or, perhaps, a tasteful Ryan Giggs mirror (nice). Distance travelled converts to merchandise cash for clubs like United and us, and that's one reason, of course, why the club suits don't listen too hard to calls from some supporters to market their clubs more strongly to *local* fans.

We have a predictable, visceral fear and loathing of this enemy. Today the Manchester bizzies are out in force, riot hats on board, because this one has got a little lively later over the past few years. Outside the ground, on the stadium apron, it's been Liverpool song-free but once inside, away from the preying hordes, it is an instant and collective release into 'Scouser Tommy' and the rest. But it is not an angry, aled-up visiting crowd, this early morning one; it is, instead, a group who are deeply resentful and frustrated by the current power, success and image of their hosts and desperate for something out of this game. There *is* envy here.

Did I imply we are sober? Because famous Reds fan, John Mackin, arrives to sit next to me, direct from a vodka-still in Salford and eyes looking in different directions. He heartily joins in the tasteless Gary Neville song, apologising for its daft anal core, and then points to the massive United banners in the Stretford End, which illustrate *their* obsession with *us*. The United Independent Supporters boys have huge banners across the distant top balcony of the Stretford End advertising the 'Red Army of Mancunia'. A blood-red 'You're not famous anymore' number has been lovingly prepared for us, turned over at half-time to reveal a more pointed 'Ten years and counting' – we last won the title, and even a match at OT, back in 1990. This now looks like a real supporters' end, has the air of fan ownership. It's hard to imagine the same at Anfield.

In the Liverpool corner, everyone stands, a sign of the importance and tension of this fixture. The Hillsborough and Munich chants which were once exchanged during the really poisoned years in the '80s have now virtually gone and we are down to: 'Shit on the cockneys' and 'Eighteen times' (cleverly) from us and 'You'll win fuck all again' (pointedly) from them. The team news favours us: United, kings of squad strength, have injuries and only one available striker, the loyal and dangerous Solksjaer, while Houllier has opted for two forwards, Owen joining Heskey. Gerrard and Biscan get the crucial central midfield jobs again. The respective benches also offer hope: we have Robbie, Gary Mac and Smicer, experience and quality in hand, while they must rely on the untried Chadwick, Greening and O'Shea. Houllier has been talking up our lack of experience and the youth of our recent formations, but we look stronger overall today.

The playing pattern becomes immediately apparent: we are happy to let United have the ball and try to catch them on the break. Heskey will try to hold the ball up while Murphy and Barmby double up wide on Giggs and Beckham, and mostly it works because they play in front of our back four for the first period. Westerveld also looks nerve-free, solid for once. Steven Gerrard is in charge of the centre, Keane strangely subdued. As the first half moves on we begin to make chances, gaining in confidence. They look edgy. With more control, Michael could have scored a couple before Gary Neville handles, needlessly, on the edge of their box on the stroke of half-time. Danny Murphy curls the free kick miles wide of the United wall and over a crouching Babbel into the corner of the goal where Barthez ought to be. He is, blissfully and inexplicably, absent.

Paul Heywood of the *Daily Telegraph* later described the sliver of Liverpool fans at this moment as like looking down the spout of a boiling kettle. John Mackin is squeezing me so tight, breathing is difficult. The lads in front are tumbling over seats: older fellahs behind are wide-eyed and beaming, shaking our shoulders in merry disbelief. Mobile phones now appear to offer those watching on TV direct access to the loud and exhausting pandemonium which is taking place here. The half-time whistle, which comes next, means that, downstairs, people are still bubbling, striving unsuccessfully to contain their joy whilst stressing over the trials still to come. Two years ago we led here until the 88th minute in a fourth-round FA Cup tie – and still lost. The utter desolation we felt then is not forgotten here, not by a long chalk.

At the start of the second half, Michael hits the bar when he should score following good work by Babbel, but the pattern remains the same. We look comfortable and we are slowly strangling them. Solksjaer has one clear sight of goal, but Sander saves well, and the home crowd is now out of it, uneasily sensing a league loss for United at OT for the first time in two years. 'Keano thinks you're wankers' we gleefully remind the silent ones. Heskey is offering vital and muscular relief for the Liverpool defence and Smicer, replacing a tiring Murphy, does the same by setting off on a late 70-yard run with young Chadwick in tow, before being yanked down on the edge of the box. Chadwick has to walk for this, applauded off by the locals who are now also streaming out, defeated. Immediately behind us a Liverpool fellah in his twenties – cropped hair, big bloke – sits trembling with his head between his legs for the last ten minutes, unable to watch. His mate cradles his shoulders and tells him it will soon be over, this psychic torture. (And football clubs call their followers *customers*?) It ends 1–0.

Being held behind by the GM bizzies in an emptying, alien ground after this kind of emphatic win against bitter rivals is no trial. We congratulate each other for 'being there' and go through the whole Anfield repertoire now, embracing, joyfully serenading the banks of vacated seats while also joking nervously about 'legging it' outside. But most of Manchester's finest have already retreated, gone to drink this bad day away. Meanwhile, the United Megastore still churns on: Christmas is coming.

BILLY BRAGG'S NEW FOOTBALL SONG

A meeting of the Home Office's new Football Disorder Group has been called to try to turn around the behaviour and image of England fans abroad. It is chaired by Lord ('call me Steve') Bassam and draws in 25 contributors, including Andy Walsh of IMUSA, Mark Perryman of the England Members Club, the grizzly Dougie Brimson, Labour peer Lord Faulkner, Mark Sudbury of the FA and left minstrel Billy Bragg. And me. There follows a wide-ranging and (largely) intelligent discussion about Englishness and identity, which ends with a general concern to wrest back expressions of patriotism around English football from today's racists and violence merchants. I wonder why we need the England Members Club at all; the concept of the 'England fan' seems unnecessarily fixed to me, part of our problem. We agree instead to revise the membership from scratch to try to root out troublemakers. You'll read about it.

Bragg is emphatic, impressively passionate about the 'problem' of Englishness. He has produced a new sports song, set to Elgar, and aimed at recalling the Corinthian ideals of a bygone age in which the English were noted for their fair play rather than their lager consumption and intolerance. Unfortunately, this new number does *sound* like a nineteenth-century English public school anthem, and it is unlikely to strike a chord with post-punk English lads. I suggest he changes the lyrics (yes, I pinch myself later). He refuses, naturally. But Billy is essentially right: the iconography and language of the England national team needs to be reclaimed. Anfield hosts an England World Cup qualifier against Finland in March, a chance to 'do' Englishness differently; let the 'No Surrender' brigade try it on in this complex Anglo-Irish city. But will scousers naturally support England, or Hyypia's Finland, I wonder?

23 DECEMBER: LIVERPOOL 4, ARSENAL 0

No one here can remember the last time Arsenal even *scored* in the 1990s at Anfield, and yet no one can forget Michael Thomas's goal in the Hillsborough season which won the title for the Gunners at Liverpool in 1989. I remember sitting late on the steps of the Kop that night, too much happening in that season to take it all in. I just felt empty.

There has been some rapid reassessment going on here recently. Within a couple of short weeks Houllier has moved (again), in the eyes of some local judges, from being a destructive foreign dunce who is obsessed with damaging rotation (Spurs, Newcastle, Ipswich) to a near-genius now astutely piloting the Liverpool revival (Olympiakos, Fulham, Manchester United). After all, as the latter camp points out, we have massive matches with AS Roma in Europe to come; 'only' Crystal

Palace stand between us and the League Cup final; we have a convincing win at OT under our belts for the first time in a decade; and now we are confidently lining up Arsenal at Anfield. Suddenly, things look brighter, a whole lot better. But because of our awful early away form we are still ten points behind United in the league, and this is what the doubters still say.

In the Flattie, for another early morning start, the talk is excited but also controlled. No one wants to be seen to be getting too worked up by *that* result. But everyone knows that defeat today will wreck the gains from last week. We need to measure up to *both* United and Arsenal, home and away.

Houllier, the Prince of Rotation, has actually re-selected the team which beat United, a first for the season. Arsenal are without Seaman and talisman Tony Adams, a man impressively transformed from oafish lager sponge to the sort of fellah Billy Bragg would like to write songs with (and about). All power to him, but we're glad the yeoman poet Adams is not around today. From the start, it is clear that the Liverpool team is really pumped up for this, like we were for Everton and Leicester, and we battle and work for openings, less affected than Arsenal by the Anfield sandy scrub we have to play over. Through sheer willpower, it seems, we take a first-half lead, Steven Gerrard screwing in a shot from the edge of the box and directly towards us at the Kop end in Manninger's bottom right-hand corner. Already it looks like this might come down to Heskey and Gerrard for us, versus Henry and Vieira for them; these are the key men.

Arsenal take over at the start of the second half, Vieira powering through the dunes and probing around the Kop goal, Henry slippery and sharp, but making no real chances. We urgently need another goal to feel safe. On the hour, Heskey makes it, shrugging off Keown on the left and forcing Manninger to parry in front of Michael, who can't miss – and this time doesn't. Soon after Smicer, on for Murphy and using his body much more positively these days, puts another marker down for those who see him, unfairly, as just a gutless luxury by cleverly putting the incessant Barmby through for 3–0. At ease, the Kop can now go through the Xmas song-book, including the Shankly-era 'Oh come all ye faithful'. This is over, and we have won.

Well, almost over. Robbie comes on for Michael for the final ten, rapturously received by all those who have been following the recent paper talk which now includes some fact: an official twelve-million-pound bid by Chelsea has been posted last night. GH has told Robbie we want him to stay but he can talk to other clubs if he wants to. But today Fowler does well outside the box in his cameo show before spotting a Keown-free channel down the left in the last minute, which

Barmby also sees. Manninger goes to ground too soon and Robbie easily floats it over him into the empty goal. 4–0.

Now we have *hammered* Arsenal; it has not always been pretty or conclusive from the start, but we *have* hammered them. Wenger is right when he says later that our more direct style and Heskey's strength has been better suited to this messy heap we now call home. But the best thing about this win is that Arsenal have come at us for half an hour in the middle of the struggle and we have been strong. We have resisted them and waited for our time to come again and then taken our chances. We look like a real team once more, a different prospect from what we saw at Leeds, Spurs and Newcastle. The Kop chants Houllier's song, as Babbel give us his cheesy 'strong man's' victory salute before disappearing into the warm darkness of the Main Stand.

In the Flattie afterwards loud cheers greet bench images of the distressed Ferguson and Wenger, both beaten managers in the past week. Arsenal, like us, now lack balance and character away from home where they look like an expensive mess of foreign imports. The whole pub simmers, briefly, for Houllier's own post-match TV interview, which is typically sober and careful, pointing to the new-found team strengths in defence and the sharp taking of chances. He also mentions, *precisely*, the average age of our starting line-up: 23.9 years. We are getting stronger all the time and lack only experience, is his message. For a few hours at least we have moved up to third in the table, our highest position of the season.

DOWNED BY THE RIVERSIDE

We are now well into what Graham Taylor calls the 'tunnel' period of the season; the sunlight and optimism of August and September is well behind, the new dawn of April and May still some way out of sight. In the darkness you need resolve and spirit in abundance to survive. But for this Liverpool a couple of good performances and results is a Signal Passed At Danger in the tunnel, and before the end of the year our recent steaming progress towards the daylight is punctured once more. At the Riverside, on Boxing Day, Terry Venables' relegation-threatened Middlesbrough defend bravely against our hesitant and witless attacking to win, Westerveld-assisted, 1–0. Houllier describes the defeat as one of the strangest of his career as Boro allow an impotent Liverpool to gently pummel them: 'We keep the ball, they keep the result,' he moans.

It is a crushing blow: halfway through the season we have already lost *seven* league games, six of them away from Anfield. So we go into the new year bloodied and confused. How far have we come? Crucial wins against United and Arsenal, certainly, but also poverty at

Tottenham, Newcastle and Boro. And we have now slid to sixth, fully thirteen points behind United. There'll be no league title, as a dark November strikes again. A Champions League place and maybe cup successes are still possible. We are, says Houllier, 'active' in all competitions and so there is still plenty to play for. Except what we all really want, and what we expect this manager, and this football club, to deliver. Merry Xmas.

4. INTO THE RED: THE RISE AND FALL OF LIVERPOOL FC

Promotion for Liverpool FC from the obscurity of the Second Division under the young Bill Shankly in 1961–62 ushered in the beginning of a completely new era for Liverpool. The ambitious Shankly had explosive early confrontations with the club's rather conservative directors when he first arrived from Huddersfield Town in 1959. He thought they were complacent and scared of radical change. Shankly persuaded the Liverpool board to modernise the poorly developed Melwood training ground in 1960, and he transformed the club's playing staff: 24 players left in just over a year after his arrival.

Shankly's ideas were very different from those of the departing and loyal previous boss, Phil Taylor, who represented stability and continuity, having been with the club since 1936. The *Liverpool Echo* reported on 14 December 1959 that Shankly was, instead, a man with a 'continental' approach to football, who would make his players concentrate on movement off the ball and on developing skills. The modern era had arrived at Anfield.

Shankly was determined to introduce 'modern' methods of training and preparation with his new club. In February 1960, for example, Liverpool players flew to Plymouth for a league meeting with Argyle, something which was hardly the style of an English football club; certainly not one in the Second Division of the league. Having recruited well from Scotland, especially with the giant Ron Yeats and the volatile centre-forward Ian St John, and with a hungry young goal-scorer Roger Hunt stepping up to replace Liverpool idol Billy Liddell, Liverpool won the Second Division title in 1962. With the major additions of a stylish left-midfielder, Willie Stevenson, and a local youngster, Ian Callaghan, in 1964 Liverpool went on to win their first Football League title for 17 years. The FA Cup soon followed, for the first time in the club's history, in 1965. With football and music to the fore in the city, Liverpool in the '60s seemed like the very centre of the popular cultural universe. Using some of the league and Cup final profits, the Anfield Road ground was also slowly transformed in order to meet the new demands of a 'European' football age.

On the coaching side at Anfield, Shankly had inherited what were to become a number of key figures in the successful Liverpool period which followed. They included the quiet but knowledgeable Joe Fagan, later the manager, and chief coach Reuben Bennett, a severe physical education disciplinarian who used to complain endlessly at the 'softness' of his players. Ex-Liverpool players Ronnie Moran and Roy Evans would join the backroom staff in time, but the most important of all the coaching staff at Anfield when Shankly arrived was certainly Bob Paisley, a long-serving Liverpool player himself, who had been offered the job of reserve team trainer by club director, and later chairman and president, T.V. Williams, back in 1954.

Paisley took over as trainer at Liverpool from the ageing Albert Shelley, who by now spent his time sweeping out the changing-rooms and swapping banter with the club's hardened professionals. Paisley, a north-easterner from a mining background, already had a 'native' interest in fitness and the body which he attributed to his father's work in the mines and to a northern working man's 'natural' interest in the performance of pigeons and his beloved racehorses. Paisley often compared players to racehorses, noting their common edginess before contests and the different temperaments which demanded different methods of preparation. He might have had players on the racing gallops, had he been allowed. Even when he became club manager in 1974 Paisley was probably most at home in slippers and cardigan and in the local bookmaker's studying form. He shared many of the 'communitarian' values and football enthusiasms of Shankly's own Scottish industrial heritage, which produced a crop of great British football managers, from Matt Busby and Jock Stein through to today's Alex Ferguson.

In preparation for his new role, Paisley had taken a correspondence course in physiotherapy, but T.V. Williams had also secured an open letter from local friend John Moores, founder of the Littlewoods group, requesting that Paisley be allowed into Liverpool hospitals to study medical methods and operations. For years the training staff and players at Liverpool trusted to this training and to Paisley's more intuitive insights into injury, but he was also aware of the lack of specialist knowledge in the sport about treatment of injuries. He was one of the few trainers in the Football League in the '50s to have any medical qualification at all. Paisley was also tactically astute, more so than Shankly. Their combined qualities of a strong, inspiring leader who hated detail, allied to a shrewd tactician and judge of a player's health, strengths and weaknesses, dominated the English game for virtually 25 years. In a total of 784 matches in charge at Liverpool together, each missed only one match on the bench – Paisley due to illness, Shankly in order to scout elsewhere.

Shankly and his staff at Liverpool were slowly evolving methods of training – substantially, conditioning work and hyper-competitive pass-and-move five-a-side games – and player preparation which were quite distinctive in the English game. Shankly thought little, however, of the football theorists at the Football Association who began in the 1960s to promote coaching seminars and a more 'scientific' approach to coaching football. For the staff at Liverpool this seemed likely to make what was essentially a simple game unnecessarily complicated. Early in Shankly's reign, the manager, plus Paisley, Fagan, Reuben Bennett and Ronnie Moran, attended an FA coaching course at Lilleshall, reporting to their hosts on Saturday evening. Paisley was unimpressed and Shankly hated it and never returned. Moran and Fagan, however, enjoyed meeting other coaches and went back for five or six years. Until the arrival at the club more than 30 years later of Gérard Houllier, formal or more scientific approaches to coaching were largely decried at Liverpool in favour of tried and trusted schemes of preparation, honed under Shankly and Paisley and passed on via custom and practice to those who followed. The message was: if it ain't broke, don't fix it.

With Liverpool now playing regularly in Europe, the club's coaches were now also being exposed on a regular basis to new innovations and lessons from abroad. Defeat by an emerging young Ajax team in 1966 alerted the Liverpool coaches to the need for far more flexibility and movement on the field, from defenders as well as forwards. After a comprehensive defeat, home and away, by Red Star Belgrade in 1973, the Liverpool coaching staff concluded that the old hulking 'stopper' English centre-backs were now outmoded and they successfully converted more mobile and lightweight midfielders (Emlyn Hughes, Phil Thompson) to these defensive positions. Experience and flexibility, rather than theory and diagrams, were championed as the central virtues at Anfield.

This surprise European defeat by Red Star occurred, in fact, during what was to prove to be Bill Shankly's last season at Liverpool. It may have influenced his decision. Soon after an easy 1974 FA Cup final win against Newcastle United, and with a team crammed with new young talent – including Ray Clemence, Phil Thompson, the university graduates Hall and Heighway, and a new Shankly protégé, Kevin Keegan – Shankly dramatically resigned. Liverpool had been through a rebuilding period in the late '60s and early '70s, but had won the league title again in 1973. It was known that Shankly's family were anxious that he was pressing himself too hard. Perhaps he had already sensed that *players* would hold more of the whip-hand in future, and that television would increasingly dominate the game? Perhaps he worried at his lack of serious European success? It seems likely from later accounts that Shankly soon regretted his decision, leaving the Liverpool club in a difficult spot with respect to how to relate to the retired genius while giving his successor, Bob Paisley, maximum opportunity to fill these not inconsiderable shoes. What was clear was that Bill Shankly, often at odds with the new coaching gurus in the footballing establishment, had been a central figure in establishing key features of the modern 'Liverpool way'.

After the Shankly years, and under the management of Bob Paisley, Joe Fagan and then Kenny Dalglish, for 16 years Liverpool football club were *the* dominant force in English football and, for seven years from '77 to '84, were unquestionably the strongest club side in Europe. Bob Paisley's homespun image masked an acute and forward-looking football brain: he predicted the emergence of a European league structure and an academy system for the development of young football talent, years before the Champions League and the FA's Charter for Excellence seemed the 'obvious' direction for the game to move in. His player recruitment – Neal, Hansen, Souness, Dalglish, Rush – and his assessment of player strengths (his conversion of Ray Kennedy from a talented but limited striker to an outstanding scoring midfielder, for example) were unmatched. Perhaps his greatest talent, however, was to produce a chemistry in his best sides which matched an unforgiving work ethic to individual brilliance which was always placed at the disposal of the collective. His teams were stuffed with good leaders and decision-makers, which meant that the great man was not being wilfully obtuse when replying to questions about what the Anfield secret was: 'Good players' was always his modest, but truthful reply.

Paisley's service to Liverpool was without parallel. Shankly may take the popular plaudits for beginning the great Liverpool dynasty from the early '60s, but Paisley's record for the club is quite stunning. He piloted the club to three European Cup wins, and told a writer in 1978, following Liverpool's successful defence of the European Cup that, in its entire history, Liverpool FC had now been winners or runners-up in the league, FA Cup or European competitions some 36 times: Paisley had been involved in some capacity in an incredible 26 of those campaigns.

Following Paisley, who retired as Liverpool manager in 1983, Joe Fagan, another reluctant man promoted to the top job from Liverpool's backroom staff, won two league titles, in 1983 and 1984, and another European Cup in 1984. Some judges consider 'his' 1984 treble-winning side (league title, European Cup and League Cup) to be the best in the club's history, boasting as it did a fearsome spine, with Lawrenson and Hansen in a cerebral defence, a young Ronnie Whelan and Graeme Souness in a talented and bruising midfield, and the incomparable combination of Rush and Dalglish up front. Paisley acolytes would undoubtedly point to the 1978–79 title team, which scored 85 goals and conceded just 16, and which relied, pretty much, on 13 players for the whole campaign. So much for the benefits of rotation.

So what happened to the Liverpool dominance? It actually survived Shankly's departure, became even stronger as a result. Even when Bob Paisley gave up the management chair, the established structures at the club helped Joe Fagan to continue the Reds' success. Fagan had already decided to step down, of course, on the morning of the European Cup final of 1985, the fateful Heysel final. Even after this awful tragedy, and with Kenny Dalglish now at the helm, Liverpool built another great side in the late 1980s, this time around the defensive brilliance of Nicol, Hansen and Whelan and the attacking talents of Barnes, Beardsley and Aldridge. But, arguably, Liverpool were already, even now, beginning to slide from their pinnacle as the best club side in Europe: the club was damaged by Heysel, left behind by Europe's élite, and was soon to face another terrible football tragedy at Hillsborough. Both in terms of commercial and administrative activities, and in terms of approaches to player preparation, the rest of the football world was moving on.

Explaining the secrets of Liverpool's success in the 1970s and 1980s may seem easy – good players, astute managers. But it is the *longevity* and consistency of this success which is so startling. What accounts for it? The economist, Stefan Szymanski, and business consultant, Tim Kuypers, have recently tried to identify what provides top football clubs with what they call 'competitive advantage'. Taking lessons from business, Szymanski and Kuypers argue that successful football clubs have, or have had, a number of *distinct capabilities*, exceptional attributes which cannot be easily reproduced elsewhere. They identify *four* such capabilities. The first they call *strategic assets* which are scarce resources which provide an advantage in competition and which once possessed by one club cannot be easily possessed by others. In a business sense this would be a monopoly over a necessary input in the production process; for example, some raw materials obtainable only from a particular location, or else some specialised equipment which other businesses just don't have.

Examples in a sporting context might be an outstanding player (Maradona at Napoli, perhaps) or more likely an inspirational and astute football manager. This description fits Bill Shankly and his coaching staff at Liverpool. At Liverpool, of course, a set of practices with regard to preparation of players had been laid down at Anfield and a coaching team had been groomed to succeed Shankly. Moreover, a group of senior players at the club were also charged with responsibility and leadership in a way which was probably uncommon elsewhere. Note how many of these key figures later went into football management (Souness, Dalglish, Neal, Keegan, Toshack, Whelan, etc.) and how many went into media work (Hansen, Lawrenson, Fairclough, Beglin, etc.).

Finally, the approaches established at Anfield also marked out the club's coaching staff as reliable early *identifiers* of necessary strategic assets, which were then purchased cheaply from other clubs. Shankly bought both Ray Clemence and Kevin Keegan from lowly Scunthorpe United for small fees. Each went on to become world-class players for Liverpool in the 1970s. Alan Hansen, Liverpool's kingpin defender for the whole of the 1980s, was plucked, at 20, by Bob Paisley from Partick Thistle for just £100,000. Steve Nicol, also a key defender, was also recruited cheaply from Ayr United in 1981.

The *second* strategic advantage identified by Szymanski and Kuypers is innovation. Successful football clubs are more likely to be able to innovate compared to their rivals, and at a lower cost. Liverpool, under Shankly and Paisley, certainly showed a capacity to buy players cheaply and to improve on its purchases. In an era when involvement in *European* football competition was limited to a very small number of clubs from each country, Liverpool's routine involvement in European competition from 1965 right up to the Heysel ban of 1985 provided exclusive opportunities for cross-fertilisation of systems and of ideas, the kind of opportunities which came much less frequently to other English clubs. This is why regular meetings with – and sometimes defeats at the hands of – some of the best club sides in Europe were vital to Liverpool's evolution and continued success at home and abroad. The club's coaches were open to ideas from elsewhere and so learned, from meetings with Ajax, Red Star and Dynamo Tbilisi, things which could never be picked up from coaching seminars or from the insular British game. For a while, Liverpool did manage to successfully combine innovative lessons from the continent on patience, passing, technique and ball retention with the high tempo, physical and mental strengths of English football.

The *third* strategic asset highlighted by Szymanski and Kuypers is that of *reputation*. A good reputation obviously makes a product more attractive to consumers: they know the quality of what they are buying. In England, Manchester United had a glamorous, a romantic reputation in the 1970s and 1980s, but the popular image of United among many top British *players*, was of a big club which was critically under-achieving. Professional players chose *Liverpool* in order to win trophies, United, perhaps, more for wages, publicity and profile. While United courted publicity and a strong media image – sacking one manager, Dave Sexton, for example, because he didn't get on with the press – at Liverpool all other issues were subordinate to the serious business of winning football matches. Okay, Shankly could charm the media circus when he wanted to, but Paisley, Fagan and Dalglish paid little heed to their dealings with the press. Indeed, Dalglish was positively obtuse towards them, something which was much celebrated on Merseyside, where United were also labelled 'the glams' because of their alleged lack of proportion in relation to the media and their unbusinesslike lack of real focus on winning titles.

All of this meant that in the pre-global football era, at least, the routine playing success of Liverpool offered the club pretty much an open hand in the choice of the top British players they wanted; professionally, few players could afford to be seen to turn down a move to Liverpool. Perhaps this is also why rather more *intelligent* football players – Dalglish, Hansen, Souness, Lawrenson, Barnes – were at the core of the dominant Liverpool teams of the 1980s. Coaches at Liverpool, especially those who followed Shankly, were also happy to let good *players* decide on basic strategies, and so they were quite unthreatened by the arrival at the club of players with ideas or strong *football* personalities. Anyone who stepped out of line would soon be brought down to earth, in any case, by the unforgiving dressing-room culture at Liverpool.

The *fourth* strategic asset offering competitive advantage to football clubs or firms is what Szymanski and Kuypers call *architecture*. This is a unique organisational structure, sometimes associated perhaps with the manager and coaches, the players, or sometimes with the relationship between the team and supporters, or with the institutions of a club. Taken together these organisational advantages amount to a powerful source of competitive advantage, distinctly associated with a club such as Liverpool, and never emulated elsewhere. The authors go on to argue that the mythologised coaching 'boot room' at Anfield was a unique and key source of institutional architectural advantage at the all-conquering Liverpool of the 1970s and 1980s. I will return to say a few things about the famous Liverpool boot room and its fate a little later. But what happened at Anfield after Heysel will give us some clues to the roots of the decline in these advantages which soon followed.

Kenny Dalglish started brilliantly as the new Liverpool manager. He was steeped in the Liverpool traditions recently established under Shankly, Paisley and Fagan: ebullient team spirit, signing 'good' players, a rejection of the star treatment even for key players, and an uncomplicated approach to match preparation and tactics and strategies. Liverpool still spent little time rehearsing set pieces, for example. There were obvious strengths inside the club Dalglish took over, but there were also growing signs of the traditional 'Liverpool way' now beginning to look a little dated, at least when judged against some of the newer developments coming on stream in the sport. For one thing, even this outstanding Liverpool outfit still relied strongly on the kind of team spirit and togetherness traditionally built by English club sides in the saloon bar.

The accounts from Liverpool players of the intense team bonding at Liverpool and the drinking cliques inside the club in the mid-'80s was also a marker on the *general* nature of the occupational culture inside many top British football clubs at the time. Ian Rush, for example, was initially astonished – and then delighted – by the pace of the 'social' side of life at Anfield, something which actually tends to put recent Merseyside 'spice boys' stories into some perspective. Alan Hansen famously teased his fellow squad members when Dalglish himself resigned by pretending *he* was the new Liverpool manager and that the drinking of the club's players would now be severely curtailed. No one was laughing. A night 'on the bevvy' was an important part of the Liverpool – and English – approach to the game. The club's players, famously, once had a session in the afternoon before a midweek league game at Middlesbrough in the early 1980s. As Rush revealed, 'You're never told what nights to stay in, there are never any deadlines put on us. If you went out on Friday night and got legless, that's up to you. Not a word would be said. But if it shows in your play – boy, you're out!'

Drinking by players was no novelty in English football and it was certainly not something confined to Liverpool; far from it. But traditional British team spirit and strength, and this kind of chaotic and abusive treatment of the body, which seemed to matter less before Heysel, was unlikely to triumph for too long in the new football era which followed. As new methods of conditioning and preparing players became more widespread abroad, foreign sides would become increasingly unimpressed by the uncompromising physical approach of English teams. Nor would they crumble quite so easily in the face of the sort of 'die for each other' fighting spirit of the British male mentality which was best forged on nights together in the bar. The top European sides would soon combine athleticism and strength with superior fitness. The drinking clubs – even the talented ones – would have to rethink.

Other things would have to change, too. Liverpool's traditional approach to major European games continued to be a crude 'fly in, fly out' strategy, which offered little time for proper acclimatisation or pre-match rest. On the related and important *medical* side of club affairs, up to now taken care of by the recently retired Bob Paisley, Ian Rush also agreed that even in the mid-'80s Liverpool FC broke all the accepted rules: 'Liverpool operate just about exactly the opposite to the way most people believe a football club should be run. We have all the latest equipment at Anfield, costing thousands of pounds, and we don't have anyone qualified to use it! It's hard to imagine, I know. Millions of pounds worth of footballers being treated with less fuss and less knowledge than your pet dog would expect at the vet!'

In fact, it wasn't hard to imagine at all, and not much further on from the days when Shankly himself, in the 1960s, used to invite dog-walking passers-by into Anfield from nearby Stanley Park so that Bob Paisley could try a new piece of equipment out on their pet. The point of this is that Liverpool changed as little as possible in what they did. After all, they were the top club side in Europe in the late 1970s. Why change? For all the native tactical and coaching awareness at the club, little was learned or imported from elsewhere on these important new aspects of preparing players. This was especially true, of course, following the European ban after Heysel.

Much of what was available, in terms of guidance or training on exactly *how* to manage at a club such as Liverpool in the late 1980s remained very much at the intuitive level. There was no blueprint, no handy job description. Kenny Dalglish, himself, for example, would have to make the overnight move from player to club manager simply with the support of the club's inspiring backroom staff. His promotion would have been impossible in, say, Italy or Germany, where football coaches were required to be formally qualified for their jobs. Houllier pinpointed this issue later as part of the crisis in English coaching. In fact, of course, Dalglish was not being promoted as a coach but as a football manager, quite different roles in the English game. Kenny's 'qualifications' for the managership at Liverpool in 1985 were that the Liverpool staff and fans loved and respected him, he was arguably the most talented British player of his generation, he had a shrewd knowledge of the game and, crucially, he *knew* Liverpool Football Club. This, it was argued, was more than enough.

But Dalglish had no idea what the manager actually *did* at Liverpool. In truth, the job was hard to describe, apart from picking the team and then telling the players to get on with it. When Jan Molby signed for the club in 1984 from Ajax, a club where players were given detailed briefings on how to approach matches, he asked Joe Fagan, nervously, what the manager wanted him to do in his first match. Where should he play, who should he mark? He was astonished at the answer: 'Play. Don't do anything silly, just play within the system.' Simple. Dalglish later described the Liverpool manager's job as 'Never complicated . . . one of the most straightforward jobs in English football.' Kenny was expected to pick the team and get results. Peter Robinson and chairman John Smith would deal with financial and most other administrative matters at Liverpool. They would also have to deal with most of the fall-out from Heysel, the experience of which had deeply affected some Liverpool players.

Technical preparation at Anfield remained minimal. Dalglish even picked as his team captain the largely silent Hansen, simply because he felt the Scot was 'lucky'. Perhaps partly because of this deceptive simplicity, Dalglish soon seemed to get on top of the job: he not only guided his squad to the club's first, and only, domestic double in his first season in charge, but he also later successfully, if briefly, rebuilt the Liverpool side around a new generation of exciting attacking players between 1988 and 1990, including, especially, the talented John Barnes. Ironically, the watershed of the dominance of the typical English football style was probably the defeat of this talented Liverpool team by a limited, hyper-aggressive Wimbledon in the FA Cup final of 1988. Meanwhile at Anfield more profound changes were already occurring.

The famous Anfield 'boot room' is widely seen as possibly *the* key to Liverpool's football success in the period from the mid-'60s to the mid-'80s. It was little more than a cubby hole at the Anfield ground, the Liverpool foremen's shop floor, where matches and players were discussed over tea and bottles of ale. This was a place where the club's lieutenants and sergeant-majors could pore through injuries and illnesses, discuss the morning's training, and run the rule over the new recruits while looking for weaknesses in the long-servers.

Dalglish described the approach of the boot room as: 'Give the opposition very little and get as much as you can out of them.' Paisley, Moran and Fagan kept detailed written records of events at Melwood, the 'Anfield bibles'. According to England international Phil Neal, a policy of custom and practice – 'Have a look, see what we did last year' – was a common response among the club staff to try to right a slump in form or an outbreak of injuries. The boot room was probably most important, however, for its *symbolism*; it stood for a set of values, for solidarity and a rough democratisation inside Liverpool – coaches and other staff 'chipping in' – as well as the idea, in an increasingly commercialised era, of the Liverpool club as a closely knit family characterised by traditions of generational inheritance about how the team played.

The boot room itself was eventually demolished, ironically, under pressure from UEFA for the provision of a larger *media* interview area at the club. But Kenny had actually already installed a bar in his own office at Anfield, thus crucially redirecting some of the important post-match drink and gossip among coaches and managers *away* from the boot room base of Liverpool coaches Ronnie Moran and Roy Evans. Whatever the motivation for this development, it was probably the first sign of a real shift in the successful Anfield coaching dynasty which had been inspired from the late 1950s by Bill Shankly.

As the exciting late 1980s Liverpool team quickly began to fade, with key players – Whelan, Nicol, Rush, Hansen – beginning to age, and Dalglish's new signings – Speedie, Rosenthal, Carter – failing to match up, self-doubt and gloom began to envelop a clearly strained Dalglish. Hillsborough was central to this. It hit the whole club hard, but the manager and his family, essentially very private people, were at the very heart of the emotional public mourning in the city, a huge strain. Dalglish hung on until March 1991 before leaving, suddenly, after a dramatic FA Cup replay with Everton, pleading accumulated stress rooted in coping with the terrible aftermath of the 1989 disaster. He looked exhausted. Ronnie Moran stepped up, briefly, into the Liverpool managerial breach.

Next, another ex-Liverpool player and Dalglish colleague, Graeme Souness, took over at Anfield. He joined a club which was, arguably, still struggling as an organisation to deal fully with the effects of the events of 1985 and 1989, as well as with the pace of change in the 'new' football industry. Six years' exclusion from European football competition had lessened critical Liverpool advantages, and it was also proving hard to cope with the very special pressures brought by a quarter of a century of near constant footballing success at the highest level. Souness entered Anfield at a critical and difficult moment.

Graeme Souness was a man of his times; he lacked the communitarian ideals of the Shankly/Paisley traditions, but his values chimed well with the free-market philosophies of the 1980s. He had an opulent style, he married an heiress and sent his kids to exclusive private schools. He had also left Liverpool as a player in 1984 simply for more money in Italy. Souness was a respected, rather than loved, ex-player at Liverpool, a man with a reputation for toughness both in sport and in business. He was a self-proclaimed 'winner,' and he had been welcomed back to the club by most Liverpool fans precisely because of his uncompromising competitiveness and winning mentality. Above all, he had a Liverpool FC heritage. He was unlikely, nevertheless, simply to fit in with the established management traditions at Anfield. It simply wasn't Souness's style.

Souness, correctly, thought Liverpool were now living too much on past glories. He had a moderniser's steely glint and he quickly moved unwanted players on and brought in new players to the club on what were, by this stage, soaring salaries. Souness was critical of the lack of real commitment from some of the senior professionals at the club who, he felt, were either already past their best playing days or were looking for a last big football payday. John Barnes was a key player here. Suffering from injury but also unimpressed by Souness's signings and his occasional teacup-throwing antics, Barnes felt little excited by the Souness project. He may already have been thinking about his own football management ambitions. Barnes remained overweight and unengaged. The new manager felt he had inherited a team which had little backbone for a fight, a shadow of the 1980s squad in which he, himself, had been a key figure.

This was also the moment when the new FA Premier League commercial boom in English football was getting under way. With established players on agreed contracts and new arrivals pocketing higher wages, this buying and selling strategy produced further disharmony in an already unhappy Liverpool dressing-room. Also, the earlier internal boot room discussions about what *exactly* the club needed and precisely *which* players the club might sign – something which had already begun to recede under Dalglish – now virtually disappeared in a much more hierarchical managerial set-up under Souness.

Finally, Souness sold good players – Staunton and Beardsley, for example – and replaced them inadequately. Dicks and Clough hardly matched up. Talented youngsters coming through the Liverpool production line – McManaman, Fowler, Mike Marsh, and the Dalglish signing, Jamie Redknapp – tempered the negative effects of these sorts of deals. In 1992 Souness underwent serious heart surgery and, crassly, sold his story on his health and his relationships to *The Sun*, a newspaper still hated by Liverpool fans for its disgraceful coverage of the Hillsborough tragedy. A Liverpool FA Cup final win in the same year, against Second Division Sunderland, did not convince all Liverpool fans, either, that Souness was on the right track or that he was the right man for Anfield. A near-comic televised exit to Spartak Moscow in the European Cup-Winners' cup later in 1992 served only to confirm the spreading doubts.

Souness, a man who had, of course, played at the highest level abroad, did begin tending seriously to Liverpool players' diets for the first time, and he moved all the club's training activities and its day-to-day focus away from Anfield to Melwood. This necessary modernisation of day-to-day routines at Liverpool also meant, however, that the collective coach ride for training, during which the vital Liverpool 'team spirit' was mainly sparked, also disappeared. Players now arrived for training alone in their cars. Boot room meetings, partly as a consequence, also became less central to the coaching and playing culture of the club. New recruits failed to impress in training or on the field: Torbin Piechnic, a Danish international, was a disaster at centre-back, while Nick Tanner, bought from Bristol Rovers, was willing but limited. Istvan Kozma, a Hungarian midfielder, was barely seen in the Liverpool first team.

Finally, Souness had taken over at Liverpool at a time when it lacked real stability and top quality on the playing side, and when it was also missing effective boardroom leadership, vision and dynamism in the area of club administration. As a business, Liverpool was falling behind its main rivals: decision-making at executive level seemed ever more tortuous. At the end of 1992–93 the Liverpool board effectively split over Souness. As media speculation heightened, the manager was absent from Liverpool's last-match 6–2 victory over Spurs at Anfield, so much of the Kop was demob happy, anticipating his removal. Instead, Liverpool director Tony Ensor, a Souness opposer, was forced to walk.

In short, the Liverpool club as an *insitution* was clearly ailing and it had been for some time. Souness had seen this, but he seemed hardly the man to bring Liverpool up to date. In the words of David Fairclough, a player with Liverpool in the late 1970s and one who had unusually, like Souness, played abroad: 'The boot room had run its course. I thought when I was in Switzerland that Liverpool, even though they were still European champions, were falling behind. I thought, ultimately, Liverpool would have caught up by the time I got back, by broadening their vision a little bit. I don't think Liverpool or English clubs were aware of what was going on on the continent.'

Liverpool had not been aware of developments abroad partly because of the Europe ban. It had also been caught up in the ramifications of Hillsborough since 1989. Liverpool could no longer have first pick of domestic players either: in 1993, future England goalkeeper Tim Flowers chose emerging Blackburn Rovers, then managed by Dalglish, over Liverpool, something virtually unimaginable in the 1980s. Liverpool fans accused Souness of trying to change too much too quickly, of threatening the club's stability. Liverpool *was* changing, but change *was* also clearly necessary. But the truth about Souness is that he had arrived at the club as its distinct capabilities were already being allowed to drain away. He was also, simply, a poor man manager and, unlike many of his predecessors, an inconsistent judge of top players. He was no Bob Paisley. Feeling the club needed more fighting credentials, he brought in hardened, but poor quality players to Anfield – Dicks and Ruddock, for example – who were happy to keep up the club's drinking schools, but who had little of the ability or sense of responsibility of earlier Liverpool players. It was a mess.

After a promising start to the 1993–94 season, Liverpool lost five out of six matches in late August and September, and continued to draw matches which really should have been won. New playing recruits were rumoured to be less than respectful of the Liverpool coaching staff, adding to concern among the club's supporters. Early in 1994 the critical loss occurred: a shattering home defeat to Bristol City in an FA Cup replay, mirroring a similar loss at home in the previous season to Bolton Wanderers. Even Souness could see his time had finally come: his resignation was eventually accepted by his close friend and club chairman, David Moores.

Still troubled by the lingering aftermath of Hillsborough and now by the public mistakes, ill-judged transfers and man-management practices of Souness, the Liverpool club turned, once again, to what seemed the greater certainty and stability offered by a recognised boot room disciple. Bootle-born Roy Evans, 20 years on the Liverpool club coaching staff, stepped up, perhaps reluctantly, to take charge. Evans was the sort of servant who personified the commitment and the collective spirit of a British football club. Briefly, at least, it seemed like his appointment might prove to be inspired.

Evans faced serious problems in rebuilding the club after its post-Hillsborough demise under a drained Kenny Dalglish, and following the chaotic reign of the abrasive Souness between 1991 and 1994. He offered a very different approach to that of Souness; he was a calmer, more thoughtful boss. Some thought he lacked the necessary steel to be a top manager. But Evans went very close, in fact, to successfully rehabilitating Liverpool. With John Barnes, Doug Livermore and long-time coach Ronnie Moran, Evans constructed a new 3–5–2 (or wing-back) system which, especially in 1995–96, came close to recapturing early glories.

Under Evans, John Barnes's enthusiasm and fitness returned, this time in central midfield. Evans bought two new centre-backs, Phil Babb and John Scales, and coaxed Mark Wright out of his depression to form a formidable and footballing new back three. With Barnes, Redknapp and McManaman to the fore, Liverpool quickly re-established their national credentials as *the* passing team in England in the mid-'90s. They kept possession of the ball better than any other side, they passed the ball relentlessly, they committed fewest fouls, and they played the purest football. Critics argued that Evans's Liverpool *over*passed, that they too infrequently went for the jugular. But on their day they could be devastating: an early away win at Tottenham in August 1995, Barnes in charge and the young Fowler rampant, was a signal of what might now be possible.

In his careful support and development of emerging young 'scousers', such as McManaman and the extraordinary Robbie Fowler, Evans reinvigorated local traditions for nurturing young players at the very heart of the club's ambitions. The intelligent and talented McManaman, especially, had eventually lost ground under Souness; under the gentler and more creative Evans he became the energetic hub of an exciting new team. For all this, though, the club's League Cup final triumph of 1995, against First Division Bolton Wanderers, represented nowhere near enough for supporters who now eyed Manchester United's emerging dominance down the M62 motorway.

Evans, a traditional English club coach, rather than a football manager, was essentially a nice man who lacked some of the cunning and disciplinary ruthlessness of his Anfield teachers. He liked his footballers, and he wanted them to like him. Evans hated the necessary cruelty of football club management. Gérard Houllier noted later how difficult Evans found it to tell favourite players they were being dropped or rested. Foreign players at Anfield also complained of the dressing-room cliques which still existed there, and how little the club coaching staff did to explain why they were being omitted from the side. This kind of basic man-management was still alien to the British tradition and it had had little place in the earlier Shankly and Paisley eras, where players were expected simply to get their heads down and work harder. For Shankly, especially, once out of the first team players simply ceased to exist. This was Evans's school.

Perhaps above all else, Evans was dogged during his time in charge at Anfield by recurring accusations about the mental weaknesses of his teams and his own laxness in managing some of his players, who attracted the 'spice boys' label because of their liking for celebrity culture and the high life. His problems were exacerbated in this area when he paid big money for the talented but perplexing Stan Collymore in 1995. Stan was sometimes deadly, frequently anonymous, but worse, he seemed almost completely unwilling to come to heel, at one point flatly refusing to play for the club's reserve team. Collymore also refused to move to the Liverpool area, citing his close relationship with his mum as enough reason for staying in Cannock. Evans capitulated. And there was more. Goalkeeper David James once explained a routinely erratic performance in goal for the Reds by saying he had been playing a computer game all afternoon before the match. What sort of ship were the Liverpool staff running? All of this added, perhaps unfairly, to the public image of Evans as a weak character who had problems managing wealthy young men and in facing up to difficult challenges and decisions.

Evans was, of course, simply following the tenets of the regime established under the Liverpool boot room dynasty, when players were never route-marched, but were treated like adults. Senior Liverpool professionals, such as Dalglish, Hansen and Souness, would be expected to keep in check their own socialising and the potentially dangerous excesses of younger members of the squad. Under an increasingly puritanical and watchful media, as new methods of player preparation were emerging, and at a time when the sport was massaging its own new image as a 'family' product, Roy Evans seemed to be struggling for good sense and judgement among some of his young 1990s stars. But he was also short of the crucial reliable *senior* dressing-room leaders. Stan Collymore was no Dalglish and Neil Ruddock was hardly Alan Hansen. Even John Barnes seemed loath to offer a disciplinary model. It just wasn't his style.

Evans's Liverpool produced some remarkable performances in 1995–96 – the kind of football which, even in the more successful Houllier period, is still remembered fondly by many Reds fans as a standard to aspire to once more. But the growth in the power of players, their alleged lack of club loyalty, the fact that young Liverpool stars seemed to be enjoying the high life too publicly and the looseness of Evans's regime, meant these displays are remembered rather less than is the poor end to the 1995–96 Liverpool league season – only three wins in the last eight matches, with the title in sight – and a terrible performance against a disappointing Manchester United in the 1996 FA Cup final. Liverpool's ostentatious cream Cup final suits and 'hit-men' sunglasses seemed strangely symbolic of the general lack of discipline and focus in the Anfield camp.

In the following season, further alleged player indulgences and defensive frailty and failures on the field finally provoked the frustrated Evans to dispense with his entire playing strategy, one which he had built up so carefully since 1994. After a cowardly team performance in Paris, against PSG in the UEFA Cup-Winners' cup semi-final first leg, Barnes himself was sacrificed. With him went the whole of the 3–5–2 passing philosophy. In came an already failing midfield ball-winner, England international midfielder, Paul Ince. The eventful and entertaining – if frustrating – Evans years as manager of Liverpool FC were already beginning to draw to a close.

With Scales dogged by injury, Wright close to retirement and Babb increasingly erratic, Evans seemed unable to replace his previously reliable defenders of 1996. His supposedly tighter 4–4–2 formation, built around Ince, also produced a team which seemed much more anonymous and much less fluent than before – and no more successful. The emergence of the astonishing Michael Owen in 1997 served only to mask real weaknesses elsewhere, especially in defence. Liverpool managed third place in the league in 1998, but it was a distant third to Wenger's Arsenal and Manchester United. At the beginning of the 1998–99 league season, and under pressure for more managerial change but *without* sacking the loyal and well-liked Evans, the Liverpool club announced a new direction. Evans and Frenchman Gérard Houllier were unveiled to a disbelieving press as the new *joint* managers of Liverpool FC. The start of a new 'continental' era to the coaching and development of players at Liverpool was about to get underway.

Following the eventual uncertainties and traumas under Dalglish, and the harsher failures as Graeme Souness struggled for more rapid change at Anfield, by the end of the Roy Evans era at Liverpool many of the core strengths of the Liverpool club were still clear and intact. The club was, finally, emerging from the shadow of Hillsborough and planning for a future in what was likely to be a new European élite of top football clubs. However, many of the distinct capabilities referred to by Szymanski and Kuypers, which the Liverpool club had nurtured, perhaps not always consciously, in the 1970s and 1980s, had effectively been overtaken by events in the 1990s and were simply no longer quite as effective in this new, globalised, more capital intensive and more 'scientific' period of the sport's development. Foreign clubs had caught up and then overtaken their English equivalents. After a weak home performance against Spurs in a League Cup tie in the autumn of 1998, Roy Evans decided that Gérard Houllier needed to pursue his own new direction with the club Evans had loved and served for all his professional life. The boot room dynasty at Anfield was over, but at least the club was now in the hands of a man who seemed to understand and respect both the traditions of the club and the new future for football.

Early in 2001, Roy Evans, the most experienced and successful *available* football coach in England, remained unemployed. He had been little talked about in relation to coaching jobs in the England hierarchy. He eventually took over as director of football at Swindon Town in August 2001, his first job since the Anfield resignation. Some would argue that his period in charge at Liverpool in the mid-'90s made him now unemployable in top level football, which seems absurd. Of course, the game has moved on and foreign coaches, including Gérard Houllier, have made their mark. The traditions at Liverpool, with which Evans is so closely identified, might seem out-dated today, but in many ways

Houllier is simply modernising the Liverpool way, rather than dispensing with it altogether.

By any measure, Evans has been hard done-by: he is a talented man and one almost universally liked in the sport, but a man who has been charmlessly treated by it. After winning a league title with Blackburn, Kenny Dalglish had a poor time at Newcastle United and an even more difficult one at Celtic, where he recruited John Barnes for a catastrophic managerial spell. Both left the club under a cloud, and Barnes now looks as unattractive a managerial prospect as his old boss Evans had once seemed. Dalglish seems happier to be out of the sport, and is often seen today as a spectator and media pundit at Anfield.

Graeme Souness has fared rather better than other ex-Liverpool bosses. After a spell at Southampton and a turbulent time in Turkey, he successfully piloted Blackburn Rovers back into the FA Premier League in 2001. His return to Anfield is eagerly awaited in the new season. Meanwhile, although Liverpool fans warm to the new Houllier era – still hoping for title success, of course – many regret the passing of a marvellous phase, 1994 to 1997, when the club once again raised passing and keeping a football to something close to art.

5. OUT OF THE DARKNESS?

1 JANUARY 2001: LIVERPOOL 2, SOUTHAMPTON 1

The hazy-headed opening gambits in the Flattie in this bleary new year are a 'state of the parties' debate on Houllier's progress. Some in this little exchange go as far as to say the current fare, win or lose, is unacceptable: simply 'shite', and not the 'Liverpool way'. Steve Kelly, editor of Liverpool fanzine *Through the Wind & Rain*, is less damning, arguing that football players, like school kids, always look for ways of avoiding responsibility and that Houllier's constant and artless assertions about how far we are still behind the Man Uniteds and the Arsenals undermines our confidence away from home and allows our lot to 'settle' for defeat. Too easily, once the opposition is ahead, we seem to accept we lack the quality or the experience to get back into matches, to properly assert ourselves. Fresh from a hammering of Arsenal and an away win at OT, we hardly looked the part at all at lowly Middlesbrough, where we should have really gone at them. Houllier's defeatist caution once more? Or is this also some strange comfort zone for Liverpool players which is rooted in the belief that this is not yet our time?

Our previously reliable defenders, Henchoz and Hyypia, have been less so this time, Hamann has lacked positive authority and vision in midfield, Babbel is noticeably playing out of position and Westerveld has conceded more than he has saved. Latterly, the admirable McAllister has also begun to look his 36+ years on occasions, while Smicer looks, alternately, both convincing and marginal. The manager has also failed so far to solve the Fowler/Owen conundrum, convincing no one that his rotation system has been about keeping players fresh, rather than about desperately trying to find some form in his strikers and to keep both of these scorers at least some way short of abject unhappiness.

The 'positives' this season have been the real progress and fitness of Steven Gerrard, the effervescence of Barmby, the muscular *scoring* talent of Heskey – who now also stands up – and the recent sturdy promise of the young Croatian, Biscan. Add to this the surprising emergence of Danny Murphy as a decent squad player and more, and the all-round reliability and scouse heart of Carragher, and this is the uneven core of our new future. This is increasingly *Houllier's* team.

I provide tickets for this disturbingly well-below-capacity meeting with Southampton for a friend and his French girlfriend. Strangely reassuring is the fact that she has never even heard of Michael Owen, or David Beckham, thus confirming the existence of a confusing world out there where football still means virtually nothing. This New Year's Day performance, as it turns out, is no place to begin one's football education. It reveals all the problems we have been churning over earlier in the Flattie.

Last season the Saints came to defend during our excruciating goalless run-in and only their lack of ambition kept the contest scoreless then. They try to do the same this time but we start brightly towards the Kop, with Robbie in for Michael. Steven Gerrard scores another early, quality goal from long distance, this time high to Paul Jones's right. The lead doesn't last long, though, with Westerveld caught, perhaps unsighted, by Soltvedt at his near post following a Saints corner. In front of a largely comatose post-party Liverpool crowd it's a decent first half and we look like we just might score more. Exclude Robbie from this, though, because it is another sluggish non-shooting show from him with Heskey, once again, playing furthest forward.

The second half fails to build on even the small promise of the first and soon it disintegrates into the sort of uninspiring, narrow and leaderless stuff we have seen all too often on tour this season, albeit less so at home. In the wake of this torpor, a flurry of home substitutes eventually brings on a lively Michael Owen and it is his run from wide on the left which sets up the corner that produces an unlikely late winning goal, a header from the hobbling Babbel. If playing poorly and winning is the clichéd sign of a good side, this performance surely heralds future greatness for us. But it is a relieving win, nevertheless.

Back in the Flattie I apologise to our French guest for the poor quality of the game. No need: apparently, she had been openly calling for more movement from the Liverpool attackers in the second half, thus proving that advanced football coaching is indeed a new national genetic trait in France. Her compatriot, our manager, says later that, *of course* we deserved to win and that the substitutes turned it. The truth is we have scraped home on a bad day. He knows this.

BEST OF THE BEST?

Following our recent blunderings and our struggle today, and Arsenal's New Year loss at Charlton, the Corporation absolutely *batter* West Ham at home for Sky viewers this evening and so truly disappear over the title horizon. Ferguson says this is certainly his best United team, eclipsing even the Cantona sides of the mid-'90s. Some journalists are now beginning to say that this United side even has it over past Liverpool teams. We need some history here.

The 1972–73 Liverpool Championship team of Smith, Hughes, Keegan, Heighway and Toshack has some claims to ultimate greatness, but won a miserly eight times away in the First Division. The 1983–84 Championship, League Cup and European Cup winners, built around the domestic core of Hansen, Souness, Rush and Dalglish, was formidable, but again struggled to win away from Anfield in the league. The 1978–79 all-British Liverpool side is worth a bigger shout, with eleven away wins. That Liverpool defence – Ray Clemence behind Phil Neal, Alan Kennedy, Phil Thompson and the emerging Hansen – I would put up against United's Barthez, the Neville brothers, Irwin and the rest at the Corporation today.

The midfield comparisons are also interesting. Would you easily take Roy Keane over the young, velvet-fist Souness, for example? Jimmy Case is probably edged out by United's urchin Scholes, but then it is the elegant Ray Kennedy and the non-stop McDermott against the very different talents of United's Beckham and Giggs. Up front, Dalglish, partnered then by a fading Heighway or by Craig Johnston, would easily hold forth against all the current impressive United crop. Liverpool used virtually 13 players for the whole of the 1978–79 season, losing only four league games, conceding just 16 goals and scoring 85. Losing to Forest in the first round of the European Cup is an irritating blemish. Comparing *squads* makes no sense here, of course: United easily. But a starting eleven? A different prospect.

So much here, of course, is about the chemistry of sides; complementing the strengths of players and using sweated workers to mask the possible weaknesses of the so-called creatives. Looking at particular players outside of the systems, teams and times in which they played makes no real sense, particularly given the way Paisley and Joe Fagan, especially, sought to build their sides as water-tight, ego-free units, something rather more than the sum of their considerable parts. Ferguson has, impressively, done much the same thing today, of course, and he has managed it in an era of football millionaires; he has fathered a talented group of mansion owners who seem to enjoy, most of all, playing selflessly as a team. Deep football engineers like Ferguson and Paisley purr in the background at the power and efficiency of it all. This is not to all tastes, of course, especially at the still star-struck OT. 'You have just seen the result of 17 years of simplicity' – Bill Shankly's words after Liverpool's first European Cup win in Rome in 1977. He meant them.

JARI, JARI

Childhood Liverpool fan, one of the global millions, Jari Litmanen, joins Anfield on a free from Barcelona – and a reported 55-grand weekly pittance. We tried to sign him before the French revolution, and Houllier also wanted the Finn two years ago, but Jari then chose Barcelona reserves, where he has been plugged ever since. Houllier says, suspiciously quickly, that this is *not* a signal for Fowler to start packing his stuff, but the Toxteth terror did also get into another of those 2 a.m. post-bar disagreements in the city this week, suspected broken nose and all. This is not an incident designed to thrill the sort of manager who feels all professional athletes ought to be snuggling up with hot chocolate and *Harry Potter* at ten. Robbie is at risk. Litmanen is already 29 and he will expect to play. Houllier describes him as: 'A world-class player who comes with a reputation that needs no improvement.' He also comes with a recent injury record which has meant just 14 games for Barca in two years. We'll see.

6 JANUARY, FA CUP THIRD ROUND: LIVERPOOL 3, ROTHERHAM UNITED 0

Ah, the magic of the FA Cup. The FA has 'relaunched' the Cup this year, the oldest and best knock-out football competition in the world. The FA Cup in some ways remains the antithesis to modern corporate football, where certainty of outcome and budgeting is all, because of its traditional all-or-nothing pitching of large businesses into the dangerous backyards of hungry and aspiring corner shops. The Cup still has the dwindling romance of the occasional dumping of pampered millionaire posers by the sort of honest postmen, teachers and meat traders so painfully featured on TV's *Football Focus*. So why the need, you might ask, to so aggressively refloat the Cup?

Well, you might also recall that the FA itself in 1999–2000 asked the Corporation, the Cup-holders no less, to play instead in a new FIFA world club competition in Brazil. United thus readily – too readily for many – ditched the Wembley trail. The FA hoped that United's presence in Rio would push grateful FIFA delegates towards England's wobbly World Cup bid. The result: United carted limply out of the FIFA beano while Germany, with no club in Rio, were voted World Cup hosts and the FA was left with plenty of the eggy stuff over its greedy and negligent chops.

Today we face gritty Rotherham, currently flying high in the Second Division and good travellers. The Flattie is virtually deserted by Reds and flooded, instead, with the aled-up boisterous post-industrial best from the scrap yards of South Yorkshire. This day out will offer 7,000 visitors a chance to sing it out on a famous afternoon, but this is not a case simply of 'Rotherham through and through', as our lively guests protest. We meet a couple of Yorkshire Man United fans here, for example, who are also off to Fulham to watch the Corporation play tomorrow. A depressing sign of the times.

Rotherham are busy and well organised but like most clubs down the English divisions, where coaching is even more limited than it is at the top, they also lack imagination and guile. Soon after half-time, Owen clearly fouls Rotherham's left-back Hurst, but is allowed to go on to pick out a cross for Heskey for a header which goalkeeper Gray first claims – and then dribbles into his own net. The expected Liverpool stroll is then briefly threatened when referee Mark Halsey sends off Biscan for a second bookable offence, a truly hopeless decision in a generally troubling refereeing season. Elsewhere today Arsenal's Vieira is nearly cut in two by a double-footed lunge in agricultural Carlisle, an offence so blatant that neither referee Stephen Lodge nor any of his officials see anything amiss at all.

As it happens, this half-hour, ten-man challenge actually livens the Reds up and also kills off the confused visitors: Hamann and Heskey score within a couple of minutes of each other to produce an ultimately comfortable win. 'We've only got ten men' teases the Kop. 'You're supposed to be at home' respond Rotherham, appalled by the lethargy of it all. The truth is that when invited to come out and play Rotherham have shown – and have got – very little.

Smicer, who has had fun on the left throughout all this, draws accusations from the visitors later about his alleged diving. On the empty wastes of the Kemlyn lower, lads in hats with designer ear-flaps concur that if the game Carragher is 'Mister 300 per-cent', then Vladdy is 'Fuckin' class'. The radio monkeys near us now let it seep out that Everton have, disappointingly, scored twice in the last ten minutes to win 2–1 at Watford. They, like us, are in the Millennium hat tomorrow.

MARKET FORCES

Alarm bells at the Corporation on the 40th anniversary of the lifting of the maximum wage. No sooner is Ferguson complaining in the press about the 'unrealistic' demands of agents and their macho posturing to each other about the deals they manage to strike for their clients when, wouldn't you know it, best boy Beckham arrives with a reported new contract demand of a cool £160,000 a *week*. Even allowing for red-top hype, this has rather raised the football wage stakes and all the top clubs will be watching the outcome of this little farrago with some interest and dread.

Beckham's claims are that he is worth more, much more, to United than just a talented right foot: he sells shirts, moves merchandise, and generally keeps the Corporation in the public eye via his glitzy doings. His 'brand symmetry' with United, claim his advisers, is worth at least three times the salary of United's current big earner, the explosive non-celebrity and top player, Roy Keane. The cold economics of this may be convincing, but the United shareholders are unlikely to see it that way. And if the market is the test, where exactly could Beckham go and have these sorts of demands satisfied? After all, even the very top men abroad come up short of this sum. But he will get this money – or something like it – you'll see.

At Anfield, only Michael Owen could make the sort of 'commercial' case outlined above by Beckham's entourage. Since Michael has recently been buying an entire street to house his relatives, he might just need the cash. But at the moment Beckham is actually *delivering* in his real job, playing well, winning football matches. Michael is spluttering. Some Reds fans, amazingly, would try to get a price for him now.

Did I say, by the way, that the Reds have drawn Leeds in the FA Cup – *away*? Revenge!

10 JANUARY, WORTHINGTON CUP SEMI-FINAL, FIRST LEG: CRYSTAL PALACE 2, LIVERPOOL 1

Michael does not add much to his future England or contract claims tonight. A truly awesome clutch of misses here means a long midweek trip with little to show for it, bar a brief and promising late start by Litmanen, which has actually helped to keep us still in touch with a possible late-February trip to Cardiff.

Our conversation down to London is all about the 'Robbie situation' and also the right-back slot. I suspect Houllier's mind is already made up and he would be quite happy if Robbie wanted to leave. But he wants that to come *from* Robbie, in order to sell the outcome to the fans. Babbel is fit, so Gerrard and Biscan start in the middle and Owen is up front. Robbie, goals surely in his locker, is left at home, not even on the bench to join Smicer. This already looks a dangerously negative move.

In the White Horse in Selhurst, Palace fans cheerily tell us that the home team are in for a hiding, so more obvious alarm bells ring. My mate Steve has a Moscow Donkey (vodka and Guinness) to quell the nerves. In the queues outside the away section on a clear and frosty night, a painful 'songs for Litmanen' competition is under way, with no obvious winners. Inside, the 'Who the fackin' 'ell are you?' rhetoricals from the *Liverpool* end tell you all you need to know about the make-up of our travelling support tonight: scousers, plus all nationalities, and with a strong south London flavour. This is one of the few major grounds now where the visitors are allocated a welcome side-view of events. But sitting down in this shed, the outlook is poor; standing up it is worse. We stand up, obviously.

The pitch is dreadful, an uneven sticky sponge, but Gerrard immediately commands midfield and Owen, and especially Heskey, soon rip into the home defence. This is going to be easy. Except Michael and Emile blast *everything* wide and high. Chance after simple chance ends up bobbling around in the home end. And slowly Palace start to come into it, raising the pace, gaining in confidence from our profligacy. Nil-nil at half-time is a joke, but things are also starting to get a little uneasy for us.

Owen and Barmby miss more easy chances at the start of the second half before Henchoz, deceived by the pitch, tries to chest down a long Palace clearance while on his *knees*. The ball squirts left and is picked up by the little Latvian, Rubins. Steve Gerrard is there and Rubins is pushed wide, very wide, a reckoned £2 million worth of not very much so far tonight, so there is no obvious danger: that is until this slight winger produces a left-foot cross shot of such power and direction that Westerveld doesn't even *see* the ball until it is bouncing around, exhausted and bruised, behind him. I'll let you guess at tomorrow's headlines. A clue: the word 'masterpiece' figures quite widely.

It's a sucker punch. We have been as wasteful as any team could be and now we have been punished for it. There is no Fowler to call on and we also know, some of us, the dreadful truth that at *no* time this season have we come from behind to win or even draw. Smicer and Litmanen now replace Murphy and the hapless Owen, but we soon allow another cross into our box, again from their left, and Clinton Morrison shows Michael exactly how by planting the loose ball from Forssell high to Sander's left. Two-nil, Palace fans joyously bobbing in loud disbelief, and a trip to Cardiff is now looking quite out of the question for us.

But within a minute substitute Litmanen shows us exactly why we chased him for so long. Thus far he has been trying outrageous little flicks and passes which have produced just quizzical looks from his new team-mates. Now he wriggles away on our right and pulls it back, expertly, to Smicer who *passes* the ball into the net as if to say to our front boys, 'What is difficult about this?' With ten minutes to go we can still get level but Palace hold out, uncertainly, for a famous victory.

A 2–1 defeat for Liverpool actually means everyone goes away with something from the night. We still think we can win through back at Anfield, and a home win after a fearful early pounding is surely more than the most chauvinist Palace follower might have hoped for tonight. But it would be crass to think we now have this tie taped. No, no way. Yet Palace, for all their guts and speed, are 17*th* in the First Division. We get back home, frustrated again, at 2 a.m. Is Robbie in bed? Is Michael sleeping easily? I wonder.

GO LEFT

At the back, Liverpool still lean absurdly to the right. Crystal Palace knew this, of course, and tried to get at the game Carragher, awkward and lop-sided on the left. The concept of achingly one-footed players, even defenders, is naturally not quite so fixed abroad. Paulo Maldini, the world's greatest left-back, was actually a right-footed right-back until his club, Milan, asked him to play on the left side of defence at the unspeakably early age of 16. Within a couple of years no one went by Maldini on his left – or on the right for that matter – and the man was the complete defender. So, in our limited English terms, Paulo Maldini, Italian male model and left-back supreme, is actually right-footed. So go on, Jamie lad, you can do it, the improbable scouse Maldini.

13 JANUARY: ASTON VILLA 0, LIVERPOOL 3

Dave Woodhall, author of local fanzine *Heroes and Villains*, and on sales duty outside Villa Park today, is worried about Villa's sinking support. Doug Ellis is not flavour of the month with frustrated Villa fans, of course, the usual complaints here being about him spending too little and too infrequently. It's the modern supporter's accusation this: a top chairman who will not release the funds needed to get a large club like Villa into that Champions League nirvana. John Russell, the Villa fan who actually called the 1968 public meeting which resulted in Ellis eventually taking control of the club, comes over for a chat. 'He has to apologise now when people find out,' says Woodhall, gloomily. Villa are drifting, divided inside the club and not convincing their supporters. The mordant John Gregory is said to fancy a move to Newcastle to escape Ellis. It *feels* like a good day to be here, as someone following a travel-sick side which needs to win away.

Since last season, a comatose 0–0, the marvellous 1920s Villa Trinity Road Stand has been brutally bulldozed to be replaced by a larger and much more anonymous brick and glass container. Beliefs that the Trinity was a listed building did little to protect what stadium buff and Villa fan Simon Inglis rightly described as the façade and entrance 'which has more pomp and style than that of any other ground'.

Nothing of the Trinity has been saved, everything brought down by the owners overnight in a facile act of real corporate football vandalism. Villa fans seem hardly moved.

No building of architectural or historic interest would now be lost if Anfield was flattened, of course, and the Liverpool Main Stand really does need to go. But that is hardly the point of recent discussions in L4 on this score. Would 70,000 seats in a proposed new Liverpool ground on nearby Stanley Park make the football experience a better one for most fans? I doubt it. And how many times would we really need 70,000 seats? So the opposers have their points. But the business agendas will out here, as they have at Villa. These suggest that if we had another, say, £100 million to spend on players we would now be right up there with the Corporation. Somehow, I doubt that, too.

Today's outcasts are Owen, Barmby, Biscan and McAllister, which means that Smicer, Hamann and Litmanen all play. But not Robbie: Fowler fails to even make the final 16, having been warned by Houllier that he will have to 'work his socks off' to get his place back. Villa parade their new £9.5 million capture, the Colombian River Plate forward, Angel. He's greeted ecstatically, as an arriving sorcerer or priest to an ancient village, but no Villa fan here has any idea if he's actually any good. He's just big money walking in civvies on the pitch: *this* is the thing they are really cheering. Reds fans make the point more bluntly: 'Who the fuckin' 'ell are you?' they blithely and predictably enquire. It's a good question.

Villa line up with young Barry and Samuel in centre midfield with the dangerous Merson and the flabby Ginola on the left. But it looks a patched-up team, with only the struggling Dublin up front, as yet Angel-free. And that is precisely how it plays. We are on top from the start, with Litmanen prominent, and an early mistake by Alpay, ignoring a call from James, gives Murphy a chance to drive a low shot against a Villa post. When the ball returns, Murphy is also the first to respond and scores.

Alpay and James now have a comical stand-up slapping row, some necessary entertainment this, because frankly the next 20 minutes are utter rubbish. Villa have no home team authority and we have trouble keeping the ball. But out of this ugly mire something of real beauty finally emerges. Gerrard, Litmanen and Murphy combine sweetly to pick up the young scouser's long, looping run from the left and Stevie boy, England's future rock, fairly thrashes it past James.

Villa shoulders now really droop and the talk at half-time in the Liverpool seats is about how this *must* end up as a routine away win. We want no scares, no last-ditch defending: Villa are a poor side and they need to be safely despatched. Significantly, Ginola and Alpay fail to reappear after the break, and they are good judges because early in the second period Murphy ties up the points with a deflected third which makes even Heskey's earlier appalling miss when clean through on James seem more excusable. The match now drains away to nothing, which is slow torture for the home crowd, and a chance for singing practice for the visitors. We chant, predictably, for Fowler, which Robbie later says warmed him in his rookery in the new Villa stand.

We have hardly been perfect, but we *have* been completely dominant. Litmanen has been impressive, playing intelligently in the Beardsley/Sheringham role behind Emile, the spot where Houllier has tried unfairly to shoehorn Robbie all season. Later, on the way to the traffic jam which slyly awaits us, Villa fans are darker still, talking in red-top headlines: 'If we lose to Man United next week,' one observes, 'we're in crisis.' Planet football keeps on turning.

OUR (BENT?) BOY BRUCIE

Could a player, a *Liverpool* goalkeeper, throw football matches for cash? The court of appeal has found for *The Sun* in its claim against libel damages awarded in the Bruce Grobbelaar case. This means, contrary to earlier *jury* decisions, that this court now judges Brucie to be corrupt and to have accepted bribes to throw games. A few questions emerge here: for start-offs, should we trust the views of three elderly members of the Establishment against those of a jury who have actually sat through all the case evidence? Second, if Brucie had taken the cash – this now seems pretty certain – did old 'wobbly knees' *really* conspire to concede goals when he had played under Souness, the period in question at Anfield?

These are not one and the same thing, of course. We, the fans, are not interested in the money; we just need to know that Grobbelaar was always trying to keep the opposition out. Mind you, some Reds fans who remember those dark days under Souness might be tempted to want to bring whole Liverpool defences to account on this score; there would be thousands of traumatised witnesses. Brucie's wild ambition is one day to manage Liverpool. I would suggest this may not happen now for some time.

20 JANUARY: LIVERPOOL 0, MIDDLESBROUGH 0

The city of Liverpool has *banned* street football. Look at those words closely and just think about what they mean. All right, life moves on and it's no longer city urchins kicking a ball of rags, and good thing too. We live in an era of floodlit astroturf play-stations. But do you think Robbie or Stevie G. or Macca learned their sweet moves simply on some spruce junior FA coaching course? Rushy, like a lot of scruffy kids, learned *his* playing in rough-and-tumble 20-a-side thrashes outside the city with kids three or four years his senior. John Cartwright, one of the few sane senior football coaches in this country, laments the loss of the English street kickabout, but actually cares much more about what happens next. Why did we fall behind the rest of Europe in adding refined skills to the inventiveness and passion which came in off the streets? The answer is deceptively simple: bad coaching: 'Methods of coaching employed in this country have so failed the game and the players that there has been a steady decline in skill levels over the last thirty years.' He's right. You know it, I know it.

Part of the reason for the recent failings in this area is the historical stand-off between the FA blazers who have controlled coaching here and the football professionals who play the game. Each have been involved in a bitter and draining power struggle over who should be in control of coaching qualifications. The result has been a professional game too slow to change, to adapt to new challenges, and a national system of coaching which lacks feeling and imagination, and which too few senior figures in the game properly respect. Only the recent arrival of foreign coaches is beginning to make us wake up to our real failings.

But there are a few good English coaches. No matter what his failings elsewhere, Terry Venables is an able coach. A couple of months ago Boro, under Bryan Robson, were a rabble, no other word for it; disorganised, disillusioned, going down. Now, and following some hard and intelligent graft by Tel, they are the form team in the league after Man United, and playing tight but inventive football. This is *not* a story about players; but it *is* one about decent coaching.

All right, a slight exaggeration above. It helps a lot if you have a talented striker like Alan Boksics, who is fit and wants to play for you, though that is also part of the coach's art. Boksics and New Caledonian eco-warrior, Christian Karembeu, today show real purpose and class in the first half and they make our four lop-sided centre-backs look slow-witted and vulnerable (which is what, by top international standards, they probably are). When the Croatian spins on our newly relaid green, and takes out three defenders with a controlled back-heel before chipping over Westerveld and just wide, most of the Kop applauds this, instinctively. Okay, it helped that the shot drifted wide. And I'm not saying that if, say, David Beckham comes here later in the season and drills one in from 25 yards we'll be turning to the Fellahs in Front to congratulate each other that we were here to see this wonderful strike. But most of the people on the Kop *do* respect real football quality.

So, we are lucky to be 0–0 at the half. Hamann and Barmby have been passengers. We have started with both Michael and Robbie on the bench, but that soon changes. At half-time Heskey goes off with a thigh strain and Michael kicks off. The dressing-room chat seems to have done its job because now we get a hold of this match, which has previously looked beyond our grip. Karembeu also runs out of steam and we do much better at isolating Boskics. But the chances we manage to make fall to Michael: and you know what this means at the moment. For a different Michael these may have gone in, but for this one Schwarzer saves both efforts. Easily.

GERMANY CALLING

In the Flattie later I get tied up with Berndt, one of the Moenchengladbach Liverpool boys, and a bit of a man mountain. Our Liverpool–German link goes back, really, to the 1977 European Cup final when, although we beat the Gladbachs 3–1, the rival fans got along mighty fine in Rome. The Germans also got strongly involved in the post-Hillsborough international mourning and fundraising and, rather like our strong ties now with Celtic for similar reasons, a real bond has grown between the supporters of the two clubs. A few games a year now we get a bunch of the Germans, red and green scarves on show, gathered noisily on the front of the Kop.

The Gladbachs themselves have recently fallen on hard times, and out of the Bundesliga, but Berndt is full of that unquenchable and irrational supporter belief that a revival is just around the corner. Berndt and a few of his mates went to a recent Cologne match armed with stink bombs (what else?). These were duly dropped in the home end while other Gladbach men raised a banner in the opposite end asking: 'Can you smell it?' This tickled Berndt. We might get them to try it soon at Goodison, where the stench of another relegation struggle is already rising. Later, I'm down at Lime Street Station when the Evertonians return from Coventry, surprising 3–1 victors. The ugly old station booms with their aled-up songs of relief. But they are not out of the woods, not yet.

23 JANUARY, WORTHINGTON CUP SEMI-FINAL, SECOND LEG: LIVERPOOL 5, CRYSTAL PALACE 0

Tonight, we are in the upper Centenary for a change, which at least offers Steve the chance to furiously miscall offsides from *exactly* the right spot. We are up here with Merseyside's Red middle classes, some of whom are nervously contemplating a February weekend off from the gardening to take young Philip or Fiona to Wales for a 'big' football match. I'm not much impressed with our 'premier' stand, by the way; it feels like the concrete has just dried, and it has none of the little architectural or design touches which might just say you are actually at the home of the great Liverpool Football Club, and not at any two-bit sports outfit with no past or future. This club and its leaders often lack real imagination and class in this – and other – departments, believe me. But at £13 in all parts tonight the match is at least a sell-out in the Liverpool areas.

Along with Kenny D., Liverpool's Ian Callaghan, 'Cally', is in the crowd tonight. He played 843 times for the Reds over 18 seasons, from 1959 until his last match in February 1978. He signed as an amateur in 1959 when the club was shambolic and in the Second Division. From there, Cally won pretty much every domestic and international football honour at Liverpool, save a European Cup-Winners' Cup winner's medal. Shanks once said of Cally that he 'typifies everything that is good in football and he's never changed. You could stake your life on him.' My dad, and tens of thousands like him, did just that, following Callaghan's entire career at Liverpool, assured that first the Red No. 7 shirt, briefly 8 and then 11, was in utterly reliable, committed and skilful hands. His like is probably gone for good now. Injuries, rotation, freedom of movement, agents, the crazy cash – it all means that no one is likely to play this number of matches again at a single top club in England. Respect.

Michael's hammy's gone – again. GH isn't wild about talking about it, describing the situation as 'normal', but Michael faces another three or four weeks out in a stop-start season, and just when we face some of our biggest games. McAllister plays in midfield with Biscan. Babbel is ill and so Steven Gerrard has had to be moved to right-back. Robbie is back, for Michael. Our bench for the outfield reads Heskey, Barmby, Hamann and Ziege: £40 million worth of replacements, which tells you we really should win this with something to spare. The danger is that Palace, 2–1 up, score early and we panic, the home crowd in uproar. But this doesn't happen. 'You spit in the air and sometimes it comes back in your face' is Houllier's less than Proust-like response to some of the Palace lads allowing themselves to be parodied in the red-tops by mocking our wayward finishing in the first leg. So no need for motivational seminars tonight, as the Liverpool players, our heroes, huddle conspiratorially before the off.

In fact, rather than threatening us, the visitors, lacking the pacy Fan Zhiyi at the back, look nervous and play far too high up the field and and too flat in defence and Robbie, front man at last, has soon cleverly reverse-passed Smicer inside Wayne Carlisle for the first goal. Within five minutes it's 3–0: firstly, Murphy volleys in a Litmanen pass and then Robbie back-heels Biscan through a defensive black hole for his first Liverpool goal. Basically, after eighteen short minutes, it's all over. You have to feel sorry for the Palace fans: a five-hour trip and confidence high, and now they already know there will be no February final. They are slunk deeper now in the Anny Road seats, revived briefly only when they remember the 1990 Liverpool v Palace FA Cup semi-final and tell us that: 'We're gonna win 4–3'. It's a nice touch. No one believes it.

Another Murphy goal early in the second half kills off all hope for Palace. The midfield has come up with goals again. The only question now is: can Robbie get his goal? He does, late on, to wild crowd acclaim. Even Houllier smiles. As we later shuffle down the Centenary stairs, all 'We shall not be moved', a huge Liverpudlian bawls into his mobile phone at some depressed Bluenose somewhere: 'How many finals are youse in, ay?' Which means, where we come from: book the hotels and get out the maps because *we* are going to Cardiff.

KIPPERED BY INJURY

Some new research on football injuries shows that a lot of serious knocks occur in training and that the quality of medical care for top players in England still leaves a lot to be desired. It reveals a general lack of specialist knowledge and care, and some players feel forced to go outside their clubs for more detailed assessments of injuries.

Of course, managers want players to play. Mostly, players want to play, too, but sometimes they also need protecting from themselves. Club medical staff need to be closer to players than to managers, and strong enough to fend off calls from above for reckless bravery and instant returns. The squad system should help with all of this, of course. These days at Anfield you sense that anyone coming in complaining of a strain is likely to be whisked off right away, no expense spared, for a full-scale check-out by some top surgeon in Germany or the USA. Steven Gerrard, worth £20 million, is especially closely monitored. But it wasn't always like this here. Shanks was famous in his scorn for players who were injured: injury was a personal betrayal to Shankly. Reuben Bennett used to rub a kipper on Anfield's injuries. Tommy Smith and others can tell you all about that now, walking sticks in hand. Most of today's players at least have a decent chance of walking, unaided, in later life. We should all be thankful for that.

27 JANUARY, FA CUP FOURTH ROUND:
LEEDS UNITED 0, LIVERPOOL 2

Is our intellectual manager cunning and strategic; or does he lack real vision and ambition? He was chastened by our 4-3 loss here at Leeds in the league: 'We were too romantic; I prefer to be more lethal.' And this is a tough draw, sure, but Leeds today are hardly in a rich vein. Big money spent, but Leeds are a poor tenth in the league with *five* losses at home already. They still have Champions League possibilities, of course, but not even sly old O'Leary expects much more progress there. Which all means that a reliable route to Europe must be found for Leeds for next season in order to balance the PLC books. Hence the significance to them, low on confidence or not, of this meeting.

Defensively, we have also turned things around in the past few months; only five goals conceded in the last 14 games. More worrying is Houllier's latest team selection. Robbie keeps his place, but looks like having to fend on his own up front, as Hamann is picked alongside McAllister to replace Litmanen. Babbel comes in for the injured Gerrard, with Biscan moving to right midfield. So our bench is a costly attacking array: Heskey, Barmby, Litmanen and Ziege. Add to these the injured Owen, Gerrard, Redknapp, Berger, Traore and Heggem, and the invisible Diomède, and Houllier has now compiled a powerful squad of twenty-odd players, almost all of whom are full internationals. This looks like a major advance, though not a massive incentive, I must say, to the local kids struggling for air in the Liverpool youth teams and reserves. But today, for this vital match, Houllier selects just *one* forward, Fowler presumably with Smicer offering support when he can. What *is* his thinking here? Again, it looks like a negative and fearful selection, when actually going at Leeds, nervy and unsure as they must be, seems the more obvious strategy.

The first half is poor, Leeds showing all their expected problems and Liverpool, understandably, having difficulties holding the ball high up the field, despite Robbie working hard against multiple opponents. Leeds try to apply more pressure in the second period, but defensively we look reasonably comfortable – despite Sander's jitters – with our main back four men mainly in charge. Viduka, otherwise becalmed by Henchoz, misses one decent chance. But Robbie is now beginning to look sharp in his build-up work and Hamann, inconsequential in the first half, begins to be more assertive in the second. And then, crucially, as at Derby earlier in the season, injury takes a guiding hand for us. First, Babbel has to give way to Barmby on the right, and then Murphy suffers in a block tackle with Ferdinand and is carried off to be replaced by Ziege. Finally, Smicer has had enough chasing shadows behind Robbie and Heskey steps up to replace him.

All this means that for the last 20 minutes or so we end up with the sort of side Houllier may well have started with had we had just a little more self-belief. And suddenly, after so much time dangerously wasted, we get into the game as an attacking force; Robbie and Heskey directing traffic with Hamann, and Barmy and Ziege really buzzing on the flanks. Leeds are now shaken, beginning to hang on a little, and in the final minutes Ziege forces his way into the Leeds box, where the ball breaks to Robbie who, like the real poacher that he still is, gently but expertly pokes it left-footed through a thicket of legs and in our direction, South Stand Upper, Row A, Seats 50–52, towards Nigel Martyn's right-hand post.

Psychologists will have some model to describe how we *see* or experience what happens next. What is it, exactly, that kicks in inside our football minds to apparently slow down the next few seconds as the ball, barely 20 yards from where we sit, hits the *inside* of the post and gently arcs across and in front of the Leeds goal-line, but behind the stranded Martyn and his defenders? And as our anguish rises and then escapes, these experts might also explain how we now become aware, peripherally to our left, of someone in red arriving just as the ball moves outside the frame of the goal.

Renewed hope now suppresses despair, meets it head on even as it rises. But Barmby (is it Barmby?) is too wide, surely, to squeeze this in: the area is just too crowded with Leeds bodies. And yet somehow our out-of-form but celebrated 'scorer against the shite', and goal-deliverer in important European ties this season, manages to thread his shot high and beyond the flailing goalkeeper and his goal-line defender, Woodgate, and into the Leeds net. Which means Liverpool have killed off Leeds' 2001 FA Cup dreams.

The Liverpool crowd – in fact everyone in the ground – knows this is the winning moment. That is why the celebrations in our end now show such wild abandon. And it is wild. It is amazing, don't you think; eighty-odd minutes of mainly rank sparring, all forgotten for this one ecstatic moment? Or is it just one? Because then, deep into injury time, with Liverpool fans still throbbing with disbelieving joy, Robbie picks up the ball wide on their left. And like a nervous tightrope walker, two steps forward, one back, he sways with the ball right on the far touch-line, gliding past Bowyer and making his opponent look a jerk, just as Stevie Mac used to do for us.

The Liverpool coaches want Robbie to just run the ball into the corner, of course, to do the 'professional' thing and waste the last few seconds, as Macca would certainly have done. No chance, because Robbie still wants to play so instead, head up, he threads a left-foot cross fully thirty yards over to Barmby at the far post. Leeds are now in disarray and Barmby has time to collect and calmly lay the ball back to the arriving Heskey, who fairly explodes his shot past Martyn.

The players and the Liverpool staff are really bubbling over this win. You can see it as they leave the field. Okay, Henchoz, job completed, disappears first as usual, but Carragher and McAllister are jigging and jubilant. Litmanen, still tracksuited, goes to each player individually, high-fiving or hugging them. Phil Thompson double punches the air from inside the tunnel. Robbie lingers last to applaud the fans, who roar their feelings for him, architect of this win. And Houllier waits on the pitch for Robbie now, arm around his striker's shoulder, like a doting dad after a hard-fought schools' cup final.

Later, GH will make his usual speech about the game being about 16 players, not 11, these days and how the substitutes turned it for us, and how he doesn't want to take *all* the credit for his master plan which has produced a vital win. And it's hard to argue with the outcome as we drain our Guinnesses in the local Wheatsheaf later with gusto and pride, among reflective and gloomy Leeds supporters. Revenge is sweet. And maybe the fresh spring in our subs' heels has turned the tide. But something still rankles: did this win really need to be this hard, Gérard – and quite this late?

FOUR COMPETITIONS

No need to look out for the Bluenoses in the fifth-round draw: Tranmere have walloped them 3–0 at Goodison, meaning more wailing in Walton. And cancel Manchester hotel rooms in South Wales: the Corporation also lose at home, to di Canio's West Ham. So when Trevor Francis and Steve Coppell, FA celebrity pickers for the fifth round, pull out Sunderland matched with West Ham and Arsenal to play Chelsea, and then ball No. 12 (Liverpool) to play at home to No. 13 (Manchester City), we are even beginning to think that this just could be our FA Cup year, too. Time for Houllier to remind us that it is early February and we are still in all four of the competitions we began. He has a point. But is it harsh to suggest – we don't think so – that this also means that GH thinks, presumably, that being 16 points behind United, two-thirds of the way through the season, means we are still somehow 'in' the league?

MANCHESTER MUSICALS

More confusion and dejection returns to the Liverpool ranks. In mid-week we go to the desperate Maine Road home of the desperate Manchester City and field one striker, Heskey. Robbie, beginning to find his best form at last and crying out for more play, is benched again for all but the final half-hour. Steven Gerrard, England's outstanding driving midfield player of the season does return – but at left-back. A flaccid Ziege, starting at left-midfield, is withdrawn at half-time. A scrappy 1–1 draw results, a Heskey header matched by Tiatto's messy equaliser. Liverpool supporters watch from the 'Gene Kelly Stand' according to a dark Mancs steward: 'I'm singing in the rain, just singing in the rain.' But this away-points drought is no longer funny. Two more have been unnecessarily sacrificed at this dank pit in Moss Side, on the altar of rotation and caution. We have now collected a miserly 12 points from 12 away league matches: one more than the calamitous and relegation-threatened City. GH will see it differently, but this travel sickness will surely cost us.

2 FEBRUARY: LIVERPOOL 3, WEST HAM UNITED 0

There is a small feeling in the Flattie, no more than that, that the London press has been selling too hard recently to the affable Eriksson the obvious talents of the young West Ham midfielders, Cole, Carrick and Lampard. This bandwagon got another mighty push last week when the Hammers deservedly tipped United out of the FA Cup. Don't get us wrong; these guys are decent players, Cole especially. But they are still a long way from international quality in terms of consistency, application and experience. And none of them, we think, are close to matching our own young Gerrard. This is our gripe and I suspect – hope – that some of this kind of press talk was stirred deeply into the Liverpool motivational porridge at Melwood this week as we prepared to face this 'future England midfield'.

A sign of the season going well at any club after Christmas is looming ticket crises. Large parts of the day can now be spent on the phone to Anfield or wondering how to get tickets for forthcoming matches in cup and league, home and away. The ground swarms with urchins wanting precious season-ticket vouchers, exchangeable for match tickets. 'It's how it should be,' say the Fellahs in Front, fully turned out on the Kop, 'It's like it used to be.' But it's another supporter's test this, a kind of sub-Darwinian scramble for stadium access. It provokes anxiety.

Rogan has also returned from the international Football Expo event in Cannes with tales of Michel Platini's unfeasibly tiny frame. All really great players look amazingly small, we agree. This could be 'Ruddock's Law', we hypothesise. The West Ham visit is sold out and we await an open and proper football challenge, a real match. Instead, as history tells us we should, we stroll it. First, di Canio decides that another trip to the north-west is just too much following his heroics last week. Titi Camara replaces him, and looks woeful: a clear result for GH. Secondly, we sit hard on their aspirant young midfield trio – and throttle them. It's a breeze.

With Carragher still absent Gregory Vignal, a 19-year-old left-sided £500,000 signing by GH from Montpellier, surprisingly steps up, another stern signal for the benched Ziege. But Smicer runs the show, and West Ham just can't pick him up. After threatening early on Vladdy blasts a swerving long-range opener past Forrest inside the first 20 minutes. Later in the first half Robbie tries from the same spot and this time trundles one beyond Forrest and inside his near post. Meanwhile, young Vignal has played brilliantly, reminding everyone here of the economy of having a decent left foot in this area, and Steven Wright, on for the injured Babbel and huge ears flapping, is doing fine at right-back, including passing to Robbie for his goal.

West Ham have five minutes at the start of the second half, Westerveld saving well from Lampard, but then the pattern resumes with Smicer still pulling the strings. And for the first time for some time we actually *play* some sophisticated football, passing and moving, pulling them apart. Litmanen's arrival at the club might have sparked Vladdy, but his form has been improving for some time and now he pulls two balls back for Robbie from one of the Toxteth Terror's favourite spots, the byline to Robbie's left, Kop end. Both end up buried, naturally, though one is disallowed by some myopic linesman claiming Vlad has tripped the ball over the dead-ball line. What, in this form? Three-nil it ends, but it could have been any score, seriously.

We now have harder tests ahead: Sunderland in the league, two meetings with Roma in the UEFA Cup, Manchester City in the FA Cup fifth round and the League Cup final against Birmingham City. Our entire season, five games, four competitions, all within 16 crazy days. It could be the mid-'80s again. If Houllier is right we will now see the rewards of his careful policies, his clever husbanding of our growing resources. But are we *really* ready for these tests?

6. THE FRENCH CONNECTION

As Liverpool's favourite boot room boy, the loyal Roy Evans, was struggling valiantly to bring the league title to Anfield in the mid-'90s, elsewhere a new generation of imported foreign coaches, players and managers was beginning to mark the wider transformation of English football. Arsène Wenger at Arsenal, and Ruud Gullit and then Gianluca Vialli at Chelsea, were in the vanguard of this development which eventually brought the arrival in England of the continental coaching technocrats. Gullit and Vialli were well known as top quality international players, of course, drawn to the FA Premier League in the twilight of their careers by the allure of life in London and the big cash rewards now on offer in Sky Sports England. Gullit, actually, was rather like a lot of English player-managerial candidates in his new role; a brilliant player, as a manager he was lazy and intuitive, accused by some players of arrogance, and he relied substantially on his own judgement and reputation to try to sustain a new career. He soon failed the test. Vialli, by contrast, was popular and eager to learn and he had success at Chelsea before being discarded by an impatient Ken Bates only a few weeks into the 2000–01 league season.

But the real head-turner was Wenger. With no serious playing record to talk of and barely known in England, except via Glenn Hoddle's recommendation because of their shared time at Monaco, Wenger had been working as a manager in the obscurity of Japan before Arsenal brought him on board to replace the struggling Bruce Rioch. Relaxed and assured of his own ability, but looking more like an FE lecturer than a top foreign coach, Wenger saw no need to make early expansive gestures at his new club. Instead, he built cleverly on the existing Highbury defensive strength and experience, brought by George Graham, and impressed the old-timers at Arsenal with his thoroughness and discipline, as well as his determination to ditch the control freakery of Graham and to treat his players rather more like mature professional sportsmen.

Striker Victor Ikpeba said of Wenger's time at Monaco: 'He was patient, listened to you, but above all you trusted him; he is a man of honour. A gentleman, as you say in England.' Not that much of a gentleman: Wenger soon got rid of the north London favourites whose dressing-room influence he distrusted – Merson, Hughes and Ian Wright – and signed a trio of little known but ambitious Frenchmen, Patrick Vieira, Nicolas Anelka and Emmanuel Petit. They took the English game by storm. In Wenger's second season, 1997–98, Arsenal did the double. This Francophile north London success had been fully and enviously noted at Anfield.

Wenger and Gérard Houllier knew each other well from their time spent together hoovering up knowledge on coaching courses in France in the late 1980s. Wenger, and Arsenal's David Dein, were a key influence in ensuring Houllier decided to go to Anfield to job-share in 1997 rather than to manage at either Celtic or Sheffield Wednesday. 'I told him Liverpool was like a Ferrari and the others did not have the same potential,' Wenger said later. Wenger's influence at Anfield did not stop there. With Liverpool giving up a home lead to a Leeds United defeat in Houllier's first game in sole charge, he turned to his rival and friend Wenger for the sort of advice which was to shape Houllier's reign at Anfield: 'In my first game we were 1–0 up and lost 3–1. I'm not sure whether Arsène rang me or I rang him. But out of our conversation came a resolve to do what I have done about our defence. If you can trust someone it can confirm what is already in your mind.' With support from his French friend and rival, Liverpool's new manager prepared to go shopping.

Like Wenger, Houllier had no great legacy as a top player to draw upon for his progress as a coach or manager. His own limited playing ambitions had been thwarted early on by his father's insistence that he should acquire qualifications in a more 'respectable' profession, so the young Houllier set out in search of training in teaching. However, his father was also the director of a small French amateur club, and the young Gérard took a keen interest in the preparation and performance of the players. From here, and with research and teaching experience already under his belt – some of it in Liverpool – Houllier made his way in the sport in France as a young, innovative coach with a reputation for meticulous attention to detail and a determination to apply a more 'scientific', an educator's, approach to player preparation and tactics.

After beginning as player-coach at Le Touquet in 1973, aged only 26, the young Houllier spent a couple of years as youth coach at Arras, before he eventually moved into coaching duties at modest Noeux-les-Mines. As an assistant there to manager Guy de Beugny, a man Houllier regarded as being possibly 20 years ahead of his time, Houllier picked up the importance of a skills-based approach to player development, something which totally changed his approach to coaching. He said of de Beugny: 'He was a thinker, he showed me things I had never seen before, despite all the coaching courses I had been on. It was a forward-thinking and very modern approach in which everything starts from skills. Even if you're working on the physical side, do it through skills. And the players improved a lot. I think the success I've had is owed to him.' Between 1976 and 1982, Houllier guided this little-known team from the fifth to the second division of the French league, using an intriguing management style which was firm but also 'democratic'. He was known in France during these early days of club management, for example, for his willingness to involve the players, and even the fans, in his discussions about football tactics.

Football folk in France were beginning to sit up and take notice of this new young coach with his new ideas and, recruited by another club from the old coal-mining region of the Nord-Pas de Calais, Houllier then took the well-supported RC Lens into the French first division and to a UEFA Cup place. Houllier enjoyed the passion for football among the working-class people of Lens. Alain Tirloy, a friend of Houllier who had also played under him at Lens, noticed a very different approach to football coaching in the young Houllier, one which focused strongly on mental as well as physical preparation: 'He's always been very modern in his approach. Back then it was revolutionary,' said Tirloy. 'Firstly, he was very specific in his demands for physical fitness. He had specific training programmes for everyone, specific targets. He's also a great believer in players having it right in the head. If the mental attitude isn't right you can forget the rest. He's a psychologist really. I get the feeling this is what sets apart these good new French managers, people like Houllier and Wenger.'

At Lens, Houllier also learned the hard way how to balance his theorising with more practical advice and work on the field tuned to the needs of hardened football professionals. 'We could see he was an intelligent coach,' said general secretary Louis Plet, but some Lens players also began to despair of Houllier's methods. 'They said it was all blackboards and discussions, not enough work on the field. It was a minority, mainly younger players, but it was a problem for Gérard. I think that was when the other coaches helped him. He knew he had to make people respect him, and at Lens he learned how to do it.' From this experience, Houllier worked on linking a highly disciplined, carefully planned, and well-organised administration of a football club

– something easily associated with technocratic foreign coaches – with a passionate, empathetic desire to connect with the 'spirit' or 'heart' at the core of a club's identity. He learned well: by 1986 Houllier was leading the under-achieving Paris Saint-Germain to their first French league title. He would later make the same formula work at Anfield.

Houllier already knew about Liverpool FC, of course. As he was leading PSG to the French title, so Dalglish's Liverpool was doing the double in England, dragging the Anfield club out of its post-Heysel despond. Houllier, in fact, had been a long-time admirer of the Liverpool club and of the city. At age 22 he had chosen to come to Liverpool in order to work on his Masters dissertation – on poverty and youth culture in the city. He enjoyed the rough edges, the vibrancy and the humour of the youngsters and the adults he met there: 'I've always liked the town, Liverpool,' he says. 'I know the town has not a good reputation abroad. I know that some people would come through various districts of the city and would say, "Well, this is absolutely ugly" or "This is dirty" and it's funny because I surprise myself because I say, "Well, I like it!" I like the people and their sense of humour, this is important, this is a part of it. This is part of the game here. I think the people here like to have a good time.'

Most of all, he loved the passion for football in Liverpool: it matched his own. Houllier briefly taught as an assistant at a Walton school, played local league football and, when he could, supported Liverpool FC as a visiting 'Kopite'. As he pointed out later, this was hardly a halcyon period for the Red half of the city: Liverpool had last won the league title in 1966 and would not triumph again in the league until 1973. *Everton* were league champions in 1969–70. Nevertheless, when pressed by football-mad kids in Alsop school – 'Are yer Blue or Red, sir?' – the young Frenchman instantly blurted out 'Red'. He immediately knew he had made a life choice. His first game at Anfield, in the company of later Liverpool first-team coach, Patrice Bergues, saw Liverpool crush Dundalk 10–0 in the Inter Cities Fairs Cup. He was much impressed by the power and pace and the 'professionalism' of the Liverpool team, as it hungrily pressed forward for more goals, when a French club in a similar position would have strolled to a smaller victory.

Houllier struck up an unlikely friendship with Liverpool secretary Peter Robinson through a mutual friend, which further cemented his own growing attachment and admiration for the Liverpool club and the values he felt it expressed. He returned to Anfield from time to time in the years which followed, and in 1986, the year of his own greatest club triumph, Houllier brought along another friend and football coach to Liverpool to share his appreciation of the English game. His name? One

Arsène Wenger. Three years before, in 1983, Houllier and Lens coaching assistant, Joachim Marx, had come to Anfield to watch a potential Polish signing in a second-leg European tie against Widzew Lodz. It was clear, as Marx recalled later, that Houllier had something else on his mind in Liverpool 4 that evening. That here, in the north-west of England, was more than just a football club:

> I could see from the start that something was getting to Gérard. He seemed very excited about something. The football, of course, was fantastic, but there was something else. It was the noise, the passion, the red-brick stadium, the little working-class houses all around. Gérard was spellbound by the whole thing. We were from an area of industrial France, where poor miners had the same feelings for the game and their team. We went to a pub nearby after the game and drank a few beers. No one, of course, knew who Gérard was, even though he was a top coach in France. He was talking football with the fans, just like he was one of them. As we left the pub Gérard made a remark to me I have never forgotten. He said, 'You know, Joachim, I would love to be the coach of this club one day.' I honestly believe Gérard never lost that dream.

Houllier's early passion for Liverpool FC, for elements of the traditional English game and its supporters, and for the English in general, is obvious. He confesses himself to being bored, for example, when he had to sit as the French national coach through highly technical but cagey continental matches. The high pace of the English game always excited him. 'For those who love football,' he said recently, 'England is a wonderful country, different from anywhere else. There is so much effort and enthusiasm on the field, such passion and pace that you can never get bored for a minute.' But by 1988, Houllier had been appointed the assistant to the French national team coach, Michel Platini, eventually taking over the job of French manager for a brief period from 1992. His 16-month spell as coach of France ended when the national team failed to qualify for World Cup 1994 after a last-minute home defeat to unfancied Bulgaria.

This crippling loss, which occurred after David Ginola had tried to dribble out of trouble but had helped launch a fatal opposing attack instead, confirmed Houllier in some of his strongest footballing beliefs: first, that teamwork was more central to success than the skills of any individual player; and second, that *all* players must take on the responsibility of defending properly as a unit when under pressure. Much later, when the talented Jari Litmanen arrived at Anfield in

January 2001 – 'A nine-and-a-half,' according to Houllier, 'a link player between midfield and attack' – the Liverpool manager made it very clear that it was the Finn's contribution to the collective Anfield cause which was more vital than Litmanen's undoubted individual skills. 'He's a good passer, who is also tougher than I thought,' he said. 'He may be a star player but to me he is a team player. That's the main thing.'

As national technical director of French football, Houllier then concentrated on youth development in France, contributing to the emergence of the 1998 World Cup and Euro 2000-winning French squads. He was by now widely respected in UEFA and FIFA circles because of his central role, as national technical director and national team manager, in the dramatic transformation of the previously moribund French game.

Houllier came to the wider attention of the footballing élite in England when he enthused an FA national coaching conference in Birmingham in May 1997 with his use of video clips and coaching drills to illustrate the power of forward-passing on counter-attack. It was clear his approach would be very different to that of the Roy Evans era: one of his drills was aimed at scoring with four passes inside five seconds when possession was gained. The importance of the fast pass forward was a theme he would return to many times later at Anfield. 'In England,' Houllier commented, mysteriously, 'the speed is high level but there are different paces. The quality I believe in is *vivacite*, the quickness of reaction, of tactics. Ronaldo is fast but he is also quick.' This last observation is actually straight Bob Paisley. Houllier would soon be coming 'home'.

The FA agreed to follow in England the lead on youth development Houllier had established so successfully in France through the Clairefontaine national football academy near Paris. Houllier was the vital cross-channel fixer of links between the English coaching élite and the French hierarchy. As a result, 'After the 1998 World Cup I spoke to the French coach, Aime Jacquet, and they told us everything they do,' enthused Les Reed, the FA's director of technical development: 'What we're doing here gives us a chance of winning three World Cups.' One, it should be pointed out, would probably suffice. Howard Wilkinson's FA Charter for Excellence, which later established youth academies at all the major professional clubs in England, has its roots firmly in the soil of Gérard Houllier's own transformation of youth coaching in France. Sven Goran Eriksson, and others who follow, ought to reap the national benefits.

Peter Robinson had recommended Houllier to Spurs in the late 1980s, and after Kenny Dalglish stood down as Liverpool manager in

1991 Houllier was apparently considered for the vacant post. The FA also thought about him as their inaugural technical director. But these ideas, to recruit a foreign coach for England or one to succeed the boot room dynasty at Anfield, were still way ahead of their time and came to nothing. But by the late 1990s, following his national football successes in France, Houllier was itching to get back into club management: 'When I became national team manager and then national technical director I could still keep in touch with reading *Le Monde* every day, reading papers, books, and so on,' he said. 'But when you are a club manager it is very focused. All that goes. Not being involved in a club, I missed what we in France call "the powder", the gun and fire. At 51 do you stay nice and cosy by the fireside, or do you go to war again? I needed to go out into the trench again!'

If not exactly in a 'trench', Liverpool under Roy Evans had come agonisingly close in the mid-'90s to returning to earlier glories without quite establishing the sort of discipline and the mental strength needed to win the top football prizes. Chairman David Moores, a 'boot room' disciple, was loath to sack the Bootle man. But it had also become clear that new thinking and a tougher influence was needed. Some top players were beginning to take liberties in training. To widespread surprise – and some heavy criticism – Houllier was brought in by the Liverpool board for the 1997–98 season for an ultimately ill-fated experiment in dual football management.

Cynics argued from the outset that Houllier's willingness to become a co-manager was him simply stalking the Evans job at Liverpool; what incentives were there, after all, to make the new arrangement work, given that Houllier would almost certainly get the job for himself if the partnership failed? This seems unfair. Houllier respected Evans and the Liverpool boot room ethos he represented. He wanted no part in undermining or replacing the Liverpool man, one of the conditions, in fact, of his joining the club. He seemed genuinely moved by his new appointment, and he appeared convinced that joint decision-making was perfectly possible at a top English football club, even one which was desperately trying to reclaim past glories in the full media spotlight. Of course, sharing management of the club, having a good look from the inside without ultimate responsibility, almost certainly helped Houllier prepare for his later period as sole manager of Liverpool. He would need less time later to weigh up the really corrosive influences at Anfield before moving on to his own vision of the future for the club.

There was something inevitable about the Evans/Houllier failure. After all, the characters and philosophies of the joint managers were very different. Houllier's disciplinary and preparatory zeal clashed with Evans's more relaxed and more intuitive feel for the game and his own closeness to the players. More importantly, the Anfield dressing-room was by no means at ease with the new regime, and was soon seeking out weaknesses in the partnership, with some experienced players resenting aspects of the new football professionalism favoured by Houllier. 'It is very difficult to share the same philosophy, the same management style. There can be only one boss at a club,' said Houllier following Evans's resignation. 'I think the main thing is that people you work with are not prepared for that type of situation and if they are not prepared for it either they make it difficult for you or they find it difficult to adapt.'

Secretly, the new man was appalled by key features of the Liverpool style of training and player preparation and the approach to work of some of the club's top players. Later he confessed: 'What surprised me when I first came here was the attitudes of one or two of the players towards their job. Earning so much money, they just wouldn't do the right thing for it. If you know that it's going to be a tough training session then you can't go out or stay up till midnight the night before. I can point to so many still here who became different players the moment others left. You have to create the best conditions, climate and atmosphere to get the best out of the players.' Paul Ince, the self-styled 'governor', was a key player here, an obvious target for removal, but when Houllier started his first full season in charge in 1999–2000, it was noticeable, too, that Babb, McAteer, Ruddock and goalkeeper David James had all disappeared from Liverpool first-team concerns. Comparing his own regime with the Evans years, Houllier observed: 'Having seen the two – and this is not a criticism – there is a different work atmosphere, a different ethic. All I know is that my team will die for the shirt they now wear; I can promise our fans that at least.' Gérard, that *is* a criticism, and it is one which was probably justified.

Press mutterings about the lack of a single 'decision-maker' at the football helm at Anfield added to the pressures on the new pairing, but it was poor performances and unacceptable results which really ended the experiment. A weak Liverpool team lost feebly at home to Spurs in a League Cup tie in November 1998, a result which finally led to Evans's resignation. By this stage Liverpool was barely competing physically with opponents at all, something which had dogged the talented Evans teams throughout the period of his management. This experience confirmed Houllier's later insistence that physical strength and athletic ability were absolutely vital as prerequisites for a successful club in the new football era. Liverpool's defensive core would need radical surgery, but *all* players would need to up their workrate and application on defensive duties.

Equally, passing for the sake of passing and keeping the ball to no apparent attacking purpose had become real problems in the Evans years, and Houllier made no apology for his conviction that Liverpool needed to revert to a more positive approach, particularly with respect to getting the ball forward earlier. In 1999 Houllier remarked: 'Two years ago Liverpool made more passes than any other team, they were the best passing team in the Premiership. But to me that doesn't mean anything. You have to verticalise, and to go deeper with passes.' He wanted to hurt opposing teams more than Evans's talented sides seemed willing to do.

A second feature of the new approach Houllier brought to Anfield was the need for football technique and skills to be more closely integrated with the evolution of players' all-round education and culture. This more 'holistic' view of sportsmen is really quite foreign to English football, where the culture is expected to produce young players who require and expect direction, discipline and supervision almost all the time. They are generally little prepared to make decisions on the field. Houllier stressed the need for players to be good decision-makers, to have the intelligence to read the game, and to adapt to tactical shifts made by opponents. Under Evans, the simple shackling of the gifted McManaman, for example, was often sufficient to stifle the entire creative emphasis of the Liverpool team. No alternative plan seemed to be in the offing. Liverpool would now also practice set-pieces, an undercooked part of match preparation in virtually all previous Liverpool regimes.

On the tactical side, Houllier favoured the tighter and narrower 4–4–2 formation or a 4–4–1–1 shape, over the looser 3–5–2 format championed by Evans. He especially liked the idea of establishing a lead in matches, and then placing two defensive barriers of four in front of opponents, inviting them on, while trying to catch them on the break with a crucial killer goal. This meant a much less attractive, less open style away from home to that favoured by Evans – but also a rather more successful one. Liverpool managed only five away victories in 1997–98, Evans's last season in solo charge. In 1999–2000 Houllier's Liverpool managed eight victories but scored three fewer goals, 23 to 26. Defensive solidity – especially away from Anfield – was to be one of the watchwords of the new Houllier era.

Houllier was also committed to a very different approach to substitutions to that established under Evans. The former manager had seemed almost frozen in the old Liverpool way, established under Shankly and Paisley, of changing as little as possible on the field, even if the team was playing poorly or losing. The same players also seemed to be withdrawn whenever substitutions were made, adding credence to fatal suggestions that Evans had 'favourites' in the Anfield camp – the willing but limited Harkness, for example – and scapegoats – the talented but frustrating Berger. Houllier, in contrast, felt that the physical and mental demands of the modern game and the increasing tactical sophistication of opponents meant that a completely new approach to substitutes was needed. Houllier even admitted that the closest he ever came to *striking* a player was when a substitute he had introduced into a match at the start of the 2000–01 season had actually made the on-field Liverpool team *worse*, a heinous crime in his book: enter the much-discussed – and not universally loved – rotation system.

Houllier's view was that the English professional had to rethink the whole concept of replacement and rotation, and to consider it much more strategically. If a British player is rested or replaced, he argued, 'They feel you think they've done badly when it isn't necessarily true, when it might be that they've worn out the opposing defenders so someone else can come on to finish the job. Why can't people accept it?' Well, because they want to *play*, for one reason, their playing careers are short. European sports cultures, unlike those in the US, are much more resistant to this sort of strategic specialisation, and to the more centralised role for the coach which it implies. Moreover, rotation only seemed a feature at Anfield for forward players: the Liverpool defence was seldom rotated. But Houllier kept on making his point in the 2000–01 season that it was now a 14- or 16- or even a 22-man game at the highest level, and that substitutes often turned matches, scored vital goals. We were close to the era of the specialist substitute. Robbie Fowler, especially, seemed less than impressed with the Anfield rotation policy as the season reached its climax, whereas Houllier, contrarily, seemed at last actually to settle on his 'preferred' team. But players on the bench could at least be assured that, under Houllier, they would be likely to get their chance. Liverpool frequently used two, or even all three, substitutes in crucial matches under the Frenchman, an unheard-of rate of exchange under any previous Liverpool manager.

Houllier's instincts have been not only to address these questions of skill-acquisition, tactical flexibility and squad depth at Liverpool, but also to address what he saw as the problems of the prevailing player culture in English football. This contrasted the well-worn emphasis on juvenile 'laddishness' in many English dressing-rooms – and in English football crowds – with Houllier's preferred emphasis upon more of an all-round education and personal development programme for the modern élite footballer.

Perhaps surprisingly for some people, Houllier soon expressed his delight at working with young players in England even over those he had worked with in France. He enjoyed, especially, the depth of feeling for the game and the enthusiasm of the English:

> The good thing about working here is that there is a lot, a lot, of tremendous assets to the English players. The frame of mind, the attitude, the enthusiasm. They like the game. They've got a big heart, they put everything into it. I would say that I prefer to be a coach for the English players than working with young players in France. It's easier maybe on some aspects of the game with the French, but from the human point of view it is much more exciting here. Because I knew the type of environment the young players used to live in, and what it would mean for them to be there in the team, nobody wants to help them more than I do. It might be easier to work with other players from a technical point of view. But I enjoy the human things about working with the players here.

But Houllier also argued, forcefully, for a commitment to a much stronger 'learning culture' in English football, one in which change is not necessarily viewed as threatening. This meant a more cerebral, a more strategic, approach to playing the game, but also a much stronger commitment to what Houllier regards as the values and principles of professionalism in sport. Central here was an attack on the drinking cultures inside English football clubs – something which had, clearly, been an important part of Liverpool's earlier period of dominance in the European game. According to Houllier, and the other new coaching technocrats, the football world had since changed: Liverpool, he reasoned, would have to change with it, or sink.

So when Houllier began to work inside Liverpool he was taken aback by what he found: it was a set of behavioural patterns among established professionals he had never come across in France. Liverpool club officials worried, for example, about taking players away for extended periods abroad because of potential problems in controlling their drinking and general high jinks. 'Let me explain what stuns me here,' Houllier said later, referring to the situation more widely in England. 'A young player comes into the game, looks the part. He's not a drinker, looks after himself. Then, as soon as he gets into the first team, he thinks he has to show he's a man, he has to drink. In probably every other country, the young player actually becomes *more* serious about the game. He'll do anything he can to improve and stay in the team.' Staying in the team in England, in fact, traditionally meant being one of the 'lads'.

This deep antipathy towards drinking among professionals is what led to tensions between Houllier and some of the local Liverpool players he valued, like Robbie Fowler, of course. Houllier was convinced that breaking the drinking culture which still existed at Liverpool – graphically outlined later by Neil Ruddock, a key member of this club – depended upon increasing his contingent of foreigners, rooting out the English drinkers, and convincing the new generation of young players from the city and elsewhere that professional pride and physical conditioning and awareness, rather than the 'team spirit' supposedly engendered by a lads' night out, was the key to modern footballing success. 'I compare top-class players to racing cars,' he said in February 2000. 'Drinking alcohol is as silly as putting diesel in a racing car. If you have a booze-up every week, you won't edge out a foreign player who doesn't. The future of English football is in the players' hands.' And so, of course, is Liverpool's future. 'There used to be a time,' he said in his second season in charge at Anfield, 'when as soon as the young go through to the first team they have to start drinking to show they are men. That's finished; if they do that they last two years. I don't think we have a booze problem. Previously, perhaps, but not now.'

When Liverpool kicked off the 2000–01 season, with a home match against Bradford City, not one of the starting line-up had been a regular starter in Liverpool's colours at the end of the 1997–98 season. Post-Bosman, the rapid movement of players through top clubs has become more generally a new feature of late-modern football. This especially, in Houllier's eyes, is what distinguishes this current era of the freedom-of-contract millionaire footballer from those overseen by previous successful Liverpool bosses. Houllier admires Shankly and Paisley, but he doubts there is too much from their approach which transfers directly to the new situation at Liverpool. Today, he argues, it is insufficient and impractical to try to direct or instruct players, as Shankly might have done. Today, players are more reflexive, have much more control over their own futures. The job of a successful football manager is more complex than in earlier periods: it is to create an environment and a future for players which is both attractive and realisable.

For these reasons, Houllier does not lament the passing of the era of the all-powerful football boss. 'Every manager would acknowledge it was easier to manage then,' he contends. 'But because it's different now, because it's more complicated, you can turn it the other way round – it's more exciting. From an intellectual point of view, and from a psychological point of view, it's better to be confronted by these problems than to have a situation where you ask a player to do something and he just does it. The most important things in this job are human management and your concept of football – and I don't think you can learn those on a course.' So, selling the controversial rotation policy to his players, and keeping his star players fully on board, was a challenge Houllier relished.

But Houllier also believed that the squad he inherited at Anfield lacked sufficient depth to compete with the best in England and Europe. He brought in Hyypia, Henchoz and Hamann to cement his defensive foundation around a 'square base' of central defenders and central midfielders whose first task was defence. Playing in front of the newly signed goalkeeper Sander Westerveld, these new arrivals conceded only 30 goals in 1999–2000, the best defensive record in the FA Premier League. Markus Babbel arrived later to shore up the right full-back berth with Jamie Carragher, a fourth centre-back, later converted to left-back. This was, clearly, a defence designed to defend, and one replete with plenty of the physical strength and height so lacking in Evans's teams of the mid-'90s.

The acquisition of 'touch' players such as Vladimir Smicer and Jari Litmanen shows that although Houllier has stressed, repeatedly, the sheer athletic endeavour required from footballers in this era, he also remains convinced that skill, not power, will win out in the modern game: that top players of the future will be technically excellent, two-footed and utterly adaptable to almost any position. This also explains his hard work with Robbie Fowler, Michael Owen, Danny Murphy and others at the Liverpool club, aimed at expanding their game, and also the rueful remark from the brilliant Steven Gerrard that Houllier reminded the young midfielder 'Every time I have a decent game' that he still has a lot to learn. But Houllier also admits that his approach with young players has changed over time as he himself has matured as a manager. In the past, he reasoned, he had been too demanding, far too negative: 'I believe in qualities,' he explained. 'Up to a certain age, you can work with the qualities, not with the flaws. When you are a young manager, you make the mistake of looking for the flaws. You are always the perfectionist, you always want more. You say this one doesn't defend enough, or this one doesn't use his left foot. Wrong! Now that I am over 50, I know you have to emphasise a player's assets, emphasise what he *can* do.'

This philosophy was useful when some Liverpool fans were initially wary of what *exactly* it was, for example, that £11 million capture Emile Heskey had to offer the club. In early matches he seemed clumsy and immature, lacking in some of the Liverpool basics. Houllier bolstered Heskey's confidence, told him to attack defenders with his power and pace and to shoot more often. He soon won his Anfield doubters over.

The manager also praised the real qualities of both Robbie Fowler and Michael Owen, but also insisted they could get still more from their game. Owen's ability accordingly began to improve, and slowly he began to trust his largely inactive left foot. Fowler learned to play in a deeper role, which emphasised his passing skills and his impressive 'joining up' play. After a slow start, it was clear that Houllier was actually getting somewhere, that he was moving the club and academy at Liverpool towards a base which produced players who were flexible and multi-skilled in their approach to the sport. Houllier has no doubt that it is skill, not power and pace, which will ultimately win out in the game's new future. He says:

> I believe in skill. The game will go with skill, I believe that. In ten years' time you won't be able to tell if a player is right- or left-footed. In ten years' time you will have to be able to do that to succeed. I believe in skill. Skilful players solve problems on the field. Take a player who is clever, can read the game, can run. The more we go on we will have more physical ability and more skill. See the difference in central defenders. In ten years' time central defenders, who used to be strong and sturdy guys who just clear the ball away, just being a good defender, you won't have that anymore. Everything will start from the back. You will need a good, passing defender; a good defender who is a passer of the ball.

When Houllier took sole charge of Liverpool for his first full season in 1999–2000, he confirmed his 'Liverpool core' approach to the rebuilding of the club by bringing back to Anfield ex-player and Liverpudlian enthusiast, Phil Thompson, as his assistant. Thompson, a player with 'sparrow legs but a heart like a lion', according to firebrand coach Ronnie Moran, took on some of the important motivational duties, a role which fitted well with Houllier's more reserved touch-line and dressing-room demeanour. Houllier was also concerned to point out, however, that his rather owlish and gentle public persona should not be mistaken for some benign 'niceness' – especially if any player threatened to disturb the all-important collective ethic he was trying to re-establish at the club: 'I'm very demanding in terms of work and spirit,' he said in November of his first season. 'I think I'm a very nice man but I can be a very nasty man if someone is not behaving right. If someone upsets the harmony of what we are trying to do, I am ten times nastier than anyone else.'

Thompson could also be 'nasty' when it was needed. One of seven football-mad children from a council estate in Kirkby, Thompson's mother and sisters were passionate Liverpudlians, his father a less committed merchant seaman Evertonian. Thompson remembers well the huge excitement of the 1960s in the city, shaped around Everton's 'school of science', Shankly and the Beatles, but he also played in the aggressive and sometimes miserly Liverpool sides of the late 1970s, when the accent on defence had the club grinding out hard-won victories away from home in the domestic game and abroad. Thompson's job was to bring the same defensive hardness and unity to the 'new' Liverpool, and to offer guidance and support to younger players of the sort he felt had been sadly lacking during the turbulent Evans years. Thompson had said the biggest compliment ever paid to him was being called 'a young Ronnie Moran' by Graeme Souness, a man who later sacked him. 'Ronnie was the disciplinarian at the club, and there was no bigger moaner in football,' Thompson explained. Moran was a notoriously hard man to please, even as Liverpool were sweeping all before them, as Thompson points out:

> We would turn up for training after a 4–0 win thinking we were the bee's knees and Ronnie would just rip into us, ignoring all our best moments and pointing up all our faults. We used to wonder what would ever satisfy the bloke, why he was like that, but now I know. You can't be on an ego trip in this job. The last game is history and the next is the only thing that matters. You take an aggressive approach because you want things done in the right way. I accept the game has moved on, and there's no point harping on about how it used to be. But I don't see anything wrong with passion and discipline, even if it makes you unpopular.

Allied to the coaching intelligence and enthusiasm of another passionate scouser, Sammy Lee, this aggressive devotion towards achieving a rooted, disciplined perfection brought a nice balance to the whole Liverpool coaching team: Houllier and his French colleague, Patrice Bergues, to offer a more 'technical' coaching and management input; Thompson to take on the defensive and motivational duties and Ronnie Moran's old moaning brief; and Lee to keep the camp buzzing and working hard, especially when spirits were low. Joe Corrigan worked with the club goalkeepers and the reserve team. The Liverpool reserves under Houllier became, once more, a successful showcase for players trying to regain fitness or force their way into the first team, not the laughing stock it had sometimes threatened to become under Evans. Some measure of Houllier's respect for Sammy Lee can be gauged from the fact that in May 2001 the Liverpool manager was furious when England claimed the talented Lee for part-time work on the national coaching staff. Houllier argued that 'team England' ought to be developing its own permanent coaching team, not ransacking clubs for their best backroom talent.

Despite the foreign imports, the central core of the Liverpool team which began the 1999–2000 season was not only very young and inexperienced, much of it actually hailed from Merseyside. This new Liverpool team struggled initially, winning only four of the first 11 games in season 1999–2000. Injuries and a necessary settling-in period for the new foreign contingent at Anfield took its inevitable toll. When Stephane Henchoz came on board in October 2000, however, matters improved in defence: Liverpool conceded just 15 goals in the following 26 league matches.

Scoring goals was rather more difficult, especially with Fowler and Smicer absent for long spells, and Michael Owen struggling to overcome doubts about his own fitness. However, Guinean international forward, Titi Camara, captured the imagination of the Liverpool public, and a long unbeaten run in the early part of 2000 seemed to point the club towards Champions League qualification. In an attempt to confirm this prized European place, Houllier bought the forward Emile Heskey from Leicester City in March, and although it soon became clear that Heskey would prove to be a vital long-term investment, with the striker soon scoring two goals to secure an important away win at Wimbledon, the young Liverpool team he joined seemed to run out of steam and ideas, losing three and failing to score at all in the last five league matches. Only 51 goals were scored in total by Liverpool in 38 league matches, some measure perhaps of the new coaching staff's early concentration on making Liverpool harder to score against, rather than making the club any sort of potent attacking force.

Houllier's early modesty for his own team was very un-Shankly-like and for some of the club's supporters seemed to offer a psychological advantage to opponents. It actually meant, he argued, that fans had to be patient with the changes he was trying to effect at Anfield: 'Evolution, not revolution' became his mantra. It would take at least five years, he reasoned, to mould Liverpool into the sort of battle-hardened outfit which might challenge Manchester United and Arsenal at home, and the large Italian and Spanish clubs abroad. This would mean playing a very limited, defensive style in key away fixtures at first, in order to frustrate or suffocate a superior opponent.

In many ways, in fact, Houllier's supposed 'continental' approach to the game actually seemed to have much more in common with established British playing styles; no one could easily confuse the very direct approach of the Liverpool of 2001, for example, with the studied ball possession and passing and movement shaped by Jean Tigana at emerging Fulham, or even the sophisticated attacking football occasionally produced by Wenger's Arsenal. Instead, Houllier kept on stressing the force of the new team spirit and the work ethic at his young Liverpool, echoes perhaps of the old Anfield boot room days. More flowing football could wait.

Most Liverpool fans enjoyed, of course, the much greater solidity and the generally better results brought by Houllier and his staff, but some were also alarmed at the expediency of the new approach, which seemed to suggest that almost any degree of loss in style was justified if it brought results. Under Roy Evans, results had, inexcusably, not matched the quality of football often played by Liverpool. But was this new direction really the Liverpool way? Clearly, Houllier would need time to see the project through, and he was dealing still, as he reasonably pointed out, with a very young and inexperienced team. Only time would tell whether his vision offered more than the new defensive solidity allied to counter-attacking pace and power. Perhaps the wily Litmanen, in tandem with the huge potential of Steven Gerrard, would become the midfield playmaker and orchestrator the Liverpool team still seemed to lack on occasions when faced with opposition of the very highest quality?

What *is* clear is that the new manager of Liverpool is a man who has a real sense of the wider social and cultural importance of football in Liverpool and a vision for the club designed to span the next decade. He has signed mainly young, ambitious players who are willing to make a personal investment in the new Liverpool project: 'To die for the Liverpool shirt', as he puts it, another nod to Ronnie Moran and the Liverpool backroom staff of the 1970s and 1980s, and no easy aim in an era when players can earn millions by just sitting on the bench, or by engineering transfer after lucrative transfer. In May 2001, Houllier even confirmed that the old Anfield boot room had now been 'revived' at Liverpool, in the shape of The Bunker, a coaches' room at the Melwood training ground. Here, Houllier's senior coaching staff, plus Joe Corrigan and the club physiotherapist, Dave Galley, now gather to discuss training and coaching issues. The bottles of ale of previous boot room eras have disappeared, but much remains the same. 'Every morning we'll have a cup of coffee and a discussion,' confided Houllier. 'Sometimes it'll be formal. Other times we'll just have a laugh, tell a few jokes. It's amazing how many things come out of it.' It could be Joe Fagan talking.

Gérard Houllier is a man who has trouble sleeping. But this problem is not linked directly either to anxiety or disappointment. Even after the exhausting and successful European performances by Liverpool in Rome, Barcelona and Dortmund in 2001 he had difficulty resting after the match. He argues he picked up this habit as a student reading his books all night. I'm afraid he'll find few English footballers or coaches who share the same distinction. Joachim Marx remembers when Houllier was manager of Lens, how this engaging football insomniac would come around to his house, late into the night, for a chat: '"Give me five minutes," he would say. Then he would immediately fall asleep. His eyes would open five minutes later and he would start talking football. He used to drive my wife mad when he rang up in the middle of the night.'

Houllier can be assured he will easily find thousands of football fanatics in Liverpool willing to entertain him well into the early hours. It is partly the fact that he knows they share his own deep passion for football, and for Liverpool Football Club, which inexorably drew him back to this vibrant and troubled city in the north-west of England in the first place. All Liverpool fans now wonder if this man who so respects the city and its football traditions can bring the really big prizes back to Anfield once more.

7. LIVERPOOL'S FIVE-MATCH SEASON

FITNESS PROBLEMS

It's dangerous on the football touch-line: Gérard Houllier is on the Liverpool treatment table. He got so excited, our owlish little French leader, that when Robbie Fowler got his second goal at home against West Ham he wrenched his knee in crazed celebration and he's now in the safe hands of the Liverpool medical staff. Of course, we will need everyone fighting fit for the trials which lie immediately ahead. Houllier has described our five-matches-in-16-days February schedule as 'crazy', culminating as it does with the Worthington Cup final with Birmingham City on 25 February. 'This is England, mate; play the games and shut yer prattle,' is the likely response from outside. Who could blame them? We have a giant squad, after all, made for just this sort of sequence, and assembled at global cost. But this crucial period will still test legs, minds and the Houllier rotation philosophy to their limits.

Some good news. Michael Owen plays, unexpectedly, for an hour for the reserves at Bradford this week, but he still looks cautious and fragile, far from match fit in either mind or body. Ziege also plays – poorly – and the press rumour now is that he is likely to be on his way from L4. You can see why. We may have to deal with the next crucial few games without either Ziege (no loss) or Owen. The truth is, too, that since Michael's head injury at Derby back in October he has seldom looked really fit – or well. He has hardly played so his sponsors must be edgy. He's featured in a five-page Umbro ad in the footy magazines this week. I still recognised him.

10 FEBRUARY: SUNDERLAND 1, LIVERPOOL 1

Keep quiet now and listen for a bit, you might learn something. Because the car to Sunderland contains Steve Kelly of *TTW&R*, Sheila Spiers, FSA doyenne and Liverpool fan since Billy Liddell first dubbined his own boots, and Paul Hyland, Reds guru, a man who followed Liverpool in the European Cup even to deepest Tbilisi in 1979 (lost 3–0) and who has rooms and rooms at home fairly clogged with vital data about the Reds. These people have knowledge. Paul has also recently seen the Liverpool youth team despatch Stockport and Charlton and we are now in the last eight of the national Youth Cup. Our last victorious team in this competition produced Owen and Carragher, so this progress is promising – and important. It needs to be monitored.

We all agree that this trip is tough: up to Sunderland for a physical battering before a surgeon's investigation in Rome on Thursday. Can Houllier and Phil Thompson really get the team focused on digging in for this vital league game in the north-east when so many other, more attractive, big games are now coming up? And Peter Reid, Sunderland boss and hard little Liverpudlian that he is, will know this. He respects Liverpool, but the first words of his team talk today will still be: 'They will not fuckin' fancy this today, this lot: they've got other big games comin' up. So let's get into them, don't let 'em settle. Fuckin' get among 'em.'

Because let's be honest, Sunderland are grubby, the discomforting Eminem of the FA Premier League. They are an ugly affront to the big conservative corporations who feel they should be dominating the game here. They get in your face, unsettle you, nag at your better players – and they are fourth in the league playing this uncompromising, gnawing and gritty football rap. They also deserve to be where they are, make no mistake about that. We'll get all of this today, no doubt, and we will have to stand up to it, or sink. If we lose badly today we might struggle in all the crucial matches which follow.

We also talk about the problems facing Houllier's rotation philosophy for these forthcoming matches in Rome and Cardiff. Okay, for Sunderland some of our guys, lesser hearts, will probably be queuing up to be rotated. Kicked by McCann and Hutch in a muddy field today, or televised and teased in a football feast in Rome on Thursday? No contest. But how does GH tell those he's leaving out in big matches over the next few weeks that there will be 'other' games coming up? 'I'm not playing you in the Olympic Stadium, *mon brave*, but we'll soon have Derby at home; you're in for that.' It's not easy.

Question: How do you make sure a new football ground is atmospheric? Answer: It's nothing to do with standing. Just keep prices reasonable, market the ground to the whole community and build it within walking distance of loads of pubs. We are in one of these pubs now, ten minutes' walk away. It is soon heaving with brawny Mackems, and it even offers up some tipsy and entertaining Norwegian women, football players, across for the match (Jari Litmanen's father *and* mother, incidently, both played for his first Finnish club, Reipas Lahti, civilised people). Rival football supporters quietly do this all the time, of course, happily mix in packed pubs before the game. We always get loads of Sunderland in the Flattie, no problem. Having a drink, fraternising with the locals, is one of the real pleasures of travel away. We'll be in here again next year.

And it is clear that the local ale fuels this ground. Like Sunderland's team, this new home isn't pretty, not remotely so: 'Like a footballing Black Museum' a national hack called it this weekend. But as the home crowd does get right into the contest, the venue positively hums. We start today with Vignal at the back, Steven Gerrard on the right to counter Michael Gray, and Robbie and Heskey up front. The in-form Smicer is injured and Michael, surprisingly, is on the bench. Ziege is, wait for it, suspended (How? He never tackles).

We know what Sunderland are about: horrible, battling midfielders; quality from Gray on the left; danger and niggle from Hutchison on the right; Quinn to aim at in the middle as he deftly fouls and obstructs all and sundry, while badgering the officials; and Phillips up front, second only to Fowler the best pure finisher in the Premiership. So they scrap and hustle from the start, the crowd howling, and the first half is a predictable, rain-sodden mess. This game, a flapping, whirling contest, has no real shape, certainly no aesthetic. We don't have the ball, can't get hold of it.

Barbara Kruger, the US artist, has an installation in London at the moment, huge verbal messages projected menacingly onto white space. Sitting in front of this contest in this howling bowl in miserable Sunderland I'm reminded of one of them now:

> DON'T YOU THINK THIS IS JUST SHIT?
> DON'T YOU JUST WISH IT WOULD ALL GO AWAY?
> DON'T YOU WANT TO BE OUTSIDE, WALKING DOWN
> THE STREET, AND FEELING THE SUN ON THE SIDE
> OF YOUR FACE?

Yes, to all these. You see, we don't yet have the quality, or the experience, to rise above this ugly scramble, though when Heskey goes off just before the half-hour, clattered by Varga, substitute Litmanen at least offers new possibilities. But at the start of the second half, a goal: for Sunderland.

Regional football correspondents who are well soaked in the local juices will report that Phillips has been 'bulldozed over' by Hyypia on the edge of the box in the (*sic*) build-up to this goal, and in this kind of hysterical climate it probably looks like the home team is always suffering some similar assault or injustice. In fact, Phillips dives as a furious Hyypia clearly pulls out of the challenge. But the baying crowd, and claims and counter-claims about this incident on the field, does just enough now to help delay the clearance from the harassed young Vignal, which is charged down to Hutchison who scores at Westerveld's near post. At his *near*, fucking, post.

Young girls in Sunderland shirts to our left now stand up to mock loudly our acute depression. *Sunnerland, Sunnerland, Sunnerland*: the ground around us rocks. Some Liverpool fans are ejected – for what? Houllier reacts: Michael replaces Steven Gerrard. So now we have Owen and Fowler up front and Litmanen prompting from behind, and slowly it begins to work. We get more shape, more passing, a little more control. Michael looks sharp and in the last quarter he cleverly finds McAllister bursting through the middle, clear on goal, with Varga, the hairy Slovakian, trailing in his wake.

What happens next sends the home lot even more ballistic. Varga, miles from the ball, goes sliding yards outside the box but he actually clips McAllister just on the edge of it. The correct decision here is a sending-off and a free kick, still scant punishment for Varga's cynicism. But this is England, right? So referee Graham Barber gets it wrong on both counts: he awards a penalty and shoos away the perplexed defender. But you also have to admire his balls here, the referee. Because all their local barrack-room lawyers are now on the case: the esteemed City law firm *Gray, Hutchison & Quinn* swoops in, dragging the ref to confer with his see-no-evil assistant, while the less cute Phillips gets booked for excessive griping. The crowd, by now, is going absolutely mental, producing enamel-stripping howling. Barber will have none of it, and nor will Litmanen who, with a little skip, calmly strokes home the penalty right in front of us.

So we have our point, and it will be more difficult for Sunderland to challenge now for third place. Houllier says later that Sunderland are actually like us; that's why we have drawn our last three meetings. He means that both clubs stress hard work and the team ethic, but it is still an uncomfortable parallel: that we could be mistaken for a more polished version of this battling crew. Anyway, for four matches at least we can, hopefully, forget grim battles like these and our campaign for qualification for the next Champions League. Instead, we have this year's outstanding cup football to think about now – with injuries already piling up.

On the way home from the north-east, Sunderland fans ring the pea-brained Littlejohn on *606* to complain about the footballing injustices which routinely favour the big clubs. It's a fair point. Littlejohn raps inanely with his female assistants. The *fans'* phone-in? Bullshit. With Mellor giving up *606* there is now only the execrable 'God bless' Littlejohn who remains to be unseated. You know how to do it: don't fucking phone.

HOME OFFICE WORKING GROUP ON RACISM AND COMMUNITY FOOTBALL

More jaw, jaw at Queen Anne's Gate, with an assortment of officials and academics. Under the spotlight: racism and the community role of clubs. The agenda here is shaped around the lack of any co-ordinated action following the Government's own Task Force report on racism in football which was published almost two years ago. We know that most clubs have done relatively little to deal with all the issues raised there, but the Government and the FA and County FAs have also been culpable. Only around 30 professional clubs have equal opportunities policies, for example, and very few of them actually understand them or make them work. The FA Premier League's new Customer Charters are supposed to be an aid to monitoring the work of larger clubs on race, but the language of the 'customer' really just hides racialised inequalities, rather than actually dealing with them head-on. This approach also invites a 'tick box' mentality at clubs, where charters and such like are too often used in place of real action.

A number of times today Liverpool FC's own overly narrow approach to community activities and the club's generally low key approach to the issue of racism and racial exclusion is mentioned by others – and not in flattering terms. Draw your own conclusions.

15 FEBRUARY, UEFA CUP: AS ROMA 0, LIVERPOOL 2

Football memories of Rome: In 1977 I travelled to the European Cup final on a Lawrenson's bus from Bootle, two-and-a-half days there, the same back. We stopped only for piss breaks and the occasional sandwich, and we had a couple of people carted off to hospital with feet puffed up like yeasty loaves. If you sit, shoes on, for four days in a hot bus it can mess up your body, believe me. Near us was the 'bus bar': a large suitcase stacked with drink brought on board by a group of older, gently mad, scousers. Each day around noon, as the previous day's hangover was wearing off, the bus barman would announce grandly: 'Ladies and gentleman, I'm proud to say the official bar is now – open.' And then it all started again, the ale and the necessary piss stops. And the jokes. When we eventually got to Rome we headed straight for the Trevi Fountain for more ale and an afternoon's sunshine and singing.

Later, outside the ground, there were piles of our fellahs too pissed to get in. Inside, it was 20,000 scouse crazies, chequered flags and stupid hats, travel stories galore. Great night.

In 1984, I flew to Rome, nowhere near the same kick, or the privations. But this felt much more ominous, a strong Roma team to beat in the final, and dangerous and unforgiving local fans to contend with. It went to penalties, of course, our first real go at the gut-wrenching pressure this sort of ending inevitably produces. We missed, Steve Nicol first up, but faced with a rubber-bodied Grobbelaar they did too – twice – and so it came down to Alan Kennedy. Apparently, 'Barnie' had been missing them all week in training – couldn't hit a barn door. But he didn't miss this. Delirium in our end, which was soon followed by sensible fear. How do we get away from here now? Where are the police and the buses? Outside it was a scary chaos: howling in the darkness, police sirens, the coaches getting pelted. A few of ours who tried to go it alone got set upon and ended up badly hurt. It was a sickening finish, but a great performance. A few of our friends who remembered this glorious but troubled night would not come back to Rome this time. This might be good sense. But *we* are here to watch Houllier's Reds in the year of 2001.

When the draw was made Houllier visibly blanched: AS Roma, six points clear in Serie A? Totti, Delvecchio, Cafu, Batistuta? You want us to play *here*? Houllier was either very cute, or there was real fear in his face when we learned our fate. I think it was fear. We are a young team, lots to learn. They are cantering the Scudetto, full of hard, star names. Fear is a rational emotion under these circumstances – but you still don't expect to see it. As for the fans, the Italian police are worried about us – about our safety. In my experience, if we have to rely on the Italian police for safe passage we are, indeed, at grave risk.

We stay near Il Vaticano, soaking up the sun and the history and art of this mad city. When Lazio president, Sergio Cragnotti, also owner of the dairy that serves Rome, raised milk prices soon after Lazio splashed out millions to sign Christian Vieri in August 1998, the rival Romanisti boycotted their morning cappuccino in protest. Everyone has a team here: the waiters, shopkeepers, traffic guys, even the thousands of clerics who prowl around the Vatican, one of whom tells us this morning that Roma will win, 2–0.

The decor at the Basilica di San Pietro has, at least, the sort of colour and flourish I had wanted inside the new, concretised Centenary Stand at Anfield. Also, seeing how pilgrims here have worn away, through their devout kissing, the left foot of Arnolfo di Cambio's statue of Saint Peter, it does make me wonder that a statue of *our* Saint Michael, back in Liverpool 4, with emphasis on slobbering devotion to his prized right foot, might encourage more on-field action from his still little-used left. The thought soon passes: we don't expect Michael to play here. Houllier will surely rely on the muscular Heskey and his experienced continental Europeans, Smicer and Litmanen.

Question: Why do they have zebra crossings in Rome? Answer: To line up the pedestrian dead. Not that these palpable traffic dangers figure much in the minds of the Reds who start flooding into the eternal city throughout Thursday. The Trevi Fountain takes some symbolic hammer as always: red flags and banners are soon staining the brilliant white. 'The Nevilles are ugly cunts' is an early stand-out, leaving no margin for misunderstanding – except for Italians. A Japanese is later playfully thrown into the waters by scousers for far too enthusiastically promoting the case of Roma's impressive Japanese midfielder, Nakata.

Bottled ale and ghostly white skin soon starts to appear everywhere on these streets – and in large quantities. It is this, plus the raucous singing and general Liverpudlian public tomfoolery, which the Italian press will make much of later in their 'English hooligan' stories. No one is really here, following Liverpool, to wreck bars or front up the locals. They are a loud and sometimes ugly discomfort, some of these visitors, it is true, but not a real threat to life and limb. That actually comes from much closer to home.

In mid-afternoon we set off for an authentic communist bar on Via de Delfini. The owner, we have heard, is also a devout Roma fan so the contrast immediately attracts. And here, as promised, there are busts of Uncle Joe, Marx and Lenin alongside photos of Totti, Cafu and Batistuta, the contemporary Roman theorists. The walls of the bar are littered with leftist and football mottos and sayings, including the gnomish: 'Lazio fans: don't ask football questions as you are not capable of understanding the answers.' A true meeting of politics and art.

Later, browsing through a book of *La Stampa* front pages over the past few decades, the headline from 30 May 1985 shouts out: '*Tragedia allo stadio di Bruxelles.*' Knowing the force and bitterness of football rivalries in Italy, the hard guys from Roma's Curva Sud will not have lost too much sleep over the victims in Heysel some 16 years ago. There is a case for saying, of course, that we in Liverpool should remember them more often, and rather more publicly, than we do today. A handwritten note on the communist bar wall, just above a smiling Batigol, says wisely: 'Ignorance is like culture: it knows no limits.'

In the early evening, at the Christmas cake monument at the Piazza Venezia – the 'typewriter' for locals – the lads from the Woodpecker pub in Kirkby sweep incongruously down central Rome, banners flying, beer cans raised and voices hoarse from a rapid trip around the

Colosseo. Now, strains of Liverpool songs can be heard from central piazzas as we build up towards kick-off. Liverpool supporters are supposed to meet for bus transport but the J4 bus actually passes our hotel and goes straight to the ground. So we take this, instead, no problems. At the other end, there is an eerie walk past the kitsch bare-arsed sporting statues which surround the warm-up athletics track outside this bowl which has been home to both Lazio and Roma since 1990.

I actually last came here in 1990: Italy v Ireland, World Cup quarter-final. Tipped off by Liverpool secretary Peter Robinson, Rogan Taylor and I picked up £75 tickets from an FAI official in a hotel in Rome. He sat in a large armchair and, typically, had the tickets in a cardboard box at his feet. We told him that Liverpool FC would foot the bill for two. He eventually bought this preposterous story and we walked out tickets in hand, scarcely believing our luck. Tonight we only have to negotiate the lines of Italian police and repeated body searches outside the ground to get into the game. A cinch by comparison.

Inside the ground it is the usual Italian chaos. There is no stewarding, so go where you like, and no one will be sitting down on these filthy plastic plates which are bolted onto concrete steps. The pitch is about a couple of miles distant, barred to us here by fences, a moat, and an eight-lane running track. Some of the local *ragazzi* are rather closer to us, but behind welcome fences to our left. Bryce Morrison of the Liverpool staff described the stadium to me later as 'disgusting'. By recent English standards he's right. Some Liverpool fans also buy flimsy 'match programmes' in the concourse here – in English, and printed in Hackney or somewhere – from a grifter Arsenal supporter who has come down especially for the business. The English are the service class of the world game: bootleg flags, posters, tickets, programmes at major football anywhere in Europe. English guys will be there, turning a dodgy profit. And he has buyers, this guy, something glossy for visitors to take back home.

Before the game there has been some real action outside the Curva Sud at the other end to us. Liverpool fans have been attacked, in a weird mob stabbing of the legs and arse: maximum pain and injury, but unlikely to be fatal. Victims later reported six or seven different Roma fans individually returning to add more injury to the initial assault, a truly horrible and scary affair for those involved. As kick-off gets closer, Liverpool late arrivals in our 4,000 strong section force the police to simply extend their cordon around the visiting area and towards the Roma fans to our left, not a great move. Welcome to big-time football, Italian style.

The lazy British press has been reporting that Roma boss Capello will leave out Totti and Batistuta, showing Roma's disdain for the UEFA Cup. In fact, Totti is in contract disagreement with the club – 'It is a matter of honour, not money,' he tells *La Gazetta* unconvincingly – and Montella is preferred to Batigol, rather like Robbie and Michael have been vying for a place at Anfield all season. Nakata plays, so the Japanese will get their money's worth. A crowd of 60,000 also shows you just how 'unimportant' the locals think this game is. For Liverpool, Houllier mystifies once more: Michael and Robbie both play, and so does the straw-hearted Ziege. Carragher returns from injury, but there is no Smicer, Litmanen or the injured Gerrard. Hamann and McAllister marshal central midfield. We look lightweight on paper, potentially fragile.

And Roma start strongly, with good movement from Delvecchio and from Montella at the far end, which is just a decent telescope away. But our defenders stand firm, Hyypia and Henchoz prominent even at this distance, Hamann working hard, and Ziege, of all people, giving Cafu an impressive early studding. We slowly strangle the game and begin to overcome our anxieties. The only real chance in a tight first half is a near-post header for Delvecchio, which arrows narrowly over the Liverpool bar. At the interval Roma fans, by now disturbingly nearby, begin openly to bombard us with coins and water bottles: we cheerfully return some of them, as a young Italian vendor sells us more ammunition. The Italian police stand between and watch. This is the miserable half-time entertainment.

Right at the start of the second half, a Roman gift. Rinaldi lazily plays a ball across the Roma box and a watchful Michael intercepts, taking the ball wide to the right and getting his body far enough outside the ball to be able to screw a low shot back and beyond Antonioli's right hand – and into the Roma net. Michael runs off in celebration to the Liverpool bench – a sign of the spirit in the whole Liverpool camp, Houllier will remark later. Can it be true: that this priceless away goal has been casually *handed* to us and that the Liverpool travelling contingent is now working overtime, singing and shouting on a team that no longer looks out of its depth, even in this hostile place? It is: and there is more.

Because Roma suddenly look leaden, disinterested. We are beginning to look comfortable. Michael even scores a second goal, a near-post header over the comically horizontal Antonioli and suddenly the prospect of being held inside the Stadio Olympico by the Italian police for *another* ninety minutes after this first one is over no longer seems quite so mind-bending. A banner suddenly appears in the Curva Sud: 'Fuck the Queen.' We cheer it, delighted at how misplaced even this insult is. John Mackin, below us, offers the only football flag ever to feature parentheses: 'LFC: People's Front of Judea (No splitters).'

Large gaps are appearing in the Roma ranks: they know this is over and are already trudging home. We have not been pretty, admittedly. But we have worked really hard, defended solidly throughout and stolen a couple of goals. We have been professional in the kind of European performance that Paisley and Ronnie Moran would have immediately recognised – and praised. We always win in Rome. And Houllier, in selecting Owen to play with Fowler, has again come up smelling of something better than what we now have to face outside.

Because being held until way past midnight in a ground which saw the game kick off at nine might lead you to think that even these local fuckwits have had enough time to sort out transport away from this pit. Wrong. At least a couple of hundred Reds travellers are left wandering, bemused, outside, while Rome City Authority buses inexplicably turn away from the stadium and return to the city centre empty. There are no Italian/English-speaking stewards or Liverpool staff equipped to inform this drained bunch about the state of play; about how they might expect to find their rooms or transport from this wilderness at this time of night when local gangs might also be expected to prowl.

Only a famous win, still hugged joyously close, prevents this from going very bad indeed. The police won't let us leave, or arrange buses to take us away. We are about three miles from the centre, so decide to walk it anyway, sneaking out, afraid now even of our own shadows. In fact, we meet just one car-bound Roma fan, who slows down only to offer us the angry continental finger when we take the bait. Bad losers, the Romans. But they are not all sad tonight. At Piazza dei Tribunali the next morning there is already a message written in a phone kiosk. It says: 'Forza Lazio, grazie Liverpool.' 'No problem, guys. Any time.

PLAYERS FOR HIRE

Think of any decent team and top goalkeeping will be a feature. We are deficient in this department, have been for years. Our current, Sander, has his strengths but he is also arrogant and vulnerable, not an ideal combination in this job. We concede, and Westerveld instinctively slashes his arms at the defence, at someone, anyone, who has 'failed' in front. Blame never rests easily on Wester's goal-line, but he has been culpable.

Houllier will not let this goalkeeper issue go, and the press has been awash with 'Liverpool search for goalkeeper' stories. This might all be media crap, and the club denies the speculation, of course, but what do players think when their positions are so publicly auctioned? They earn bucketfuls of cash, fair enough, but the uncertainties must also be crippling to them and to their families. They have feelings, insecurities, for God's sake. Andy Gray, Sky TV ex-Bluenose, has a telling story about how the Everton manager, Howard Kendall, came sheepishly to Gray's brand new Lancashire house in the mid-1980s to tell the big man that he was, in fact, about to be sold to fund the purchase of Gary Lineker. Gray was happily putting down his new carpets. Kendall ended up helping him: he couldn't tell his favourite striker the grim news. But Gray had to go.

Players also know the score. Managers have to be liars here, inevitably: after all, they often have to depend on players they no longer really want, until a suitable replacement is found. And they often have to fish around in very public pools for the coming heroes. It is ugly stuff. Houllier, himself, says you can't stand still in football, that nobody's position is truly secure. So the football bosses sagely pooh-pooh these kinds of press stories: 'Absolutely no truth whatsoever.' But the searching still goes on.

18 FEBRUARY, FA CUP FIFTH ROUND: LIVERPOOL 4, MANCHESTER CITY 2

Des on ITV? It's still not quite right, is it? Jon Champion and Big Ron do the commentary/analysis for ITV, so you know this is no seminar which lies ahead. We worry that City might come hard and determined to make their season here, while we still have our own heads stuck in Rome. But it doesn't work out that way. One entirely expected feature? A powerful post-match Joe Royle whine, naturally.

In the Anfield studio, Des is now desperately looking under his suspiciously black eyebrows for ways to shape up a shock result for the uncommitted viewer. He calls on expert advice for help:

> DES: 'Terry, you took four points off Liverpool this season. What is it City must do today?'
> VENABLES: 'It's a tough one. No matter what attacking players Liverpool use today, City have got to cut down the time and space in which the Liverpool midfield can manoeuvre the ball. They must frustrate them. The Liverpool back four like to play close. So City have to get at them: spread them wide and try to get some spaces in the middle for men coming from the midfield.'

So now you know. Work hard, pressurise and spread the game wide, high up the pitch if you can: open up the spaces in the Reds' rearguard. This is the way to undo Houllier's Liverpool. But even with Owen, Fowler and Barmby all on the Liverpool bench today, City cannot stay level for long enough even to try to make this simple plan work.

Instead, Smicer steals an early penalty from City goalkeeper Weaver. Jon Champion guides Litmanen safely through the spot kick at the Anfield Road end in true Ron Manager style:

> Jari Litmanen is six minutes into his FA Cup début, a vast footballing CV behind him. He is faced by six thousand visiting supporters. A test of nerve. A new experience. Goal.

Within minutes, Smicer and Litmanen are at it again. The Czech this time robs Wiekens – 'There is a golden rule for midfielders,' says big Ron, sagely. 'Don't get caught in possession.' – and from Smicer's short pass Litmanen, on the centre spot and his back to the City goal, chips an instant curling ball threaded around his left shoulder down the side of the City defence for Heskey, who has read this and is a vital yard ahead of Spencer Prior. He finishes well, too, low to Weaver's right. And so within ten short minutes we seemed to have rolled up and casually tossed away this potential FA Cup banana skin in the middle of a very tough fortnight.

But City have plenty of spirit and battle back, as we are happy to sit. And on the half-hour the niggly Tiatto clips a corner out to Kanchelskis on the edge of the Liverpool box and the old Bluenose threads in a low shot through a gaggle of players and in off Westerveld's post. So, this may not quite be over. And it is a godsend for the guys in the TV studio, of course, this goal, because they can now float a very different half-time prospect. 'Can City do this?' becomes the theme. Litmanen has been the star, the studio bods all agree on that: 'If you give him half a yard, he'll kill you with a pass,' says the chirpy McCoist. As if this is a major insight.

So it is a disappointment that the Finn fails to appear after the first half – a calf strain. Barmby gets on, instead, but the pattern remains the same. After seven minutes Smicer plays a simple exchange with Ziege down the City right and is put free wide in the box. Free, that is, until Weaver hurtles out and mows him down. Penalty number two. The truth is, Smicer has actually seen Weaver coming and has slyly waited for him. 'Reckless goalkeeping,' tuts Ron. 'Weaver took the bait,' says the more worldly Tel. Vladdy himself scores from the spot. Game over – again. Babbel glances in a fast Ziege near-post free kick near the end for 4–1. Gormless Goater still has time to score again for City, deflected in off Carragher, but it is strictly a consolation. And not a sweet one.

'City were outclassed,' says Des, twinkling again now in the studio as the Anfield mist rolls in outside. 'Their only hope was that this fog might come down and save them,' he chuckles. Overall, Smicer has been the key, though Big Ron, mysteriously, gives the MoM to the battling Carragher. 'The first penalty was fiction,' says Joe Royle later, gracious to the last. What *is* fiction now is Manchester City's chance of winning the 2001 FA Cup. We, on the other hand, still have our hopes.

CASH CRISIS

Hull City from Nationwide Division Three face a winding-up order in the High Court with reported £500,000 VAT debts. To top it all, The Tigers are also locked out of Boothferry Park by the hard-faced tennis millionaire and ex-club chairman David Lloyd. The city council in Hull have just approved outline planning permission for a new 25,000-seater ground to house football and rugby league in the area. But will City still exist when it springs up, this new sporting idyll for the East coast? Potential buyers, as usual, hide in the shadows but nothing is certain here.

Nor is there much certainty at the more monied end of the game. Thirty per cent, or £500 million, has been wiped off the value of British football clubs listed on the Stock Exchange in the past six months. Even the Corporation's share value has plunged, ironically just as the OT cash machine announces a massive new transatlantic commercial partnership with the New York Yankees, for God's sake. Economists call this sort of deal 'horizontal integration', and United are no doubt eyeing up the millions of 'soccer moms' in the US. Steve Kelly, from *TTW&R*, thinks the Yankees, for their part, are setting their sights on exploiting the booming – and inexplicable – demand for sturdy baseball bats in Manchester's Hulme district.

22 FEBRUARY, UEFA CUP, FOURTH ROUND, SECOND LEG: LIVERPOOL 0, ROMA 1

Following the FA Cup win over City and since the first leg in Italy, the quality press in Britain has been stuffed with 'return to glory' stories about this new Liverpool. GH has tried to stem the feeling that this UEFA tie is already over – but it is a tough job. In the Flattie tonight, believe me, no one is taking this return lightly, though the Liverpool 'Scandies', who are prominent here, are both lively and optimistic. This crew are actually Norwegians from just outside Bergen, and we saw a couple of them in Rome. Some were, apparently, set upon by Curva Sud boys.

One of the younger Liverpool Scandies always wears a Liverpool quilt cover which has been made by his mum into an LFC boiler suit. He has been in here with an old air-raid siren before so you can tell, all round, that he is a bit of a dickhead. His girlfriend tells us it costs about £200 to travel to a home game here, but they stay with mates in Anfield Road so it is manageable a few times a season. With Bjornebye, Kvarme and Leonhardsen all recently in the Liverpool team under Evans, this Norway branch made some sense, but under the Francophile Houllier it is now stretching a point. But Norway still has wall-to-wall Premier League TV coverage and a huge Reds following: even the assassin Solksjaer was still in the Norwegian branch of the Liverpool Supporters Association when he first moved to OT. The Liverpool Scandies are actually sprawled in our Flattie seats tonight: 'How do you say "Move your arse" in Norwegian?' asks Sheila. They get the message.

Tonight is also a Bob Paisley Flag Night at Anfield, so the Kop is awash with old European banners as well as new offerings, partly in honour of the great 'wee uncle'. My mate Steve suggests that all Kopites should be made to attend wearing cardigans, slippers and Bob's flat cap. Tactics. Do we defend tonight, try to consolidate and counter-attack? Or do we go out strong to try to kill the tie off? Paisley would relish the challenge. Roma have also been stung by criticism after the loss in Rome, so we should expect a stronger showing from them here. And we get it.

But we also play into their hands. We start timidly, like the kid who has punched the school bully on the nose and is now skulking in the playground fearing the worst. And we allow ourselves to be intimidated by their battle-hardened troops. Heskey, big baby that he still sometimes is, gets pushed and pulled around by the imposing Zago and the Argentinian Samuel, and Roma combine this physical power and cynical shirt-grabbing with real technical skill in a way which make us look like the European rookies we really are. The visitors dominate, and a dummy by Nakata puts Delvecchio clean through midway through the first half but he shoots wide. Michael Owen soon misses from the same spot for us, and in the same hurried way. We can't keep the ball, so we are glad – and a little lucky – to be still 0–0 at half time.

After the break, it is more of the same, except the Spanish referee, Jose-Maria Garcia-Aranda, suddenly latches on to the fact that Zago and his mate Zembina are still both trying to get inside Heskey's shirt and he awards a surprise home penalty for some routine wrestling at the Anfield Road end. This should really be the finish but Michael's body language, even as he fetches the ball, tells you all you need to know about what happens next. Smicer is actually preparing to come on to replace Owen, so why not bring him on now to take this kick? The Liverpool bench probably thinks this is a step too far – and so watches, instead, as Owen shoots meekly to the keeper's right for a simple save. Smicer then comes on – and so, soon after, does Batistuta.

So now we are wishing this match away. Ziege has started to flounder, as only he can on the left, while Barmby has never really been involved on the right. Only the defence is holding strong, with Hamann also battling away. But at least Roma are not really making chances; they are expertly playing in our half, keeping the ball and threatening something, but we don't quite know what. So when the goal comes, from Guigou, with 20 minutes left, out of nothing and from distance on our right, we look again at Westerveld. Maybe we expect too much from him, but Sander has had decent sight of it and is guarding the side of the goal which is breached. Maybe we just don't want to see this go in and so we look for easy scapegoats. We are demanding, critical, fans after all. But I would want him to save this, our costly Dutch international. Instead, it is now a real siege – and we must survive it.

Despite the Liverpool penalty, Señor Garcia-Aranda, a typically southern European referee, has thus far been rather more to Roma's liking than to ours. He has missed most of the off-the-ball stuff and we think he has been lenient with booked Roma players who continue to foul. But now, in the final minutes, he is the central figure for us in a crucial incident. Montella, who has been a powerful presence for Roma all evening on the left, tries to bend a cross around Babbel but, instead, the driven ball hits the turned defender's elbow. Now in the real world, this is not a penalty, no way: Babbel is not even looking at the ball when it strikes him from point-blank range. But we have seen them given, these crazy penalty decisions, and this referee appears, to the Kop's horror, to point directly to the spot.

My guess is that he has not really seen what has happened here, and that his first response has been simply – blindly – to support Roma's claims. But Batistuta is obviously out of this particular loop, because he takes the ball to the corner flag, even as his colleagues are excitedly working out who will take the spot kick. And now the referee, for the first time with some certainty, points to where Batistuta stands – for a *corner* kick. Now this kind of thing has happened to me, of course, when refereeing on Sunday mornings – maybe to you, too. I have been unsure and weakly waved something, whilst actually waiting for the players to sort it out for themselves, as Batistuta has done. Later the referee will say, with a smile, that his original signal was actually for a goal kick. No one believes him.

In the few wild minutes which follow, the Roma midfielder, Tommassi, his frustration boiling over, is sent off: he politely shakes the referee's hand in departing. And then the final whistle eventually goes to huge home applause, which is released like a massive sigh, because this has been very close. We have seen the real Roma tonight and, with real defensive resolve, we have just about survived the exhausting, testing experience. Quite another kind of football exam now awaits the Anfield Reds in deepest South Wales.

SVEN'S 31-MAN SQUAD

The new England manager has named 31 players for his first England international, a friendly versus Spain. This already looks like an ill-advised fixture in a crowded season, but the new manager does need at least to meet his players before crucial World Cup matches loom. Powell, from Charlton, and Sunderland's plodding McCann are also included, the latter presumably to give the rest confidence by comparison. Robbie, Michael, Emile, Barmby and Carragher are all involved. Steven Gerrard is left out, rested.

The British hacks are torn about Sven's approach: is a large, inclusive squad like this good for morale and for contact with players, or a sign of a real lack of focus and direction? They are also irked because, unlike Keegan and Hoddle, Sven isn't really that interested in talking to the press. This urbane Swede has not crossed the British press boys yet: and he clearly has no idea just how ugly all this can become. Jeff Powell at the *Daily Mail* seems ready to lead the poisoned disbelievers. But for now at least Eriksson has some respite: he is the guest of honour, after all, for a big Liverpool match which is coming up in Cardiff.

25 FEBRUARY, LEAGUE CUP FINAL, MILLENNIUM STADIUM, CARDIFF: LIVERPOOL 1, BIRMINGHAM CITY 1
(LIVERPOOL WIN 5–4 ON PENALTIES)

We travel down early to avoid the Sunday traffic jams. South Wales police hold up their hands on this road chaos: they had no idea football fans owned cars. Other scousers are also early arrivals in Wales, naturally, and a number of them are impossibly but good-naturedly pissed, with us, in a small town outside Newport on the Saturday night. This, we agree, is a good base from which to launch an early morning assault on the Millennium site because we have managed to score some freebies from the Football League for this match. Which also means we get the free drinks and pre-match lunch, and a bit of mixing with the commercial grifters, stuffed shirts and the sought-after ex-professionals in the plush stadium suites before the big match kicks off. And, let me tell you, quite shamelessly, that all this easy parking and flannel and feeding at a big game like this is, well, *fantastic*.

Sod's law, however, means you normally end up at one of these beanos talking to the regional head of some god-awful sponsorship firm about football products or 'branding' or the new market value of clubs and players, or such like. But the Football League boys have done us proud today, because as I check the table numbers to try to work out who I'm paired with for the Chardonnay and Welsh lamb and spuds, I can see the gently shining dome of a familiar figure in the distance seated at my table. Which means I'm not sentenced, after all, to polite chat on faceless football business. Instead, I have a two-hour seminar ahead on the inner workings of the greatest winning machine in English football history. 'Err, can you pass the salt, Ronnie? Thanks. You don't mind me bothering you with these questions do you? You see I don't always get this much time to talk with a great Liverpool coach like – Ronnie Moran.'

> Ronnie Moran's greatest Liverpool team: Clemence, Nicol, Thompson, Hansen, Byrne, Callaghan, Whelan, Souness, Barnes, Dalglish, Rush.

Ronnie is patient and charming, in fact quite unlike the fire-eater we were used to seeing on the bench and whose job is now done just as ferociously by Thommo. His wife says Ronnie still 'worships' Kenny. I sense he also has the greatest respect for Ian Callaghan, Cally – two players, he says, approvingly, who would barely stir any room they entered. He contrasts these two shy men with Stevie Mac, and quietly acts out Mac's public 'swagger' to illustrate it. But he still respects Mac – 'An intelligent player. A very bright man.' He doubts that players in the '70s and '80s would stand for today's 'rotation'; they wanted to play every game then, were worried about losing their place. Ronnie himself worries about changing a winning team even now, but acknowledges times have changed and that players get used to being left out, to being rested, today. He talks at length about Shankly's well known aversion to injured players – and says we only ever injected players with water, never cortisone. Hmm.

Ronnie actually almost signed for Everton back in the 1950s. His wife and daughter now watch Liverpool's home matches: they couldn't do it when Ronnie was involved. He also still goes to Melwood a few days a week and talks to the current players about the old days and the future. He's impressed, especially, with the discipline of the new regime – and with Hyypia, the defensive rock. He thinks Liverpool are on the way back. Have I died and gone to some distant coaching heaven, I wonder?

Rick Parry comes in to say hello, bringing with him the team news. With Litmanen and Murphy still injured and with Michael and Gary Mac both playing home and away in Rome, it is pretty much what we expect. Rick thinks this is actually GH's current favoured eleven and formation, which is some news. It reads, in a 4–3–1–2 line-up: Westerveld; Babbel, Hyypia, Henchoz, Carragher; Gerrard, Hamann, Biscan; Smicer; Fowler, Heskey. This looks a strong side, but it also has a narrow shape. It means Steven Gerrard playing wider, not his strength, and the steady Biscan, not Barmby, playing on the left, where his pace is suspect. But it also puts the clever Smicer up in support of the front two, thus showing our real attacking intent. This team has more than enough to win, for sure – if the legs hold out.

The Millennium Stadium is the business: a simple but effective design and serious atmospheric qualities. Two-tiered and built rectangular and upwards in the very centre of Cardiff, it is the antithesis of the single-level, out-of-town bowl that is the decaying Stadio Olympico. The roof structure here is a little like the San Siro and the Ajax Arena, so there is legitimate concern about the qualities of the pitch, and it looks patchy and heavy today. But at least everyone in the ground can see and is reasonably close to the action: every seat in 76,000 has a decent view. Which doesn't stop supporters on the bottom tier behind both goals standing up, of course, for the whole two hours and more of what turns out to be an unexpectedly turbulent and dramatic contest.

Early signs are that Birmingham will work hard, but that we will win this with something to spare. Lazaridis is fast and elusive on the left, sure, but City's two main strikers, Horsfield and Adebola, look ponderous and well held by the Liverpool defence. We start to get control and to pass the ball in midfield, and Robbie and Smicer begin to threaten, though Heskey is having problems holding the ball up and getting fully involved. Which doesn't stop him heading on a Wester clearance to Robbie on the half-hour, for Fowler to volley instantly over Bennett and high into the Birmingham net.

Robbie, delirious, heads for the Reds' bench, clearly a new Liverpool trend this, but misses out GH, who is hailing a cab, aiming instead for the injured Redknapp and Murphy. Heskey then puts Smicer clean through and Vladdy shows us again this vital absence from his game: a killer touch in front of goal. He has another clear chance in the second half – and misses – and Heskey and Robbie are also at fault in this important department as the first hour now fades from view. Houllier says later that his only criticism today is that, once again, we have missed too many chances.

At half-time Birmingham take off Adebola, replacing him with the seriously quick Andrew Johnson, who now starts to worry our four centre-backs with his pace and workrate. Steven Gerrard is also starting to struggle with cramp and is eventually replaced by Gary Mac. But before this we seem to settle for a solid 1–0 win. City have not really looked threatening and as we move, wearily, into time added on, the red and white ribbons are already tied securely somewhere onto the Worthy Cup. Until, that is, Martin O'Connor, Birmingham's tidy midfield leader, forces his way into the box for virtually the only time in the match and is comprehensively upended for his cheek, knee-high, by

Henchoz. Penalty: no arguments. Purse keeps his nerve well and scores in front of his mates, and so we get another half hour's worth – which is not really what we need.

Even with O'Connor limping like an old-time Cup hero, Birmingham are now on top and even have another plausible penalty shout narrowly turned down by David Elleray in the first extra 15. Hamann hits a post late on, but we still don't go too hard for a winner. So Elleray blows up with the teams still level at 1–1. Karen Brady, a few rows behind, looks frozen with tension. Which means we face a bit of a lottery on penalties – and a sour taste. All right, I want us to win here, but I'm not going to be dancing around now if we squeeze past the Brummies in a penalty shoot-out. But as Ronnie Moran tells us later, 'Shanks would say: "In the record books it just says: Liverpool, League Cup winners." That's all that matters.' Houllier also says that the first trophy is the hardest to win: so you have to accept any victory. A professional's view, and in the harsh world of top-level sport, he's right, of course.

Penalties are gut-wrenchingly tense affairs, though. We have yet to lose a shoot-out, and we are notionally ahead from the moment that the Liverpool end is chosen for the kicks and especially when Grainger misses their first one, saved by Westerveld. And even though Hamann surprisingly misses for us, our greater experience should really still see us through. Heskey, our main striker, remember, is in line only after the ball-boys have their go. So, after McAllister, Barmby, Ziege and Fowler have already done their nervous work, it is the yeoman Carragher who steps up to take the vital sixth Liverpool kick. He charges in from somewhere just outside Swansea before bravely and unexpectedly *placing* his shot high to Bennett's left.

Young Johnson, who has actually turned the game round for Birmingham as a substitute, now has to score. But he looks diffident, already crushed, as he slowly carries the ball towards this lonely white spot at the very heart of 30,000 whistling, howling, screaming scousers. Westerveld is there, waiting at the penalty mark, eyeing him up, trying to intimidate. So you sense it looks bad for the baby-blond Johnson: that before-bedtime tears are probably just around the corner for him. And so it turns out: Sander easily saves his weak shot. Which means that the Frenchman, Houllier, has won his first Liverpool trophy: in Wales, on penalties.

After this is all over and we are back, drained, with the suits for tea and sandwiches, we manage to sneak my daughter Zelda, with her mate 'Diesel', a big Liverpool fan, into the afters. Diesel, a guy in his mid-20s, is initially a bit wide-eyed at all this hob-nobbing, but he's soon off collecting autographs and is happily chatting away to the likes of Eriksson and big Jack Charlton. I kid you not. Before, that is, he spots Ian Rush, who still looks just about as fit and alert as a fast robber's dog. Diesel now arrows directly towards his old Liverpool hero and he soon comes back, glassy-eyed, clutching one of those ghoulish miniature Rushie figurines, bouffant hair, muzzy and all. You see, he always keeps this little Rushie figure in his pocket, does Diesel. Never goes out without it. This is all news to us, of course. And he has said to the real Ian Rush, when pulling out the little Rushie figure: 'I always carry you in my pocket, Rushie. Can you just touch it, please?' And the real Ian Rush, probably fearing by now that Diesel is some sort of mad stalker, has uneasily smiled and gently touched this grotesque little Rushie figure. And now Diesel has something rather more than just a miniature Ian Rush to carry around. In fact he's smiling, insanely.

Over this exhausting series of vital games during the past fortnight, when we have been buffeted by Sunderland, prodded and stretched by Roma, held City comfortably at bay in the FA Cup, and been taken to the wire by Birmingham, our record is that we have won two, drawn two and lost one, scoring eight, conceding four. We have seldom been brilliant during this period, but we have been resilient and hard to beat, and we have eventually gotten the results we needed. We have stood up. So real praise is due to GH and his staff.

We have our first silverware since 1995 ready to make dust rings in the Anfield trophy cabinet. It would be easy now, of course, for us to succumb to a mini-slump, a negative reaction to the incredible intensity of the past 15 days. Instead, we have to be strong to the season's end, especially after the painful lessons of last season's capitulation. As Alan Hansen puts it: even when we don't play well, Liverpool's attitude has to be right. There is, after all, much more still to win.

8. FOR GOD AND ST MICHAEL

In the build-up to a new football season you try to keep the fears you have under wraps – at least until the first crippling loss. Then, the recriminations and anxieties come to the fore. There was the usual fretting among the club's supporters and critics about the 2000–01 Liverpool squad, and indeed about Gérard Houllier's general approach to playing the game. Failure to qualify for the Champions League taxed the patience of those who pointed to Houllier's spending and the flaccid ending to the 1999–00 season. But no issue was more taxing, or more potentially divisive, than that concerning the fate and form of the two brilliant young strikers, Fowler and Owen, that Houllier had inherited from the brimming Liverpool youth system.

These two young men also seemed like footballing chalk and cheese. The older one, Fowler, is a raw-edged natural striker hewn from the craggy outcrops of the city's toughest streets and loaded with talent *and* trouble; the other, Owen, is a solo flying machine from a stable middle-class football background and groomed from the youngest age to be the sort of football product which agents, sponsors and the new school of football managers can but dream of having access to. Throw in the fact that serious injury stalled the career of the troubled older star, who then seemed likely to be usurped in this fêted role by his upstart, clean-cut junior, and also that their manager, Houllier, seems almost religiously opposed to playing the two rivals together in the same side, and the scope for tension, intrigue and rumour seems almost limitless. Nevertheless, we in the Red half of the city of Liverpool are truly blessed that we have lived in the age of both God and St Michael.

If your club has struggled, as Liverpool had, by our own standards, over the past few seasons, it is sometimes much easier to exist in the past or the future rather than in the present. Who is in the reserves?

Who is coming up through the youth team? Who will save us? We ask these questions all the time, and sometimes you can track real talent all the way into the first team and on to the England set-up. Robbie Fowler, for example, we had heard about in the Liverpool junior teams, but when the England Under-18s won the World Youth Championships at Nottingham Forest in the summer of 1992 you could see what a talent we already had stored up in Robbie. I went to the final just to watch him play, a true *left-footed* striker, though he played infrequently and deeper in this England set-up, ironically a place Houllier had in mind for him in the modern Liverpool side. Even then Robbie had real class, oozed it. In November he scored three against Switzerland, outshining his young colleagues Beckham, Campbell and Gary Neville, but he still only started one Under-18s match in 1992–93.

The word from inside the club was that we had a real raw talent here but, like Rushie before him, Robbie never really let go in the reserves. Bob Paisley told the young Ian Rush that he wanted more selfishness in his second-team play; he was, after all, a striker, so why not try to score goals? Rush complained that the staff at Liverpool always stressed the importance of *passing* the ball – that he was getting two confusing messages, which were messing up his game. None of this ever concerned or confused Robbie: he *always* wanted to score. He is, you might say, goal-fixated, once saying, 'I hate watching live games, no matter who is playing, in case they're 0–0 and boring. You've sat down for an hour and a half and not seen nothing.' He learned from Rush his constant movement and lateral prowling along the shoulders of the last defenders. Also, like Rush, Fowler was unwilling or unable to theorise what he does on the field, afraid that too much thinking about what comes naturally will lead him to somehow 'lose' his game. He once told a frustrated interviewer: 'You leave the office and you don't want to talk about *your* work. I hate talking about football: I just do it.'

The thinking among the Liverpool coaches at the time was that the better the quality of player around Fowler the better he would perform, a sign of a real finisher whose work-space is around the six-yard area and who thrives on high-quality service inside the box. Two non-playing substitute roles in 1992–93 preceded Fowler's first-team introduction, away against Fulham in the League Cup, a big moment which naturally produced a Fowler goal, swept high into the Cottagers' net. But the return, Robbie's home début, was what made football people in the city and elsewhere really sit up. Okay, Fulham were a very ordinary Football League side, but in front of a half-full Anfield and a still-standing Kop this puppy-fat Liverpool kid showed what was far from ordinary. He scored all five, an unprecedented start. We buzzed. Moreover, we could tell later from his nervous guttural talk that Robbie was certainly one of us and, we would soon learn, warts and all.

In 1993–94, at 18, and incongruously wearing US basketball legend Michael Jordan's No. 23 shirt, Fowler started 27 league games and came on as a sub once, scoring 12 times, a figure bettered that season only by the still predatory master, Rush. Fowler also missed two months of the season with an ankle injury. This departure from the traditional 'Liverpool way' of gently easing a young player into the side was a sign both of Fowler's own precocious talent and of the real problems faced by a beleaguered Graeme Souness in trying to shape a successful Liverpool team – and save his own job. From 1 September Liverpool went five games without a goal, losing four, including Robbie's first league start, at Chelsea. Fowler scored his first league goal for Liverpool against Oldham at Anfield in October, and by December was already the club's established penalty-taker, scoring from the spot against Tottenham in a fraught 3–3 draw at Anfield.

After Liverpool crashed out of the FA Cup to Bristol City in January 1994, Souness finally resigned and Roy Evans took over managerial duties. Against Everton in March, Rush and Fowler, frightening names for defenders if thankfully for them drawn only from briefly overlapping eras, each scored to secure a derby win, a breathing space for the new manager. But only two wins from the final nine league games – including an emotional and losing farewell in front of the standing Kop, to Norwich City – pointed to the bigger challenges ahead. Fowler was ready. In 1994–95 he doubled Rush's own goal tally, scoring 25 in the league against the Welshman's 12, including an extraordinary four-and-a-half-minute hat-trick against a struggling Arsenal, future Fowler favourites, and still a Premiership record.

But following the signing of the ultimately ill-fated Stan Collymore in the close season, and faced with a problem which would later be all too familiar to his successor, Gérard Houllier – how to fill two strikers' places from three top strikers – Evans lost his nerve and started the 1994–95 season with the experienced Rush and Collymore for the first two league matches, with the young Fowler itchy on the bench. Managerial sanity was soon restored, however, and Fowler appeared close to the height of his goalscoring powers, eventually totalling an astonishing 28 goals in 36 league matches, followed some distance behind by Collymore on 14. In consecutive matches in December 1995 Fowler scored twice at Old Trafford against the champions and the fearsome Peter Schmeichel, and three times against Arsenal at Anfield. Bolton Wanderers suffered a worse fate: four Fowler goals at L4 in September.

Even at this early stage, most commentators were predicting a sparkling future for Fowler: it wasn't difficult to see why. Although he wasn't especially quick, he always seemed to have time, even amidst the frenzied action in and around the box; his timing of striking the ball was incredible, he barely scuffed anything with his dinky size sevens, which meant he could also score startling goals from distance; he also hit the target from anywhere and from any side, frequently taking shots very early on his so-called weaker right foot, and he was also brave and strong in the air; and finally, and biggest attribute of all, Robbie, like Lineker and Solskjaer and only one or two others, somehow 'knew' where the final position of the ball was likely to be whenever it came into the box. No one can teach this: this is vital striker's intelligence, given by God.

Occasionally, even the cod football analysts would focus on this last, unimpeachable skill in Fowler's repertoire. In the FA Cup semi-final against Villa at Old Trafford in 1996, for example, Fowler, already having scored a suicidal diving header, scooped off Gareth Southgate's bootlaces, then watched a second-half Liverpool corner into the Villa area whilst, almost absent-mindedly, backing-off apparently outside the danger zone. But he had sensed, somehow, that the ball would only be half cleared from the Villa box. When it duly arrived, as if drawn by unseen magnets at his left foot, Robbie then hit a controlled lofted drive over probably 16 or 17 players which faded in off Mark Bosnich's right-hand post. This exquisite goal was for a crucial 2–0 lead and it came out of *nothing* and in a tight FA Cup semi-final. The Villa boss, Brian Little, who was standing right behind the line of the shot, said later that as soon as Robbie struck he knew the game was up. It was; and Fowler, pure and simple, was the difference between the teams. With this kind of sorcery in your armoury, at that time anything seemed possible for the new Liverpool regime. Bosnich later said of Fowler: 'He often shoots early, he doesn't mind where he shoots from, but he seems to get late fade on his shots like a golfer. He usually gets ten out of ten shots on target, and with nine out of ten he hits the corners.' He was, in short, unmatched.

Playing under Roy Evans in the mid-'90s in a wing-backs formation, McAteer wide on the right and Rob Jones or Bjornebye on the left, with McManaman behind the front two and with the perplexing Collymore playing left striker, for a short while Robbie cleaned up. But it didn't always work out with Stan – there were occasions when the two front men barely spoke and Colly, never happy to be anyone's strike partner, could easily simply drift off into his own closed world. But Fowler, never the quickest forward, also thrived on the deliberate, slow, passing movement of the early Evans teams and the eventual flat delivery of the ball on the ground or in the air from wide positions, left and right. He was fearless and deadly when the ball was crossing his body, a low centre of gravity helping him withstand fearsome blows in the opposing box.

In the mid-'90s, emerging Bootle-boy Steve McManaman, university-sharp, scouse-tongued, and a couple of years older than Robbie, began to hold court in Merseyside clubs and bars – with the media and the young Robbie Fowler in tow. This double-act – Mac, the eloquent wide-boy, and Robbie, the innocent but inflammable genius striker – had its own attractions. It involved playing with the conventions of the media in Sky TV post-match interviews, for example, as these two carefree scallies hammed it up; or Mac and Robbie checking imaginary watches if Fowler (always Fowler) had managed an unfeasibly early goal. Robbie could also simultaneously draw laddish aggression *and* maternal sympathy. Birkenhead's Elvis Costello says about Robbie: 'There is something vulnerable about Fowler. He looks like he is struggling with something, but he is easily the best striker Liverpool have when he is on form. It would be a tragedy if he left and proved it elsewhere. I was out for Sunday lunch with my mum when we bumped into Robbie and Steve McManaman. Robbie was kind of sullen. He was just coming back from injury and my ma got into him, saying, "Are you all right, are you looking after yourself?" He was all shy and taking it. It was like a double act, with Macca having the lip. He was the one with the lip who can always talk his way out of it and always gets the quiet one into trouble.'

And Robbie *did* get into trouble. He drank too publicly in the city – and probably too much. He had tabloids chasing him after a much-trumpeted stylised 'romp' with an MP's daughter. 'The papers seem to forget footballers are normal people,' he once said, 'Normal people do stupid things and some footballers do stupid things. The public have a right to know what you're doing on the pitch, but not off it. When you're a footballer people forget you're actually a normal human being and think you're public property.' *On* the pitch, Robbie cheekily bared his arse during a match at Leicester, producing a stuffed-shirt FA fine. He celebrated European goals by revealing a T-shirt in support of the striking Liverpool dockers. It was McManaman's idea, of course, and it brought Robbie plenty more respect from most of the working men and women from the city who followed the club. UEFA were less impressed, ridiculously slapping a fine on Fowler for this blatant use of the football stage for allegedly 'political' ends. The real story, of course, is that this sort of thing gets up the noses of the sponsors and the TV companies. The former pay good money to get their products centre-stage, the latter have their own advertisers to satisfy. Players are allowed no agendas of their own which might, after all, distract from the lucrative commercial semiology of the modern football stadium. So much for popular action.

Later, in March 1997, Fowler famously argued *against* a penalty awarded in his favour for a foul by England colleague David Seaman in a match at Highbury, a severe contrast this with the approach of the new generation of strikers including, at Liverpool, Owen and Heskey who were regularly criticised – if not by club staff – for sometimes going to ground too easily in search of free kicks. (Notably, too, Fowler never tries to claim goals he knows he hasn't scored, those which ricochet in off defenders, for example.) Perhaps Fowler was actually afraid that the referee might send Seaman off when little contact had been made? But no matter: FIFA offered Fowler a sportsmanship award. According to Reds fans at Highbury that night, Fowler, his footballing morality clearly affronted by the injustice of the penalty award, allowed his own kick to be saved by Seaman, playing for a rebound to McAteer who followed up to score. The perfect solution, then, to a difficult moral question. Robbie in his pomp.

In 1996–97 Fowler managed 18 goals from 32 league appearances, to Collymore's 12 in 25. But the cracks were already starting to show in the side, even as Liverpool seemed well placed for a serious title bid. Collymore was regularly being substituted by now, usually it seemed for lack of effort, and a run of just two wins in the last seven matches effectively killed off Liverpool's championship hopes. In desperation, and with 16 minutes to go and 2–0 down in the club's penultimate league match at Wimbledon, Evans introduced a new young scoring sensation, the tiny 17-year-old Michael Owen. He had frightening pace – and scored in his first game. Ian Ross, chronicler of Anfield times for *The Guardian*, wrote presciently at the time: 'Owen, who turned 17 only last month, has been variously described as the next Kenny Dalglish, the next Ian Rush, and even the next Robbie Fowler. The last comparison is ironic since Fowler, another former boy wonder, is still only 21.'

In the following season it was Owen, in a new-look 4–4–2 Liverpool, who doubled an injury-troubled Fowler's own league goal tally (18 goals to 9) and who was beginning to attract the sort of press which suggested that, even at just 22, the greatest natural goalscorer seen in the English game since Jimmy Greaves had already been overtaken at his own club by a kid who was yet to wet-shave. In February 1998, having scored 91 goals in 160 Liverpool league matches, but in the middle of a period of an avalanche of goals for the lightning-quick Owen, Fowler collided sickeningly with Everton keeper Thomas Myhre, suffering a cruciate ligament injury which threatened his very career. By the summer of 1998, following *that* goal by Owen for England against Argentina in the World Cup finals, no one outside Liverpool was really talking any more about Robbie Fowler. St Michael, it seemed, had already usurped Anfield's God.

Both Michael and Robbie were staunch Evertonians as kids – Michael's dad even played and coached for the Goodison club. Both were attracted to Liverpool as youngsters, they said, by the quality and friendliness of the coaching staff and, let's face it, by the long-term success of the Liverpool club. 'Sure,' said Fowler later, 'I was an Evertonian, but I wasn't stupid. Deep down, though I would never admit it, I always knew Liverpool were the better side.' Robbie's dad played for a well-known decent local team in the city, Nicosia, but when his young son played for Liverpool schoolboys the professional club scouts dutifully queued. The young Fowler even played a few games for Everton's Under-17s – reputedly when he was just 14 – but the clincher for Anfield may well have been an old youth coaching trick: Reds manager, Kenny Dalglish, was cleverly recruited by Heighway occasionally to drop the schoolboy Fowler off home after training. The sought-after young striker was so full of his brush with the great Dalglish in school the next morning it was clear that from this point on he was always destined to sign for Liverpool, despite his deep Blues leanings.

Michael was and certainly is *admired* by Liverpool fans, perhaps especially by younger supporters, those who have managed to escape the clogging poverty of local housing estates, and by those drawn to the club from outside the city. But Owen, unfairly, is not *loved* – or criticised – at Liverpool by many of the locals quite the way the sometimes errant Fowler still is. If Owen is a boy band – all straight lines, shiny and marketable, a national icon – then Fowler is the authentic local face of rock, more imagination and substance and more than a hint of undisciplined unruliness and danger. Most Kopites could see themselves in Robbie. They would claim to understand his emotions and uncertainties – which is one of the reasons why even now, whenever the Kop chants a Liverpool striker's name which isn't 'Fowler', Robbie's own chant soon follows, even if their hero is only on the bench or is even sitting gloomily in the stands.

The unproven allegations and rumours (from among Evertonians) which persist in the city about Fowler and substance abuse don't lessen his appeal here, as they might, say, for Michael Owen. Owen's packaging and promotion is of quite a different order and, after all, everybody in Liverpool knows that it is excess ale which really puts an athlete's body to the sword. Robbie, of course, has been there, too, though he also says he knows the costs. Under Evans, players were trusted to get to bed before matches, but 'sensible' drinking *was* on the agenda: 'You can't stay out with your mates all night drinking,' said a young Fowler at the time, 'otherwise you're not doing it as well as you can. You've just got to be sensible.' We knew we could trust Robbie. Not.

Robbie is also *from* Liverpool, of course, from troubled Toxteth, which meant the sort of special reverence afforded a local player, a real scouser, raised through the ranks especially when set against the reckless purchases of the Souness years or the £8.5 million splashed out by Evans on Stan. There is also the *frisson* which came from the fact that Fowler, the Liverpool urchin, seemed constantly at risk, both on and off the pitch. Fowler, with his wilful socialising and gentle, shy lack of deference, seems so obviously to come from a different era – and a different place – than the squeaky clean and brilliant but rather colourless Owen.

Like most fellahs in the city who would quickly warn about the dangers of 'killin' yerself' in your job, under the relaxed Evans regime Robbie was healthily wary of the work ethic, a stark contrast to today's disciplinarian set-up. 'I hate training,' he said in 1996, 'I hate running. At Liverpool everyone's quite relaxed over training, but if you're not doing it in training they'll let you know and give you a bit of stick.' When Houllier arrived at Anfield he was astonished at the lack of 'connectedness' between training and playing at Liverpool: as if training for some players was approached simply to 'fill in' time between matches. He also later wondered aloud whether a back-from-injury Fowler really understood exactly how much the game had moved on even in the time he had been away; and how hard Robbie would have to work to get back to his best form.

Committed Reds followers knew of the rise and rise of woollyback Michael Owen, all the way through the Reds junior teams and from his amazing deeds for England schoolboys. Owen, in fact, had been a football star since he was seven years of age, the local press in the Chester area running stories about his goal-scoring deeds from the earliest moments when he played among kids three or four years his senior. For Deeside schools Under-11s he scored 97 goals in two seasons, 25 more than Ian Rush. He was *designed* to be a top player, came from an established football family, and United, Arsenal and Forest all showed a strong interest. He even spent two weeks at Old Trafford, but by this time he was set on Anfield. The reason? Steve Heighway always saw him right when he was a kid for new boots and tickets for big Anfield matches. 'Just the little things that keep you happy,' said Owen. His idol, predictably, was Everton's unfeasibly nice Gary Lineker.

Sky Sports showed Owen from 14 years of age slicing through foreign defences, huge pace, scoring outrageous goals. He scored a dramatic televised last-minute winner from the kick-off at St James Park against the Scots, who had, themselves, just equalised. England's response was to give the ball to Owen, who ran from halfway through the entire Jock ranks, the fastest kid in the playground. Michael could have had his own show on Sky. By the age of 14 he already had a sponsorship deal tied up with Umbro, who have pumped millions into the Owen home ever since.

After attending the football forcing house of the FA School at Lilleshall, Owen scored a record 12 (out of 20) goals for the England schoolboys team in 1995–96 and scored on his début in *all* England age ranges up to and including Under-21 level. Unusually, he was already scoring 'adult goals' at schoolboy level, according to England schoolboy manager, John Owens. Michael scored 11 goals in just five games in the Liverpool FA Youth Cup-winning team of 1996–97. Even so soon after unearthing the amazing Fowler, the word at the club was that this new boy, intelligent, disciplined and focused only on football success, might be just as good – or even better.

In the Flattie before matches in the uncertain Evans years in the mid-1990s, and especially when Fowler was injured, we Liverpool addicts used to ask each other from time to time 'How old is Owen now?' as if simply talking about the prodigy could help him age and grow, help him sprout and come and rescue us. The only real questions about Michael were: could he survive the big boys' game, this fragile man-child? And could Evans get Michael into the side soon enough to salvage our title hopes and the Bootle man's own job? Michael made it at 17 (he looked 12), though it was already too late for Evans and for the 1990s Liverpool. At 18, of course, Owen was scoring World Cup goals that had the whole planet on its feet. If he could stay fit, we thought, he looked a potential world-beater. Who could possibly match this fuel-injection pace and replicate his icy finishing? No one. Except, perhaps, Robbie.

A Fowler injury at the start of 1997–98, and Collymore's close-season transfer to Aston Villa, meant that, like Fowler before him, Owen would have no calibrated or measured introduction to the harsh world of the English professional game. With the experienced Riedle brought in from Dortmund as support, and with barely a grounding in the Liverpool reserve team, the 17-year-old Owen led the Liverpool line with a refreshing freedom and enthusiasm rarely seen at the professional level. If Fowler's engaging simplicity was in his uncomplicated goal-poaching, Owen's was in his schoolboy joy in performing and in his startling bursts of pace. He had few tricks, this wunderkid: why did he need them? His extraordinary acceleration, pursuing a ball pushed past defenders, and his trademark burrowing under the armpits of brawny centre-backs and around into space beyond the back four, seemed enough to unhinge most defences.

He looked as if he should be simply brushed aside by towering, horny-browed English defenders, but the new FIFA changes in the laws favouring and protecting attackers and Owen's own innocent bravery and rubber-ball elasticity meant he seemed invulnerable even to the gruff enforcers who patrolled the penalty areas in the English Premier League. Anyway, how could you deal with him physically? He was just a kid. Few were ever able to catch him. In an early meeting at Highbury, England captain Adams could only laugh, good-naturedly, at Owen's vim. He fairly brimmed with desire to do well, with positive ideas and hard work, and was less instinctive, less 'natural' a striker than Fowler. 'As a striker,' he says, 'you've always got to be an optimist. You've always got to think: "If he misses it, I can get in there" or "If he runs there, I can run in his space", always looking for an opportunity to get in. If there's a through-ball on, you make a run. If you don't get it, you make another.' Simple.

In his first full season in 1997–98 Michael soon began to overshadow Robbie in the English sporting public's consciousness. After all, he looked and sounded like every middle-England family's favourite sporting son. He was fully in tune with the media demands and promotional possibilities for a top player, just as clearly as Fowler and McManaman had been trying gently to subvert them. 'We were taught to be keen and competitive in everything we did,' he said, 'but Mum and Dad always stressed there was a right way of doing things – both on the sports field and off it. They brought us up to be considerate and polite to others, especially to our elders, and I think those early habits we were taught have lasted us through to our adulthood.' He was an advertiser's dream, and became the youngest player in the twentieth century to play for England when he started against Chile at Wembley in February 1998. Immediately afterwards, at Sheffield Wednesday, Owen scored his first senior hat-trick for Liverpool, and was applauded off the field by home spectators as a sporting *national* commodity and hero, something to which his partner Fowler has never aspired and is even less likely to achieve.

With Owen by now lauded as a likely successor to the fading Alan Shearer as the new most marketable and iconic figure in the English national football team, Michael's first career and 'image' crisis occurred. This boyish enthusiast was sent off – *twice*. First, in 1997, for an alleged head-butt in an England Under-18s match in Yugoslavia, and second in a hard-fought televised clash with Manchester United. Having already scored, Owen launched himself two-footed, high and late at United defender Ronny Johnsen. Johnsen was carried off. Owen was inevitably red-carded and was no longer quite the national blue-eyed boy.

It was, likely, a rush of blood, an overly committed display in an important fixture, or even a determination on the part of the diminutive Owen to show he could box his weight, even with the giants who towered over him. It showed, more than anything else in the eyes of Liverpool supporters, that he also had the required steel. Owen seemed unfazed, treating the incident as if putting a realist marker down, saying later: 'The manager likes you to have a bit of grit. If you are a winner, you show it sometimes, and accidental fouls, bookings and sendings-off are going to happen. Certain players have that, and maybe it is no coincidence that they are at the top. I think fans and managers recognise it if you look like you are willing to die for the team.'

At just 22, and with a goals record unmatched by virtually any other player in the Premiership, stories now started to circulate in the press – and in Liverpool – that, compared to the rampant and responsible Owen, the injury-troubled and feckless Robbie Fowler had put on weight and was already 'finished'. With Fowler injured and out of World Cup contention, England manager Glenn Hoddle wondered publicly not about Michael Owen's grit or temperament but, mysteriously, about his lifestyle – which seemed exemplary – and whether he was really a true goal-scorer and so, against popular opinion, he omitted Michael from England's first World Cup match in France against Tunisia.

Starting on the bench in match two, Owen came on with 17 minutes left as England fell adrift of Romania in Toulouse. Owen, effervescent and positive, scored (naturally) but a late defensive mistake still cost England the match. By the time Michael had scythed through the gasping Argentine defence in St Etienne, running for 25 strides with the ball to score what some observers describe as the best individual goal ever scored in the World Cup finals, no one wondered any longer about his goal-scoring capabilities. Pele even wanted him as an honorary Brazilian. Commercially, Owen was also about to go through the roof: Mark McCormack, at IMG management, said that Owen was the only footballer in the world capable of making as much from endorsements as the global sports don, Michael Jordan. At just 18 years old, Owen had truly arrived in the global sports marketplace, his projected career earnings being estimated at some £80 million.

After becoming, at 18, the youngest ever BBC Sports Personality of the Year in 1998, and being treated by the locals like a pop star at Liverpool's first away fixture at Southampton in the new 1998–99 season, Owen then virtually single-handedly destroyed Ruud Gullit's chances of an extended 'sexy football' stay at St James Park by scoring a typically brave and explosive hat-trick in the north-east in a televised 4–1 Liverpool rout, before scoring four at Anfield against Nottingham Forest. Owen was hot, unstoppable it seemed. As one writer commented at the time, no emerging English talent was now likely to alter the new England tactical plan for the foreseeable future: 'That has become very simple. Get the ball to Michael.' It was also, increasingly, getting this way at Anfield, previously Robbie Fowler's exclusive kingdom.

But Liverpool's 1998–99 form was inconsistent; when Fowler returned from injury in September he looked sluggish and unsure of his role, apparently confirming his critics' doubts. Despite his still lauded status at Anfield among Kopites, few Liverpool supporters were completely sure he was now worth anywhere near the reported £50,000 per week deal his agent was still supposedly trying to negotiate with the financial wizards in L4. In the earlier Evans years Robbie had been *the* key Liverpool striker, served by a marauding midfield and the mercurial Collymore. With Owen now well established in the team, a one-man strike force in his own right and more inured to the team notion of feeding *another* striker, it was unclear who was going to supply Fowler with the necessary ammunition. The big question was: could these two slight forwards play together in the same side?

As Roy Evans departed Anfield in November 1998, the two Liverpool strikers jockeyed for position and for public approval in Liverpool. Owen pleased most those who prized ambition, compliance and real application; Fowler was more the choice of the football romantics, those who liked their footballers both naturally talented and occasionally wayward. Owen was already trying to reshape his game as defenders, inevitably, began to adjust to his devastating pace. Fowler was trying to get into better shape physically for the new challenges ahead. Owen also seemed much more attuned personally and professionally to the *national* cause, something which irked some Liverpool fans from the city who see all England affairs as a poor second to those at Anfield. Owen ended with 18 league goals, Fowler with 14 (from only 23 starts). Towards the end of this transitional season each player faced vastly different sorts of problems, problems which said something about their very different vulnerabilities. Robbie may have to leave Liverpool, it was suggested, in order to solve his.

Firstly, in February 1999 at Chelsea, Toxteth city boy Fowler provocatively 'offered' his arse at Graeme Le Saux, the Chelsea full-back, implying that the rather studious and middle-class Chelsea man was gay. Le Saux went ballistic, assaulting Fowler with an elbow. So, too, did the FA, with the image of 'new' football very much at stake. While the hysterical public fall-out from this incident rumbled on, Fowler, in imperious two-goal form, then led Liverpool to a rare home derby win over Everton, responding to taunts from visiting Evertonians about his supposed drug habits by appearing to 'sniff' the white pitch lines in a bizarre (and funny) goal celebration. McManaman's mischievous influence seemed in play here once more, and Gérard Houllier's post-match response was near-surreal, suggesting on TV later that Fowler was 'pretending to eat the grass', an old Cameroon goal celebration and something he had apparently picked up in training from Rigobert Song.

The FA's fury here was difficult to read. After all, Fowler was hardly *advocating* drug-taking; this was, surely, more of an ironic response to the sort of vicious abuse he routinely received from the betrayed Blue side of the city. The authorities saw differently: taking both incidents into account, the FA dished out a £32,000 fine and a six-match suspension, four matches for the cocaine spoof and two for 'insulting' Le Saux. Fowler's season – and maybe even his Liverpool career – was over.

Owen's own difficulties stemmed less from his still air-brushed public image or his on-pitch demeanour than from the physical stresses on his body as a result of his non-stop playing as a youngster and his free-running and combative style. In April 1998, Matt Dickinson of *The Times* had commented on the booming Owen phenomenon: 'It is hard to see what will stop him. There will be those who try, of course. If there are fears, they concern his whippet's frame, which has taken a battering in several games from behemoth defenders who know that, once gone, they will never catch him.' Almost exactly one year later, and soon after signing a £2 million BBC TV series/book deal with HarperCollins, at Elland Road Michael hurtled to the ground clutching a hamstring as he chased a ball behind the gasping Leeds defence. It looked, and clearly was, a serious injury, especially for a young footballer little used to injury and one who staked so much of his game on incredible pace and utter confidence in his own movement. Owen was haunted by the injury and was later shipped off to back injury expert Dr Hans Muller-Wohlfahrt in Germany, who recommended a massage realignment of Owen's pelvic muscles and work on correcting a pelvic tilt. It sounded like a chronic problem.

It was a long haul back, five months of careful repair work and hours of painstaking preparation and fitness training. When Owen did get back in the Liverpool side he was almost unrecognisable, at first, from the ebullient, free-moving and dynamic force he had seemed only a couple of years before. He looked uncertain and unwilling to stretch out in his old way, no longer trusting his body to face up to the test of top-level sport. His confidence, so impenetrable before, had visibly sagged and he also began to register physical reactions to his injury. On the Kop, the crowd increasingly watched his displays with a dark foreboding, hearts collectively in mouths for any signs of a recurrence of his condition and alert to every signal – and there were many – that his once scorching pace had now deserted him. Above all, he looked *troubled*, a once sunny young man whose personal sky had suddenly and dramatically become clouded with storms.

So Houllier's key young strikers, £40 million worth of goal potential, each struggled against demons when the new manager began to take real control of the Liverpool club in 1999. Added to this, Houllier's vision of the new Liverpool meant less of the 3–5–2-based deliberate build-up and width which seemed so well suited to Fowler's game, and more the sort of fast-paced narrow attack which seemed much more attuned to the work of a fit Owen and Houllier's new striking acquisition, the powerful Heskey. Owen's troubles seemed less wide-ranging than Fowler's but were, perhaps, more serious. With so little real guile in his game – his left foot was rarely in play, for example – Owen's extreme pace was absolutely crucial to Michael's success. So, too, was his mental strength. Neither seemed quite so assured now. The truth was that no one was really sure that Michael would ever get back his physical and mental equilibrium.

Houllier *liked* Robbie Fowler, as he did almost all the Liverpudlian players at the club, and he was impressed by his talent. He was also well aware of the emotional bonds between the Liverpool crowd and Fowler. But after the clear-out of Ince, James, Babb and Ruddock and the departure of McManaman, Robbie was also one of the last lingering memories of the drinking culture which had been established at the club originally under the successful regimes of Shankly, Paisley and Dalglish, as well as under the less successful ones of Souness and Evans. Houllier was determined that the new football future lay with quite different approaches to player preparation and professionalism. He was frustrated with Fowler's sometimes overly relaxed approach to training and his city-centre dust-ups, even though Fowler was becoming more settled and a little more domesticated, with a new partner and young child, and was soon moving out to Blundellsands to the north of the city. Houllier was also worried that Fowler's sometimes languid playing style needed adjusting to meet the changing pace of the modern game, which had quickened even since Robbie's serious injury in 1998. He thought Robbie perhaps lacked the sort of conditioning and flexibility needed for the new era. Weighing up all these doubts, and with captain Jamie Redknapp on the long-term injury list, Houllier decided to go for broke and made Fowler first vice-captain and then his active match captain, ignoring the much more obvious choice for the job, the imposing Finnish defender, Sami Hyypia.

Robbie, the Liverpool captain, was an interesting move, a not-too-sophisticated attempt by the French manager to instil the sort of responsibility and professionalism in the still-adolescent Fowler which Houllier felt was now required from *all* Liverpool footballers. It was also a useful strategy for other reasons. Houllier wanted to short-circuit, for example, any possible local criticisms following his recruitment of a 'foreign legion' of new signings before the start of the 2000–01 season. Fowler would be a key figure in his assertion, partly for local consumption and partly because he really believed it, that although foreign talent was necessary, the heart of the new Liverpool had to be drawn from the city in order for the club to be successful in the English game. Moreover, the captaincy might be expected to motivate and involve Fowler, especially on those occasions – and there would be many – when he wasn't actually in the team. Thirdly, if Fowler did have to be sold sooner rather than later, Houllier could hardly be accused now of isolating and freezing the local favourite out of the club. You don't easily sell your appointed captain. It was a smart move, giving Fowler the armband, and Robbie publicly welcomed it as an important part of his own personal development.

Dealing with Michael's problems was both easier and more difficult for Houllier. Owen, unlike his captain, needed little schooling in the sort of 'professional life' Houllier demanded from his players: 'If you want to be a top player,' Owen once said, 'you should want responsibility.' He played like a keen schoolboy, but thought more like a headmaster. But Owen also needed assurance and support and, more than this, wise words about the importance of patience, especially when things looked bleak for him during the difficult months of 1999–2000 and even at the start of season 2000–01. In February 2000, Owen faced an overhaul of his daily routines to correct a posture problem which was supposedly contributing to his continuing hamstring trauma.

Houllier was well versed, of course, in the sorts of attritional injuries which were likely to be suffered by over-played youngsters in the very physical style of play championed in junior football in England. He also knew that some of the routine medical and physiological back-up which was now common in France was less likely in England to have picked up the sorts of chronic problems which affected both Owen and Steven Gerrard. He could do little here. More important than this, however, he wanted to work on the mental and skill-based side of Owen's game by stressing the importance of improving on the player's obvious weaknesses – his first touch, passing, heading and his left side – and thus lessening his overall reliance on individualism and sheer pace. 'I have discovered a different Michael Owen,' Houllier said in September 1999. 'He's stronger and more solid in the face of tackles now and skill-wise he has improved too. His movement and link play is also better, and he is more consistent over 90 minutes: there is no dropping-off now.'

Houllier's rotation policy for Liverpool strikers also eventually offered more time for his younger players to rest and to recover from strains and niggles. Houllier's calm, 'scientific' approach and his utter confidence in Michael was undoubtedly good for both the mental and physical trials which still lay ahead. Even when Owen was failing to deliver during phases of 2000–01, Houllier professed his core belief in his prodigy. 'I thought he was fine even when he was missing some chances. At least he got himself into position to score,' he commented, before isolating one of Michael's key attributes: 'I'm not worried about him because he's strong willed. He's a winner in his soul.'

Meanwhile, the 1999–2000 campaign was a personal disaster for Fowler. Two ankle operations limited him to just eight Premiership starts and three goals. Michael managed 11 in just 22 starts, with the whole Liverpool team claiming only 51 league goals. Fowler had effectively lost virtually two years of his career, just as the game in England was changing. Towards the end of the 1999–2000 campaign, Emile Heskey's arrival at Liverpool suggested another new striker's dawn and it dredged up the usual press reports about Robbie's imminent departure from Anfield. Michael, innocently, spoke of his own 'good understanding' with Heskey forged in the England Under-18s side. Ironically, Heskey's arrival could do little to prevent a late Liverpool goal drought which crippled the club's Champions League hopes. With Liverpool desperate for goals, Fowler never even made the trip to the vital last fixture at Bradford, with hints of disciplinary problems being quashed by Houllier, who stressed instead that Robbie simply lacked the necessary fitness. Within a few months Houllier was saying privately that Robbie 'is not half the player he was'.

In January 2001, and with both Owen and Fowler's form inconsistent, each partnering the more regularly selected Heskey, Jari Litmanen's arrival from Barcelona spelled more trouble for Fowler, according to the press. In the same week, Robbie had been assaulted, again, in a late-night fracas in Liverpool. Some press reports suggested Houllier had already accepted a cash bid from Chelsea for Fowler in December 2000, and now Aston Villa were also in with a bid. This latest incident seemed to be the last straw for the manager who, tellingly, left the decision on a possible move to a clearly bemused Fowler, who commented later: 'There was a lot of talk but nobody was saying anything to me so I was a little confused. I didn't know what was happening.' Fowler was left out of crucial Liverpool games, with Houllier explaining that, 'He has lost his place because he was in the wrong place at the wrong time with the incident last week. He knows that.' But Fowler, a Liverpudlian with little experience of any life outside the city, had few real choices: he stayed.

The Fowler/Owen conundrum continued to divide many Liverpool supporters, even as the 2000–01 season reached its dramatic conclusion. Their respective goals/appearances records for the club were quite staggering: by the end of 2000–01 Fowler had played in 313 matches in total for Liverpool – increasingly under Houllier as a substitute – and scored 167 goals. Owen had played some 162 games for 83 goals. Despite these similarly impressive strike-rates, these players still offered clear character contrasts, and rumours persisted that the two forwards were at odds with each other, though both had also been struck hard in their short careers by injury and mental crises. Owen, even at 21 and with notable World Cup exploits behind him, had already been written off a number of times by press commentators and 'experts' inside the game, something with which Fowler was also all too familiar. Part of this unease connected to Michael's wider marketing as a national youth (more properly pre-teen) icon. Had he taken his eye off the ball?

Owen's second published book *Michael Owen: In Person* was consciously aimed at the teenage market and actually offered a rather depressingly dull picture of a young man with little apparent sense of himself outside of his own body (that hamstring again) and football. A survey of English kids in 2000, nevertheless, found most girls wanting to be Britney Spears, while most boys favoured Michael Owen. Commenting, in December 2000, on the national unease and recent backlash at the pace and scale of Owen's early success, James Lawton of *The Independent* focused, with some insight, on the very real problems of easy fame in tabloid Britain. He reasoned: 'We are left with a nagging sense that our failure to nurture and appreciate Owen's young talent is representative of a wider, and perhaps more tragic, failure in this country – that is, the inability to draw a line between merit and celebrity, to distinguish between show and substance.'

In terms of his *playing* style Owen seemed, finally, to have recovered his confidence, which had been so routed by injury, and to have extended his game under Houllier, especially as Liverpool began to develop a 'one forward, one withdrawn' approach for their strikers. Owen began 2000–01 well, but Liverpool did not. Houllier recognised his value: 'To be honest,' he told journalists, 'Michael Owen saved us a couple of times. He was the goal-scoring machine we needed when we weren't doing well. The quality of our game had to be improved drastically in a short period because otherwise we would go bust.' A serious head injury at Derby County had stalled Owen, but in March 2001, after Liverpool had won in Rome with two Owen goals, Houllier also commented pointedly on the modern game and on Owen's very necessary new talents. He said: 'When you play against good teams, one of the strikers has to help in midfield as well as link up with the other striker. Michael understands the need to build his game. I don't want him to be defined only as a striker who, in a split-second, can go for goal because opponents can counter that by putting on cover and dropping-off. There's more to Michael than pace. He's intelligent.'

Robbie Fowler was also adjusting, both to the real frustrations of Houllier's rotation system, and to the demands of sometimes playing rather deeper than he was ever used to under Evans. He had also coped mentally rather better with the crushing pressures produced both by his early success and injury problems, and also the almost immediate and rude (some would say cruel) emergence, to deafening public fanfare, of Michael as the 'new' (and improved) Robbie Fowler. Fowler had suffered quite desperate damage, to the posterior cruciate ligament, a potentially career-finishing injury and he had bravely fought back, despite all the brickbats. He was also nearly forced out of Anfield by his own demons and the pressures of being a local scally living in a media goldfish bowl in the city.

Under the new puritan regime at Liverpool FC, even Fowler was apparently reassessing his approach to football and now, with a prospective wife and two children, to life itself: 'You're not in the game for long,' he said in February 2001, 'so when you've been out for two years you tend to treat your career differently. Nowadays, football is much quicker. I noticed the change even in the time I was injured. It's important to look after your body. You can't afford to go out living the life of Riley, drinking all the time. It just can't be done. The fitness of modern players is frightening, and if you want to be a top player you've got to be fitter than most.' This might have been Houllier himself talking.

For some Liverpool supporters and Fowler devotees, this looked perhaps a little too much like the sleek modern game: like a large dose of Michael, in fact. A completely reformed Robbie Fowler? Few Liverpool fans, even those who howl at his night-time escapades and his 'laziness' and uncertain first touch, would want *all* of Robbie's glorious wrinkles ironed away. So it was something of a curious relief when he also told a broadsheet journalist, reassuringly, towards the end of the season: ' I wouldn't say I've changed. I'm 26 this week, still a young lad. At that age you are going to go out, aren't you?' You see, while many Liverpool supporters wonder at the brilliance and the exploits and earning power of the marvellous Michael Owen, they still identify with and *fear* for another Liverpool hero, Robbie Fowler: which is, of course, in these bland sporting times, part of his still magnetic attraction.

9. FOR LIVERPOOL AND . . . ENGLAND?

4 MARCH 2001: LEICESTER CITY 2, LIVERPOOL 0

Jaffa cakes and wine gums: Leicester City's secret. The home changing rooms are full of them; I see the evidence in a pre-match tour today of the sacred areas of the Filbert Street ground. Two old *Reds* heroes, Alan Kennedy and David Fairclough, act as hosts for Leicester's sponsors for this match, the local City Council, who *always* invite me as one of their VIP guests because they slyly enjoy the humiliation which they know, and I know, lies ahead for Liverpool supporters here. 'Barney' Kennedy arrives with an agent-cum-stand-up comic mate, a large and jovial Geordie. These two now tour with a stage double act of football and comedy aimed at golf clubs, sports dinners and 'charridee' events. Loads of ex-players do this now, recycling, sometimes abusing, the national football heritage. You can get Barney and his man for £750 a night. Geoff Hurst charges five grand, apparently. Victoria Wood won't look at you for less than £10K, but then, hey, what has *she* ever won?

Kennedy is a decent guy, and even a man with two European Cup winner's medals – and two winning goals in finals – has to eat. So we probably have to live with this caramelised and cabareted version of some of our greatest sports history. He's also an acute reminder that the last time the Reds were *really* in the big time most players earned a decent wage – Barney himself was on £400 a week at the end – but hardly one to cover the daily expenses of today's 'stars'.

Okay, one full week after a cup final win, the Liverpool backlash starts here. But let me first say this: that we have had a really hard past few weeks, got decent results, and most of our fellahs have also been off with international squads until Friday of this week. Leicester have been on easy street and lost only Taggart to internationals – a 4–0 defeat by

Norway, so *he* must have been trying hard. All this means that the Leicester meat-eaters have already been sniffing (our) blood all week. And let's be honest, they *fancy* us here again, and who can blame them? We have no wins at Filbert Street since 1996, and given our recent away league form everything points to them. Except that coming here and doing well is supposed to be one of the true measures of our recent progress. Houllier came in, after all, on a 'help us beat the little guys' ticket as much as anything else. And league points are crucial to us. So, doing well here actually matters.

Football systems: an idiot's guide. And it takes no more than an idiot, believe me. So let's talk now. Barney Kennedy, like me, still favours the width-of-the-pitch, 3–5–2 formation Liverpool used under Roy Evans more than what has followed – though we still struggled at Leicester, even playing this way. Today we get another chance to compare our current Houllier version of 4–4–2 (or 4–4–1–1) away, to Leicester's 3–5–2. And it's not great news. We know what GH wants from us by now: solidity, a strong 4–4 defensive line, and a teak-hard central defensive core from which we can counter-attack. We aim to get the ball forward early and fast with midfield support. At home, where we must push on more and our opponents quake, this has worked well, but away it has been a disaster, ultra cautious and hugely wasteful.

Without Litmanen or Smicer it also *looks* arcane. We often play ugly, in short. But 4–4–2 doesn't *have* to be like this: look at the imagination and scope at a Man United or Real Madrid. El Tel's recent words on how to beat this Liverpool 4–4–2 are also worth recalling here: work hard, stretch us wide at the back and get your midfield men through the holes, at pace. Boro have played 3–5–2 against us this season – twice – and picked up four points. Tottenham did the same in north London – and also beat us. Perhaps we should listen.

Critics of 3–5–2 describe it as an overly defensive five-at-the-back system: I don't think so. You *can* have five there if you need them, but the trick here is to be brave and try to control and *stretch* the opposition midfield in order to get wide and behind, or to get your own runners moving through the centre onto defenders who don't expect, or like, runners doing just this. You can also adjust your wing-backs to suit your needs: Leicester, for example, have two strong but *footballing* defenders who start wide here today (Sinclair and Davidson) but they also have wide forward converts (Impey – who is soon on – and Guppy) as ready back-up on the bench. To make this system really hum you need players who work hard, who can pass and keep possession, and you need good organisers at the back. Leicester are not brilliant, but they have all of these – and a massive will to win. So here's how we line up against the locals today, the two systems engaged and compared. City actually use a 3–5–1–1, also a slight variation on their usual.

```
                    Leicester City (3-5-1-1)
                           Royce
              Rowett      Elliott      Taggart
     Sinclair   Izzet     Lewis    Savage    Davidson
                         Sturridge
                          Akinbiyi


                 Robbie        Emile
          Super Ziege  Gerrard  Gary Mac  Barmby
          Carragher    Sami H.  Henchoz   Markus
                         Sander
                    Liverpool (4-4-2)
```

Why does this approach work so well for Leicester against us? Well, it's not rocket science, look for yourself. City know we like to play narrow, so they have few fears about our pace down the outsides of their back three – a big danger for the 3–5–2 system. Our only 'wide' player, Barmby, in fact stinks again today after a great personal show for England in midweek, and Ziege has no real pace (or determination) on the left, so there are no worries for them there. What also concerns any manager of a 3–5–2 formation is the danger of allowing too much attacking freedom for the opposition's potentially unoccupied full-backs (Roberto Carlos, for example). But as *our* full-backs are actually pace-free *centre-backs*, this is also no real threat. Leicester know this. Also, Heskey seldom comes deeper in this game – the midfield is so crowded – and so he doesn't get to run at the bulging Taggart. So we don't ever get at Leicester wide or from deep with any real pace.

Meanwhile, either Izzet or Savage is able to get *ahead* of the ball and into the channels which are opened up between our centre-backs and full-backs. And these midfield guys have good movement, real pace. Now, *this* Leicester approach has solidity, spread, fluidity and some danger. What *we* play here, as a response, is a cautious and rigid system, with little width or penetration, in which our midfield never really gets forward, and is outnumbered four (I'm counting Ziege here) to their five, sometimes six.

And we just don't adjust – except to try Michael, wide right, when it is already too late. Houllier, our foreign guru, our Graduate International Professor on Advanced Football Coaching Studies, is not offering us too much of a tactical revolution so far away from Anfield in the Premiership this season. In fact, too often he looks more on these visits like an uninspired Englishman, an accented limey in French clothing. This may be European football science, but it is not what we were promised – or expected.

To top it all, Robbie gives the first goal away after a tepid first half, defending appallingly on the right and then playing *onside* the City attackers. Akinbiyi, possibly the worst striker in the entire Premiership, scores it. And this is really the crucial moment, a goal down against Leicester in a tight game.

The second Leicester goal comes late on, precisely from one of those lung-bursting midfield runs from Izzet. In between, we are truly *shite*: no ideas, no penetration, no chance. City's Matt Elliott says it is one of the easiest 'big club' matches he's ever played in. Houllier blames post-Wales celebrations, but he also says later that he thought we had *deserved* to win. This is deeply troubling on any one of three counts: either Houllier has lost his mind (which is quite possible); or he says this simply for the PR value back in Liverpool (which is plain dishonest); or he actually *believes* this rubbish (which is even worse). This, in fact, is now a 'normal' away league performance from us this season. A bad one.

As I leave the Leicester City reception area later, still angry and the worse for a few sherbets and dragging my long white mac, as I slope off into the gloom a young Leicester kid chases me – for an autograph. Amused, I ask him who he thinks I am. 'Mr Eriksson?' he suggests, now more uncertain. I smile. But could I – or you – collect *fewer* points away from home with these players than Liverpool have won recently? Two wins in the last nine away. Or is this, as usual, just the ale – and the misery – talking?

FROM THE BOTTOM, TO THE TOP

FIFA and the EU have finally agreed on new international transfer regulations. Nobody really understands them. What we *do* know is that players will still be on contract, and breaking contracts will mean a four-month suspension before a player can move on abroad. Clubs will be policed to make sure they are not inducing players to leave when under contract. Transfer fees under these new rules will be in the form of compensation payments for the training of players up to 23 years of age. Don't ask how these fees will be calculated – a minefield. The European player's union Fifpro is less than happy at these remaining chains. The struggle goes on.

While this circus wheels away, at the other end of football's food chain, at Lilleshall in rural Shropshire, youngsters who have been released by Premiership clubs are paraded in front of prospective employers; both a doleful and a hopeful exercise, a costly cattle market. Few youngsters who have tried it out at an Arsenal or Liverpool are happy to give it a go at, say, Rotherham. Not all are good enough to, not by any means. Alan Smith, manager at Palace, calls for an Under-21 league here, as in Scotland, to replace reserve team football and in order to give youngsters more chance of breaking through. Why not?

Young Liverpool players Peter Crookes, a keeper, and midfielder Stephen Torpey are both here looking for work. Torpey, especially, had been talked of as a future star at Anfield. Now they are the inevitable casualties of the new Reds regime. 'Liverpool are a big club. They can go out and buy international players,' says Torpey. 'I'm disappointed it didn't happen for me. Maybe it was not the right time. Hopefully, they will pick me up farther down the line.' Not unless you turn Croatian or French in the meantime, son. It's a sad tale, although a couple of our recent youth team heroes, Parkinson and Roberts, will turn out against the Reds for Tranmere Rovers in the FA Cup this weekend. You see, for some there really *is* life after Melwood.

THE MAGIC OF THE CUPS

Two cups, two different countries – different *planets*. The Liverpool UEFA Cup quarter-final first leg in Porto is a monumental Euro-bore in the rain, but produces a decent result, 0–0. Porto, like Olympiakos before them, make a poor joke of their 'great home record' European hype. They lack creativity and real bite and pace up front, showing again how the smaller European leagues have truly been ransacked for talent since Bosman. They get booed off. We play solid, with Robbie and Michael together again up front, but no more than that. No more is needed, though GH is, quite rightly, shooting dark looks later towards anyone who suggests this job is now done. Suddenly, dare I say it, this endless Euro-slog, the UEFA Cup, now even starts to look winnable.

On Sunday, it's across the water to Prenton Park in the FA Cup, a very different challenge for a different Liverpool team. Here, rotation shows its own logic. We field *eight* British players (compared to four in Portugal), including Stephen Wright at right-back: Henchoz is injured. Emile misses out again, apparently injured, but Murphy and Barmby are back. Ziege is told he will not be needed; there may be tackling involved. We also get mental help on Saturday from Wycombe Wanderers, who only go and *beat* dogged Leicester City in the quarters at Filbert Street. So Houllier gratefully flies this 'underdog' red warning flag to his own players – relentlessly. Which means we come out competing from the start against Rovers, as we need to. This is no classic; we dig in, English-style, with Hyypia and Gerrard outstanding, and we try to use our extra quality and pace up front to nick goals. And it works, Danny Murphy and Michael scoring for 2–0 at half-time.

We know that if we survive the next 20 minutes unscathed that this is finished. We don't get past one. Yates heads in at the far post, and so it is tin-hat time. Except, soon after this we also score a 'Tranmere' goal, Gerrard crashing in and scoring from a near-post flick-on from a Gary Mac corner. This is now, in fact, part of who we are; a dangerous side at set-pieces, a real heading threat. But Robbie, obviously, thinks this is all too easy at 3–1, and so calmly back-passes daft Wayne Allison in for Tranmere's second. Then, for the next ten minutes or so, Hyypia's head acts like a giant blond lightning conductor for the garbage which is now lumped in from all areas. Until, that is, Gary Mac slyly suckers Yates to trip him on Rovers' right side: penalty. Scored by Robbie.

In the end, we rather like 4–2. And our reward for this winning pragmatism is an FA Cup semi-final at Villa Park – against Second Division Wycombe Wanderers. GH warns about this tie, too, but he can barely keep the excitement and the relief off his French chops at this prospect. But hold on, just for a second, that gunslinger Wycombe manager's face also looks chillingly familiar . . .

A FAN'S LIFE

A letter from a parent to the Liverpool FC matchday magazine, 15 March 2001:

> One of your biggest fans, Liam Cunningham, suffered from Batten's Disease, a generic degenerative disease that turned him blind at an early age. Liam was a mascot for the club in October 1989 when we played Wigan. He scored a penalty past Bruce Grobbelaar, the highlight of his young life, and to the day he died at the age of 24 on Friday, 9 February 2001.
>
> A season-ticket holder until he was unable to walk any more, Liam worshipped Liverpool FC and it was at the centre of his whole life. The family would just like to thank all of you at the club and all the fans for giving him that special something in his life. His last six years were spent in Tadworth Children's Trust Hospital, London, but his room was always decorated with LFC memorabilia and he was kept up to date with the team's progress: he insisted on it.
>
> Without Liverpool FC, Liam's life would have been very different. As it was, everyone loved Liam and loved his passion for the club. Thank you all once again.

Only a game? I don't think so.

15 MARCH, UEFA CUP QUARTER-FINAL:
LIVERPOOL 2, FC PORTO 0

Let's face it, most committed football supporters are miserable bastards. Consider this: we have already won a trophy this season, are on the very brink of a place in the FA Cup final, stand to move into the last four in the UEFA Cup tonight, and lie a games-in-hand fourth in the FA Premier League. And so what is our animated conversation about before this vital game? Subject: can we call this a succesful season, a new dawn? Are we even headed in the right direction? And there is real disagreement.

The two dominant schools of thought on this important question look like this. The positive case is that, following the Evans era, GH has added necessary discipline and purpose not only to the team but to the whole club. Players prepare properly for games today and have a real pride in playing for Liverpool once more; the coaching staff are back in charge. On the field, he has tightened us up at the back and has produced a team which is playing pragmatic, cautious but effective football, which is carefully matched to the challenges posed by our opponents. We are winning important, tight games and we will pick up perhaps a couple of trophies this season and, ideally, a Champions League place. Eventually we will move on to play a more expansive style of football, more suited to the traditions of LFC, as our still young team matures. The signing of Litmamen is astute and also shows that GH favours a more cerebral football style. We will make a real assault on the title next season, but the defensive base is being established first.

The counter argument to this is that what we see now is also the future. That Houllier *is* a pragmatist, first and foremost, and that the anonymous style of battling football that we have now is what he really favours. We have been focused and also *lucky* in the cup competitions because we have had reasonable draws, and a much better guide to the manager's capabilities and ambitions is our away *league* form – which has been woeful – hence the massive points gap between ourselves and the Corporation. We are further now from a championship-winning team than we were last season, when we at least *won* matches away from Anfield, and we will not qualify for the Champions League this season. The signing of players such as the willing Biscan shows the manager favours limited, hard-working, disciplined performers, not real artists. Swapping the talented Matteo for the indolent Ziege also raises serious questions about his judgement.

All of this evidence is heatedly dissected and debated in the Flattie before this latest UEFA Cup meeting. Is Houllier really a force for good or a limited pretender? A few of the anti-Houllier combatants are probably secretly planning the first events in a nascent 'Houllier out' campaign. They won't expect to get immediate mass support. But there are standards to think about here.

The *good* thing about tonight is that we do at least play at a high tempo; we are aggressive and positive. GH decides we need our 4–3–1–2 formation again, with Smicer playing centrally behind Robbie and Michael, and the recently impressive Hamann playing between Gerrard and Murphy in midfield. Henchoz is back in defence. But the big news is about Michael, because this looks a little more like the Owen of two years ago, the ears-pinned-back, free-running and eager version. He *terrifies* the Porto back line with his pace and direct approach and full-back Secretario is eventually forced blatantly to bring Michael down wide on the right and in front of the Kop. Fearing a card from stern referee Neilson, the Porto defender decides to have a little lie down, pleading life-threatening injury. For three or four minutes he pleads for attention under the ref's wagging finger. By now the Kop is in angry hysterics, warming to this piece of comic theatre until the stretcher-bearers eventually glumly arrive to cart him off. He's back on in 90 seconds flat, of course, magically restored. Great laugh, true stuff.

Steven Gerrard playing frantically, like a hyper-active child overdosed on E-numbers, turns the tie in the last portion of the first half. First, he hits a great flat cross at pace from the Liverpool right which finds Murphy unattended at the far post and Danny pokes a gentle shot past goalkeeper Espinha which is chased into the far corner of the Porto net, pantomime fashion, by the lumbering Ricarda Silva. Gerrard then floats in a cross to Owen, who heads the ball downwards and *over* Espinha, who turns to flap uselessly at the ball as it loops into his goal. Westerveld is G. Banks by comparison.

Two-nil means Porto now need to score at least twice to go through; which might be a possibility if, say, we were forced to play two or three men short for a continuous 24 hours for Comic Relief. Under any other conditions there is more chance of Walter Smith getting his round in. Hyypia is utterly dominant at the back, Wester makes one serious save. So the rest is a bore, no test. And we are in the semis of a European competition for the first time since 1996. We will expect something rather better than our supine showing in Paris five years ago.

STAN – NO LONGER THE MAN

Among those who really *stunk* for Liverpool in Paris back in 1996 – and there were many candidates – was one Stanley Victor Collymore. I think he was subbed at half-time, something of an occupational hazard for Stan around this time. In the end, Stan was one of the major reasons why Roy Evans eventually went under. I raise Stan here because after being shown the door at his next two clubs, Aston Villa and Leicester City – more high jinks in the reserves, ending in fisticuffs – and than at Bradford City, Stan *then* went flying off to Oviedo in Spain and played barely a game for his new club before announcing just this week that, at 30, he was retiring from the sport. Oviedo knew nothing of this, of course: Stan couldn't be bothered to tell them.

Perhaps Stan was too sensitive and introspective to be a top player. He was certainly unhealthily self-obsessed, which might be the key, of course, to his later illnesses. And, worse, a man like Stan could wipe out, at a stroke, your most important managerial asset – togetherness, the collective sense of wanting to play for your team-mates, which is so crucial for any sort of success in the tough fight which is the English game. Football is a crude and unforgiving workplace sometimes, and this *is* a waste at just 30, but in the end Stan could never be the real deal. The new Liverpool under Houllier has run a distance from this sort of individualism and divisiveness. Stan now says he wants to go into the movies. It's more bullshit.

17 MARCH: LIVERPOOL 1, DERBY COUNTY 1

Ah, the league. But no one gets properly focused for this Sunday sunshine stroll. Anfield is dead in the first half, the Kop barely raising a groan or a discernible cheer in anger. We the fans, cheat the team, for once. 'Everyone's just talkin' about how to get to Barcelona,' is John Mackin's matter-of-fact, but plausible, half-time explanation for this morgue. We have pulled out Barca in the UEFA Cup semis next month, a *big* draw and a major local talking point. So everyone here seems to be checking on flight plans, the cheapest trips, the craziest journeys. We have had all this in the Flattie before kick-off, maps at the ready, *EasyJet*-a-go-go. Even the Kop's elderly resident prankster Dr Fun is finding it hard to get over-excited, to get engaged, by today's events. You might think that this grown man in red tails and top hat with his hand up the back of a ventriloquist's dummy, 'Liverpool Charlie', and with 'Hi Yea Kids' embroidered on the back of his scarlet tails, has got more things to worry about. But he's as nonplussed as anyone down in the Kop concourses at the interval. He's a fixture here, an important local figure. No one disses him.

GH has stressed that this is the most important Liverpool fixture of the month (yeah, right), but his latest rotation has hardly helped matters because today we have Biscan and McAllister playing wide in midfield and a very nervy Heskey to accompany the newly frisky Owen up front. Litmanen is there to offer central inspiration, but it is the lack of pace and drive in the middle and on the flanks which we worry about. We have only 'fanny merchants' wide today, according to the Fellahs in Front. And with good cause.

Derby are well organised and tidy, with Powell stamping around angrily in midfield, and they even sneak an early goal, the lively Burton bundling in a flicked-on near-post corner. We offer little in first-half response – certainly not a real sense of urgency. But we do pick it up in the second half, and when Gerrard replaces the ponderous Biscan, he, Babbel and Owen start tearing away at the right-hand side of the Derby defence. Michael scores from a Litmanen pass from the right, and then he and Steven Gerrard start playing like they are back together in the old LFC youth team, with Steven carving out chance after chance for his little mate to miss in front of the Kop. But these are *good* misses, mainly born of ill luck in crowded corridors, from a forward who is showing chirpy confidence and a desire once more. And real *speed*. Emile, meanwhile, looks only clumsy and tense in comparison, unsure of himself and perhaps damaged by Robbie and Michael's partnerships up front and his own recent lack of goals.

LEAGUE PRETENDERS?

This is two important points lost, no doubt about that. Back in the 1970s and '80s Liverpool players laughed at 'cup teams,' arguing that they lacked the necessary balls, the mental strength, to win the league, to face the *big* challenges. Back then, winning the domestic cups were pleasurable, sure, a nice day out for the fans, but no one in Liverpool confused these tasty snacks with the main meals, the cordon bleu of league titles and European Cups. Today, finishing third in the league is regarded as a triumph, a real target, and yet this current squad can't get focused on picking up the sort of points we need to challenge even for the bronze spot. Ipswich, Sunderland and Leeds all win *away* this weekend, increasing the pressure on us. So maybe this is what we have become: football fly-by-nights, pretenders in the league but a decent cup team. Or rather, a *squad* of good cup players. But only the t-shirt traders and flag sellers, and the young kids outside the Kop today who bark at you 'Are ya gonna use voucher 28, mister?' (FA Cup semi-final ticket tender) would be really comfortable with that label. Even *three* cups won this season will not completely convince the hard men here that the new Liverpool regime is really on to something. It's a harsh judgement, I know, but they are right.

ENGLAND, SOCIAL INCLUSION, AND LORD BASSAM'S BARMY ARMY

What do you think about the England national team and actively supporting England? After a few years of miserably trailing the 'no surrender' brigade round the flesh pots of Europe – and worse – it is not high on my list of priorities. Still, I'm hauled down to the FA to talk about ways of reforming the England Members Club. And there are decent people here, trying to turn around the image of the followers of England. Mark Perryman, head of the England Members' Club and football style guru, wants a new set of more 'playful' national symbols to denote Englishness abroad – he suggests Stonehenge sponge hats (I'm not kidding). The problem, of course, is that the locals abroad – and their police forces – lie in wait for the England groupies, and all of these combatants now happily assemble, usually in full battle gear, to entertain the world's media. It is cheap and lively TV drama, you have to say that. And a guaranteed result. Untying these sorts of bonds is no easy task, but we give it a good going over. Someone suggests we even call in the editors of the British gutter press and tell them to stop doing bad things. It's a thought: a stupid one.

We also have the launch this week of the Home Office's new report on Football Disorder. I'm one of the working-group members, you will recall. Now I don't know about you, but having a couple of chaotic round-table discussions down in the HO lair in Queen Anne's Gate is no real basis, to my mind, for producing a Government report with 54 (count them) recommendations aimed at the various bodies and organisations in football. I thought we were just clearing our throats. But, hey, it's election time so here it is, four months on, all sparkly and new and Lord (call me Steve) Bassam is extolling the report's virtues for a gathered audience at the Barbican. It's not convincing, not for a minute.

Trevor Brooking, for Sport England, does a pretty good job here, reminding everyone of the parlous state of the funding for public sport in this country. And does this new document, which is also aimed at delivering 'social inclusion' through football, God save us, offer any resources, perhaps? No, not a sovereign. Another well meaning but wasted opportunity. Adam Crozier, FA Chief Executive, is down to speak at the conference on 'Football and Social Inclusion', following the launch. People have travelled far and paid well to hear him. He doesn't show.

24 MARCH, WORLD CUP QUALIFIER, ANFIELD: ENGLAND 2, FINLAND 1

Live on French TV this week a marvellously angry *Monsieur* Eric Cantona said to a group of gaping French football journalists: 'I piss on the lot of you.' Admirable, and I know just how he feels because we have had a full week of media spin and mischief-making before this strange Merseyside fixture – and what else should we expect?

First, Steve McManaman, facing his first return to Anfield, is described in press interviews as an under-achiever here – a slacker, a 'dilettante' – who had to go to Madrid to become a real player. Which is complete crap, of course. Arguably, in the mid-'90s Mac was *the* best club footballer in England, and one of the most influential and hard working. The London press pack, like a few tosser Liverpool supporters, had Macca down instead as some lazy poser and this image stuck, especially when he struggled with injury in his last season at Anfield. You can call Mac for being badly used by England, and for leaving on a 'free' under Bosman and not dealing straight with the club on this last number. But you can hardly accuse him of not putting it in for Liverpool – he barely missed a game. He'll get a great reception at Anfield today from locals for what he did in Liverpool, and not for what he's supposed to have become.

The second press story with the high bullshit quotient this week is the 'Will Beckham and his United pals get abused by the Liverpool Kop?' For one thing, this suggests that we have a poisoned Leeds-like obsession with United – which is actually untrue. For another, Beckham himself says: 'Walking out with the England team, looking out to the Kop end and seeing all these thousands of England supporters cheering for the team is going to be something special.' Which suggests that maybe he realises, at least, that the Kop is not actually the concrete and plastic and steel structures which are there mainly to prevent the ball ballooning into the Walton Breck Road behind.

The Kop is, rather, the thousands of Liverpool supporters who will be mainly absent today because they have given up their prized seats for one weekend to white shirts from places like Wigan, Wolverhampton, Plymouth, Portsmouth, Carlisle and Exeter: the same guys who are filling the Flattie at lunchtime with demands for bottled lager, and with shaved heads, strange tattoos and accents, and even stranger songs. In short, this is predominantly an England and north-west crowd, not a Liverpool FC one. So no one here will lay into delicate David, and the *real* Kop deserves no credit for that. But nor did it deserve the original stupid press scare stories either. All the usual pro-Liverpool/anti-United stuff will come next week at Anfield, when the Corporation visit, as it should.

I'm struggling today with club and country loyalties. Actually, that's not really true: I have *few* strong country loyalties. My Liverpool ties are about ideas of locality and belonging which stretch back over the development of the club and its players. Following England is 'part-time' by comparison – and often ugly. What I'm really interested in seeing is what an England game at Anfield is *like*. I also want to 'support,' as best I can, all six Liverpool representatives today – including Sami and Jari for Finland – plus Macca, of course, so I'm all over the place in my sympathies, like some sporting liberal nerd. I cheer every Hyypia header and each Owen thrust. There are thousands like me.

So the thing which is missing for me from an England crowd – apart from tolerance and humour, I hear you say – is any real sense of context or tradition. I know that following England is the only opportunity most English football fans get to follow a Beckham or Adams, or a Michael Owen. And I know some England fans do try to make a 'club' tradition out of following the national team for this reason. But there is still a lack of any really regular emotional and personal investment over time here, some sort of story of support of the sort which is so central to crowds.

So today, for example, gone from our Main Stand are the older grumblers and moaners of LFC, the hardy men and women and the codgers who have served their time and can tell you, importantly and at the drop of a beanie hat, that *none* of the current staff will ever match the Stubbins's or the Liddells or the St Johns of earlier Anfield eras. Few people in the entire ground are over 50 today. Instead, this irascible footballing gerontocracy, which every true football crowd needs, is replaced by an army of 20- to 40-year-olds who have been gathered, just for the day, to do the apparently important job at a football match on behalf of Her Majesty's Government of reassuring us that there will indeed be 'No surrender' to the IRA. Good work, boys. Your country needs you.

But this is a little unfair. Because I am also rather proud to report that at Anfield today there is actually much *less* of the crass nationalism and casual racism and abuse which is a defining feature of the southern core which follows England, reinforced as it is by the young English rednecks drawn from towns in the south-west, the north and Midlands explicitly for this purpose. The Finnish national anthem is allowed some uninterrupted air-time here, for example. Which is also why moving the England team around the country, even when the new Wembley is finally built, makes some sense. But this will not happen, of course, this necessary England-for-the-regions strategy, because crude economics will dictate where England plays in future. Our own FA will carefully see to that.

I have Emlyn Hughes directly behind me today in the Paddock. And it is not pleasant. Yosser was a key figure for us, of course, but he was not the favourite drinking partner of many of the Liverpool squad, even when he played with them back in the 1970s. A big admirer of both Thatcher and *The Sun*, apparently he's still left out of the Liverpool player reunions today. Perhaps it is not surprising. Tommy Smith famously thought Emma to be a loud-mouthed gobshite and a management sneak, and once loudly congratulated

Chelsea's Ron Harris, while on the field, for cutting Hughes in half with one of the Chopper's 'special' tackles. There's no substitute for team spirit, eh?

Well, sad Emlyn is publicly performing his 'today's England are rubbish' act for his small party, loudly hammering any stray home pass or missed tackle. It's crippling. An early misdirected Steven Gerrard cross-fielder, for example, produces: 'No, no, noooo. For Crissake, you're not ready for that yet!' Charlton's Chris Powell is positively *berated* at left-back, Hughes's old England position, of course. It's a Talksport masterclass, the highlight of which is the half-time: 'Beckham, the England captain? I'm not sure he should even be in the side!' Beckham, of course, is *easily* England's best player, and he goes on to score the winning goal in a loose and open second half. I point this out to Emlyn later but, after all, *he* is the one with all the medals and England caps, not me. He leaves, mercifully, way before the end followed by a string of camel coats and a female friend who wonders if it really matters that Finland had already netted before her own chosen first scorer, Michael Owen, had obliged for the whites? England win, 2–1. Just.

Back in the Flattie our nationwide guests seem more than satisfied. England have come back from a goal behind, after all, to win a vital game. Michael scores – with his *left* foot – and Emile and Robbie both get on near the end to give England a decidedly Liverpool look in attack. Before being hauled off, Andy Cole misses a stone-cold sitter in front of the Kop – the stand, not the crowd – which means he's *bound* to score a hat-trick next week, of course, when the Corporation come here on league business. After a slow start, Steven Gerrard has started to boss the midfield, but Litmanen has also been prominent, probing and scheming, showing Eriksson that England has no comparable central playmaker at the moment. They could yet make a nice partnership for us, Stevie boy and clever Jari. But not this season: Jari breaks his arm today and so will miss the Liverpool run-in.

In a TV interview later, young Gerrard says firmly that he definitely won't be travelling to Tirana if it endangers his fitness for forthcoming club matches. Steven's growing pains will thus be suffered in L4, not on a plane to distant ex-Maoist territory. Some of the differences will probably seem marginal to him, but with big games ahead it is likely to be important to us.

UNITED – TEAM OF THE 1990s

By the early 1990s Manchester United had a collection of outstanding young players in search of a conductor, a muse. In 1992 Leeds United won the Football League Championship, denying the Manchester club its first title since 1967 by four points, with a late run inspired by a maverick Frenchman who had been exiled from his own country because of disciplinary problems. At Champions Leeds, the young Frenchman soon ran into his own problems and became unsettled once more. A French coach allegedly tipped off the frustrated Alex Ferguson that this inspiring young foreigner might yet be coaxed away from Leeds for a nominal fee. Ferguson went to work and the deal was done, over the phone, for £1 million. Manchester United, lifted by their new talisman, then won four out of the next five league titles, and brought on a shoal of young stars. The French player: Eric Cantona, of course. The helpful French coach? I'll let you guess.

31 MARCH: LIVERPOOL 2, MANCHESTER UNITED 0

Young players coming into the side – an Owen, or a Fowler – you usually get flagged-up in the briefings which come from those supporters who report back from time to time from the reserves' front lines. Important work. Steven Gerrard was different. We had heard about him, sure, but only in that hushed way when fans and coaches sometimes talk about real talent at risk: a young player who had everything, but one who had suffered terribly with injury. A stress fracture of the back was the one usually mentioned. Here was a potential Emlyn Hughes, and more, whose career may already be over as a junior, broken on a weak frame.

Then I saw Gerrard play, on an open field at the academy barely six months before his full début. A crowd of about 50 people watched, no more. Steven came on for about an hour against the Manchester United kids and gently went through his work before Heighway and his staff quietly ushered him away. It felt like the match had been staged just to offer this scrawny Liverpool kid a chance, unmolested, to stroke a few footballs. And youth team football is often like this: two elevens are needed to give one real prospect a chance to make it. It was hard to know then, nevertheless, that we had been watching a player, on that windswept space in Kirkby, who would soon be compared, by good judges, not just to Hughes, but to the legendary Duncan Edwards.

And he has good attitude, this young scouser: 'That's the good thing about our staff here. They help to keep your feet on the ground. You can't argue with them, can you? They've been there and won most of the trophies that we're playing in, and when they're trying to tell you something to help you you've got to listen. As long as you prepare yourself, and want to keep learning, you shouldn't have a problem.' And although we have already seen it all before from Steven Gerrard, here we are just a couple of years on from his academy stroll, again against United, but now in front of 44,000 and against the top team in the land, maybe in Europe.

And this is the complete event, the real McCoy, the dog's bollocks, the top bazooka. We have not completed a double against the Corporation for 22 years: only Arsenal and Forest have done it in the past *decade*. We have not beaten United at Anfield since 1995. And yet this sprouting Huyton suedehead, with a hammer in his right foot and a tackle like a bulldog's snap, who can also pass the ball so crisply and sweetly over any distance on a football field, this kid, now positively *ruins* United. He decimates them – and it is a thing, let me tell you, of some beauty.

Sixteen minutes: Fowler picks the ball up in his deep striker's position in midfield and flicks it inside for Gerrard 35 yards out. A few steps and Steven simply thrashes the ball from *within* his stride, rising past Barthez's embarrassingly optimistic dive. The goalkeeper has seen this shot every inch of the way from over 30 yards and yet is still utterly, hopelessly defeated by it. We have followed it from the Kop and seen the same thing. The ball shows virtually no rotation through the air, it is so violently and perfectly struck. One-nil. Delirium. We are kissed by the Fellahs in Front.

Forty-one minutes: A Babbel throw-in on our right near halfway, down the line to Heskey, who steps back with the ball and around Irwin, allowing Gerrard to chip a cross first time into the box over Gary Neville to Fowler, just as the defender slips. Robbie stretches to bring the ball down perfectly and half-volleys a left-footed shot past Barthez from 12 yards. He does all of this so quickly that the keeper has no time to even get set for the shot. Robbie now shrugs off the returned Patrik Berger's attempted celebratory cuddle and instead trots slowly and deliberately in front of the Manx, gently and repeatedly shaking his fist in cool, provocative celebration. Two-nil.

And that's all there is. Except that Heskey messes up fancied young Wes Brown so badly he could have had three goals himself. And Gary Neville handles so clearly in the box in the first half that even daft Graham Poll might have been expected to see it. And that red-carded Danny Murphy makes us play for the last 25 with only ten men, just to see what United have left (which is nothing). And Sami Hyypia says to their eleven anyway: 'Throw it all at me, boys, because nothing gets by me today.' And it doesn't. And the Fellahs in Front all want more hugs and ecstatic back-slapping from us before we stream home, punching the air and smiling those huge satisfied grins which remind you why, despite all the shit and the hype, why you want to be a football fan at all.

And even we can see real hope (again) at last, we one-win-in-six-

Premier-League-games, fucking-know-it-all Houllier doubters. Because through all of this, Steven Gerrard and his posse play against Beckham, Butt, Giggs and Keane with no respect. Absolutely *none*. Which means that Manchester United have lost just three league games all season, but two of them are to Liverpool, and they cannot even claim a goal against us. And the real bonus? We have cut their lead over us in the league to just . . . 21 miserly points.

DON'T SACK THE MANAGER

Ruud Koning, a Dutch academic, has looked at the effects of the sacking of football managers in the Dutch league over a period of five years. Far from a positive 'shock effect' of a new appointment, his conclusions are that there is no real proof that a new man necessarily improves results or performance – though a new manager can improve *defensive* qualities. Which shows, I guess, that it is usually easier to stop goals than to score them. And also that, after some initial buzz, a new coach is usually left with the same sorts of deep-seated problems which got the previous one sacked.

Not that this will save the managers of failing football clubs, because the stakes are too high to wait around these days. Peter Taylor, England coach and Leicester City boss, for example, has moved from being a football genius to a coaching dunce in four months. Leicester can't buy a win and now look shite. Next season he's already at risk. He's not the only one. Gérard Houllier says 'Judge me on my league performance' because a Champions League place next season is vital for Liverpool in his reasoning. Winning cups this season is fine for the present, but it won't help in the recruitment of the sort of talent Houllier regards as necessary in order for us to play with the big boys. So we need to finish third at least, because he needs that bargaining chip for next season's shopping and contracts talk. We still have work to do.

10. MONEY, MONEY, MONEY

Football clubs like Liverpool face an extraordinary new economic future. And the new economics of top football clubs get ever *more* extraordinary. In 1999, Alan Shearer at Newcastle United, England captain and centre-forward, was the highest paid footballer in England, reputedly earning a cool £28,000 a week. At that time we thought this was vast, crazy money. Top players at the world's richest club, Manchester United, such as David Beckham and Ryan Giggs, then earned about £18,000 a week. A little later Roy Keane came along for more, a reported £50,000, but compared to top sports stars in the USA, where transfer fees for top sportsmen are absent, this sort of cash was strictly peanuts. NFL and NBA equivalents routinely talked in terms of tens of millions of dollars, even for short deals.

The earning power of some of these guys in doing other things off the court or field – selling sports shoes or Big Macs on TV, for example – was just immense. The Chicago Bulls' Michael Jordan was the US sports kingpin, of course, Nike's cash cow and the world's favourite global icon. Jordan took sports stars into a different place, as far as the commercial exploitation of global sports markets was concerned, and he was keen not to let politics get in the way of business. Jordan once refused to get pulled into potentially controversial civil rights territory, for example, reasoning that 'White folks buy sneakers, too'. Tiger Woods has since followed Jordan on to the Nike sports gravy train, becoming probably the world's most marketable sports star as a result. Manchester United followed, too: a £300 million kit deal with Nike over 15 years from 2002, £20 million a year and easily beating the £7 million per annum deal between Nike and Team Brazil, the previous highest world sports-kit deal.

Although they still fell short of the earning power of some of the big

USA stars, during the 2000–01 football season in England something really began to change concerning the earning potential of top footballers. A few things were important here. The first was the general ratcheting-up of the transfer value of top players, where transfer or compensation fees still applied. TV money, scarce talent, and wild business practices were behind this. The top clubs in Spain and Italy were the key players, with Real Madrid spending £37 million for Barcelona's Luis Figo, whose own club invested more than £25 million in a replacement for Figo, Arsenal's very moderate Mark Overmars. Lazio lashed out more than £35 million for Argentinian striker Hernon Crespo, and back in England Leeds United broke the British transfer record by spending a mere £18 million on West Ham's still inexperienced Rio Ferdinand. The world seemed to have gone mad.

Transfer spending, even on this scale, is not in itself a 'bad' thing. It can mean, for example, that money circulates in the game for spending on player replacements or indeed on other items; many clubs in the past have used transfer income to renovate the home stadium or build a new stand. At Barca, the Overmars deal was money brought in by selling Figo: what goes around, comes around. But in the post-Bosman era, inflated transfer-fee spending also translates easily now into player valuation for salaries at the completion of contracts. This means that players at the end of their contracts can begin to prepare to sell themselves *back* to their own club – or to another club – when their current deal runs out. Except now their new salary includes the estimated transfer fee which might have applied under the old system. So the message to clubs is: forget investing any big transfer-fee income in some new building; in future this sort of cash will, increasingly, end up outside the loop and in the pockets of top players and their advisers. Cute.

In this country back in 1998, Steve McManaman started this new era off, of course, with Liverpool FC as the unfortunate patsies. For months, the club tried to hold new contract talks with Mac, but nothing ever seriously got off the ground. Most Liverpool fans were horrified when Roy Evans had Macca flown off to Barcelona well ahead of the end of his Liverpool contract to try to strike a transfer deal for the player for a move to Spain, for a no more than useful £12 million. After all, Macca was *the* key player in the Evans era, and this deal looked too much like cutting our own throat, flogging our best asset to a potential European rival with no obvious replacement in mind. Macca also didn't even want to leave Liverpool – certainly not before his current contract was up. What the hell was going on? (We were not Bosman-literate then.) As it turned out, Barca were playing their own sweet trick on Mac, trying to use him as a rookie bargaining chip in order to sign the Brazilian

Rivaldo. So our man came back to Anfield, after all, and sat on his hands for the final season of his contract. Macca was saying nothing, even then, about actually wanting to leave L4; but that was part of the problem, he was just saying *nothing*.

Evans, rightly as it turns out, knew that Mac *would* leave, and that Liverpool would then get nothing for him when he did. When Gérard Houllier took over in Mac's last year the new manager simply accepted the inevitable as 'just part of the new situation for players' and carried on picking Mac for the side when he was fit. The business of knowing Mac was already leaving for Spain at the season's end soured his last few months at Anfield for some supporters – but he still got a standing ovation in his last match, when GH cleverly brought him off early just for this reason.

In any case, though our coaching staff had invested a lot in Mac as they brought him through from when he was a kid, we had had pretty good service from him. When Mac did eventually go, to Barca rivals Real Madrid, he moved from earning about £12,000 a week with us to an unprecedented (for an English player) £63,000 with Real – who simply computed the cost of the total package as if a fee had still been involved. On this basis, Mac arguably came cheap, very cheap, for them – and he helped the Spanish club win the European Cup in his first season.

Move on a couple of years, to 2001, and the huge hike in international transfer fees, plus the new FA Premier League TV deal which was now on the horizon, helped take this whole transfer-fee-becomes-salary issue into new and uncharted waters. Sol Campbell was the man doing the rowing, here in England. Like Mac, but with rather more front, Sol-boy's advisers had cleverly strung along the Spurs board as he neared the end of his contract. 'My heart is at White Hart Lane. I really want to stay. The numbers have to be right.' We got all this from Sol's side. But when push came to shove Spurs made an offer they simply had to refuse. His own club became just one of a number of potential Sol buyers, which at the time also included Liverpool.

Spurs had just brought in a new manager, Glenn Hoddle, and under their new owners ENIC were trying to win over their put-upon fans for an exciting new beginning for the club. Campbell was central to their plans, and keeping him a test of their virility in the new market for selling and buying top players. Tottenham have been out of the top rank for a few years now, so this was quite some test. Spurs ended up offering Campbell a massive £80,000 a week to stay in this end of north London, crashing their own wage structure and pretty much that of any other club in England. He turned them down – flat. Instead, Sol's men threw something else into this new pot: their man also had to be playing in the Champions League now, because new England guru, Eriksson, had told him he needed more of this sort of special competition in order to keep his England place. In these new reflexive times for players, his financial people wanted him there too. So add this to the new future: top players will increasingly demand Champions League football from their clubs as a minimum requirement for their own career development.

So Sol would stay at Spurs – *if* they paid him an equivalent £130,000 a week, and *if* they allowed him a clause in his contract which would let him leave the club after one season if Spurs had not qualified for the Champions League. Now, I'm a bit of a fan of the management skills of Glenn Hoddle, but even the new Spurs hotshot corporate owners blanched at this condition. Mind you, all ENIC's talk about Campbell's lack of 'loyalty' stuck in the throat. After all, this company has business interests in a number of clubs, not just Spurs. So Sol was shown the door, off for £20 million to Arsenal.

The figures here actually make some kind of crazy sense, even if Campbell is not out of the very highest drawer, which he isn't. Campbell's men do think their boy is a better player than Rio Ferdinand – who cost Leeds £18 million *plus* wages, say another £15 million over five years. Liverpool FC – or anyone else with a Champions League calling card – can have Sol for £6.7 million a season in wages, roughly the same deal. Except smart Sol gets *all* the dough. But then how much more money could Liverpool player-of-the-season Sami Hyypia then reasonably demand to play alongside this expensive acquisition, if he came to Anfield? And we haven't even started to talk about new deals for Gerrard, Owen and Heskey and all the other young guys who would be busting a talented gut alongside payday-Sol. Because this new arrangement means you eventually have to pay out a transfer equivalent for *all* your players, not just the ones you sign from elsewhere. And who, in their right minds, would pay Campbell *more* than either Gerrard or Owen? You don't think Michael's men will already be thinking about this? That's what he pays them for.

Of course, Gérard Houllier knows that Liverpool will need more players of the quality and experience of Campbell to launch a realistic Champions League challenge. This is certain. But if we do go down this particular route, Rick Parry and his partners could soon be looking at maybe an £80- or £100-million, or even higher, annual wage bill to find, and we would probably *still* have some players in the first team earning literally millions less than some of their own team-mates. And if we did find the £80 million or more, what are the guarantees that the next round of player contract deals will stop there? I think you already know the answer to that.

Call me old-fashioned, but this doesn't look like a great recipe for long-term economic well-being or better team morale. It's hard to see this as a sensible way ahead. Which is why, or course, soon after Campbell's demands UEFA's Mike Lee has uttered those dreaded words (for players) once more – *salary cap*. Capping a player's salary is currently illegal under European law, but a salary cap on *clubs*, or on leagues, thus applying no limit to the earnings of a particular player, well, that's another matter.

Although this looks like a possible UEFA initiative, the so-called G14 top European clubs would probably have to be the collective movers of a European-wide players' salary cap, in the unlikely event it ever got beyond the talking stage. These are the only clubs which can now afford – and might be willing – to pay these sorts of crippling sums. Agreeing on a cap might save them hard cash, and it might even induce more loyalty in some of their star players, but it would also remove the adrenaline rush, the competition of the market-place, which so drives some of the guys who run these huge concerns.

Would a club president at a Barcelona or a Real really want a salary cap if these are currently also the guys with the deepest pockets, the competitive edge? We also know, from the experience in other sports, that salary caps come with a hundred ways – legal or otherwise – of sweetening the pot for any player you really want. So this would mean more under-the-counter corruption – definitely. So let's not go all dewy-eyed about the potential egalitarianism of the salary cap arrangement: it isn't going to happen that way. And anything which threatens the world domination of the larger European clubs – even if it saves them money – is unlikely ever to breathe the air you and I get by on.

This issue, about the relationship between the G14 clubs (which include Liverpool) and UEFA, is crucial, of course. Think about UEFA as a bumbling, well-meaning international public-sector provider, trying to satisfy its stronger, more affluent citizens and consumers, while at the same time offering modest redistribution and support to its poorer residents. UEFA has been looking recently, for example, at remedying the imbalance in TV markets for European football, a tall order.

Under this sort of pressure, some of the G14 group think instead: *privatisation*. After all, why do we really need public services, when they fritter and give away our money, and when we can look after ourselves rather better in any case? Or at least a threat of 'going private' is proffered, unless UEFA hands over more of the collective cake to the richest, rather than the poorest, clients.

UEFA's response to such threats has been to try to do what their richest clients want. More recently it has also suggested a proposed new licensing system for the clubs in its competitions: more, not less, regulation, though this might also damage smaller clubs if they are required to have large stadia, healthy finances and UEFA-qualified coaching staff, for example, in order to be eligible for UEFA events. The G14 response to this unwelcome prospect is to search for commercial alternatives to UEFA, to propose fewer inconvenient international matches, and to argue that national associations start picking up some of the tab on the wages top clubs currently fork out for their international stars. The G14 group recently also called for the restructuring of the Champions League format, as crowds and TV audiences for matches fell, and the physical pressures on players intensified. The move to this format originally came from these same clubs, of course. We live in interesting times.

It is not far-fetched, of course, to imagine the G14 lot – or a new G28 or G36 group – offering up an independent new competition, funded by TV and excluding UEFA. The so-called Atlantic League clubs are already talking about an alternative to current UEFA arrangements, and the landslide could start there. How national governments or the EU might respond to these sorts of changes is a good question. UEFA also has effective control over national teams of course, another sticking point for potential breakaways. At Liverpool, Rick Parry's view is like that of many top clubs: we're not for it, but if it happens we must be in it. In other words, a kind of policy by paranoia. It is also one of the reasons why Liverpool is so keen at the moment to push its plans for a new 70,000-capacity stadium. The big European cheeses may decide that a 45,000-capacity ground backing on to crumbling terraced houses, and so evocative of Liverpool for Gérard Houllier back in the 1980s, is not what the game needs in the new century. You cannot afford to fall behind in this race, this is the thinking. Fear of inertia and exclusion drives on the big football businesses.

So escalating transfer fees, the Champions League and the new TV money have all increased the financial leverage of the top players in England. So, too, has the 'brand value' of a small number of selected players: Beckham at United claims he has a 'brand worth' for his club above and beyond his worth as a player. He brings in business for United by being Beckham, is his argument. He probably shifts a lot of posters, for example, and plenty of other bedroom stuff for quiver-legged young girls – and a few young boys, too. Only Michael Owen at Liverpool could claim the same thing. Judging by the number of young kids in the city and outside who wear the 'Owen 10' shirt, and the amount of other Liverpool merchandise which carries Michael's image, he'd have a strong case. He may be making it soon. Steven Gerrard, as a good comparison, will only ever really sell football stuff, and deliver on the small matter of winning football matches. Michael's range of commercial activity is pretty much whatever you want.

And this, really, is the era we are in, where the talk is about brand maximisation and global markets, intellectual property rights and the new internet markets. Which means the commercial interests of players and those of their clubs will not always coincide. Players have their own sponsorship deals but also 'belong' to clubs: Owen is an Umbro man, but plays in Reebok, a deadly clash of signs. It also means that sponsors and manufacturers become some of the important new power-brokers in offering popular access to top footballers. The football glossies in England are already used to players only being offered to them for interview if sponsors are agreeable, if certain issues are off the interview agenda, if product placement is to the fore and, in some cases, only with full editorial control. So what you read about Michael Owen, and how you see him, may well be only what his various sponsors *want* you to hear and what they are happy for you to see. This is routine business these days, part of the new way of promoting products, commodities, not flesh-and-blood footballers.

This also means that talk of European qualification, of winning cups, or of surviving in the FA Premier League, is now pretty much all money talk: How much will we make? What will it cost us? Can we afford it? What will we lose? Thirty years ago, the only real commercial advantage the Manchester Uniteds and the Liverpools had over their First Division rivals was the size of their own home grounds: bums on seats. Right up until the early 1980s, the away club even got a share of the home gate, and pretty much an even share of the (derisory) TV income. This was one reason, of course, why a provincial club such as Nottingham Forest could be such a thorn in the side of the northern giants as recently as the late 1970s. Not any more: at least not without the kind of benefactor who might be available at a Blackburn Rovers or a Fulham today. From that moment on, and accelerating more quickly recently, the combined effects of clubs no longer cross-subsidising each other in this way, the massive new TV income for top clubs, the boom in global markets for particular English clubs and their products, the arrival of profit-oriented PLCs in football, the focus on stadia as income-generators, and the increasing power of football players in the market-place, all these have produced a very different cultural and financial landscape for football.

Even if the publicly floated football clubs in England have hardly become the cash cows that the City once anticipated, the symbolic and financial appeal of the big English clubs is huge. Early in 2001, Reds chief executive Rick Parry flew out to the Far East to discuss plans for the Liverpool team's summer tour and to establish a Chinese-language website dedicated to Liverpool FC. The new English-language Liverpool website already receives two million hits a day, many of them from the Far East. Around the same time, the Future-Brand consultancy surveyed fans across Europe about their loyalties to sports and sports clubs and assessed the capacity of sports and clubs to make profit outside their core sports activity. Their research suggested that the Liverpool 'brand' was worth some £58 million, the seventh most valuable sports brand in Europe, behind Manchester United, obviously, and also behind Ferrari Formula One and McLaren Mercedes, but ahead of Williams BMW and Jordan Honda.

Football and sports cars are the valuable new sports signs in the virtual market-place. How clubs like Liverpool now balance their determination to exploit their powerful brand value, both in Europe and the Far East, set against the interests and concerns of the club's active supporters in Liverpool and elsewhere, becomes a critical question.

One of Liverpool's 'big moves' here has been to use the club's new partnership with investors Granada Media to show Liverpool matches over the internet. For £20 million, plus a 50/50 profit share and using the technical expertise of Granada, Liverpool are the first club to take advantage of new agreements with TV investors which now allow clubs to sell coverage of their own games on the net. The club will sell to subscribers worldwide full delayed match coverage, highlights and live audio commentary, as well as an on-line betting service, on-line shopping and memorabilia auctions. The service is planned to be available in Britain in 2002, though its real aim is to build up a worldwide subscriber base. The new Liverpool website is aimed at using broadband technology to show sharp-focus TV images and will take four or five years to develop. Fans will pay either by pay-per-view or by subscription, and the club's prized Chinese market will soon be able to have their commentary in Mandarin.

The logical commercial move which follows from this, of course, is that the Liverpool club will soon sign a Chinese player. Recently Crystal Palace signed two Chinese, partly to open up that huge country to Palace merchandise. Italy's Roma signed the Japanese midfielder Nakata, and suddenly had a boom of Japanese interest in Roma TV games and the player's No. 8 Roma shirt. Good business. Little Stockport County recently toured China and are bringing over 14-year-olds they hope might develop into talented – and cheap – professional players. Liverpool may well look at opening up youth academies in China and elsewhere. FIFA recently warned against the global trafficking of schoolboy players: for a tiny few the new global markets for footballers offer unimagined possibilities. For others the dangers of dislocation and disillusionment – and penury – are very real. It was also suggested in

2001 that the routine mid-day kick-offs of increasing numbers of Manchester United games might not be simply to satisfy BSkyB's own European TV schedule: kicking off at noon here sets one up for lucrative TV audiences in prime time in the Far East. Sky also has big interests here. When we talk of 'the fans' these days, in the context of the Uniteds and the Liverpools, one is no longer talking about *stadium* fans or even national fans. The *global* club fan base also demands regular stroking.

Rick Parry's approach to the new global era seemed both reassuring and potentially alarming for the club's active supporters. 'At Liverpool our supporters come first,' he said at the new deal's launch. 'That means keeping them up to date with the latest news about the club. This pioneering project will enable us to provide innovative, entertaining and informative service to our supporters.' No problems there, then. He went on: 'If we get this right, Liverpool FC Broadband could become more valuable than the club itself. It's a proper dotcom business that we could float on the stock market in years to come.' Float on the stock market? More valuable than the club itself? He means £sd here, of course, but the phrasing could still have been better. Much better.

Indeed, one of the most interesting things about the coverage of the 2000–01 Liverpool season by football journalists in this country was the way in which the club itself was still talked and written about during this period. In an era when the general perception is that large PLC-owned football clubs are now too much like businesses, that their corporate persona and commercial policies dominate, broadsheet journalists kept on talking about the fact that Liverpool FC still felt like a football club: that football, not shifting units, or making profits, or selling insurance or pushing credit cards, was so clearly, and so importantly, still the main activity of the club.

In some important ways, these same writers also indicated that the club had managed in recent years to become much more commercially astute than perhaps it had been in the 1970s and 1980s, when it fell behind its competitors by resolutely failing to move with the times. But, importantly, the recent commercial revolution at Anfield has not been achieved at the cost of compromising ways of 'doing' the core business, or by crudely substituting the language and practices of business for those of sport. The most important man at Anfield, these journalistic accounts suggested, is still the team manager, Houllier, as it would have been Shankly in the 1960s and Dalglish in the late 1980s. The story is not always the same elsewhere, where chief executives, parent companies or greedy shareholders demonstrably hold more of the whip hand. Ask Alex Ferguson.

Some of the signs of this continuing emphasis on traditions and the game are actually very simple – but important. Liverpool FC still has relatively little of the commercial 'hard sell' at the club's home matches, for example. Apart from having to sit, rather than stand, the rituals of watching football at Anfield have hardly changed at all over 30 years, and they are strikingly different to the more commercialised or 'gentrified' approaches elsewhere. The club may be leading the way in exploiting internet markets, but it still has no electronic scoreboard or 'jumbo' screen for interviews and highlights, before or during games, for example.

There is little, if any, naked commercial promotion on the match PA or at half-time at Anfield. Even the club's new matchday magazine (an obvious revenue raiser) has very little non-Liverpool FC commercial advertising; but it does carry quite stirring, reverential and informed accounts of the club's history and great player and managers. Also, the club has no strong policies on managing the home crowd: its approach, broadly speaking, seems to be largely non-interventionist; that supporters themselves will establish their own acceptable norms for watching games. Ticket prices, naturally, are spiralling at Anfield: but they start from a lower base than elsewhere and still compare very favourably with other FA Premier League equivalents.

This balance, between the necessary requirements of 'business' in the new era and the broad separation of the experience of watching football from the marketing and selling of the club 'brand' and its products, is a difficult one to maintain – and it may well change in its emphasis if, and when, the Liverpool club leaves for a purpose-built new ground in Anfield or, more likely, somewhere else in the city. Parry has talked well about the potential role of the club in regenerating the Anfield area, but the feeling persists that, for infrastructural and commercial reasons, a new ground on transport routes in the south of the city is a more likely prospect. This 'motorway exit' option will not excite most Liverpool fans, but Liverpool FC has tried harder than most large clubs thus far, I would suggest, to not second-guess its core supporters, or to try to convert them simply into 'clients' or 'customers'.

The club's watchdogs, the excellent LFC supporter fanzines, which 'police' the current club policies and curate the history of the club, lament what they see as the increasingly corporate approach of Liverpool FC, of course. The McDonalds golden arch on the Kop, the Carling sponsorship of Shankly's statue, the Reebok stamp on the stadium seats, are all considered a step too far. The club's supporters are continually, and rightly, on their guard. As Liverpool FC were faced, at the end of the 2000–01 season, with the possibility, for the first time in a generation, of playing in the premier European club competition once more, the challenges of bringing in the top players and remaining a *real* football club, while also engaging in the new 'virtual' football business, remain acute. We will all be watching.

11. RUNNING ON EMPTY

BLIND DATES

Fixture congestion – the English disease, we're told. Twenty years ago a 60-plus match season was looked on by British football professionals mainly as a manly badge of honour, a sign of a successful campaign. *Then* it was: roll your sleeves up and battle on, a marathon not a sprint. Houllier said recently, and with only a hint of a smile, that the Liverpool club's previous heroes must have been 'supermen', but then, more seriously, that the game had moved on, become faster and more taxing mentally, since the Paisley era. Preparation for matches has certainly changed over the past 20 years. I wonder how much we really *cared* about opponents' strengths under Bob, Joe Fagan and Ronnie Moran? The new technocrats are different, they like to leave nothing to chance, and so when we are faced with a wall of crucial fixtures spanning burly and ambitious Wycombe, as well as cunning and brilliant Barcelona, GH is loath, for once, to play ball.

So we have eight vital games in 24 days, three competitions, and all matches highly meaningful for our opponents. It is another critical phase, and GH is furious with Ipswich Town and the Premier League for not switching our Portman Road fixture to a date later in the season. George Burley and his buddies sit tight in Suffolk: they are also battling for the crucial league third spot after all, so who can blame them? We would do the same in their position: protect our own interests. This is another test but for now, at least, we can forget the English league for a few days – because we have to travel away to face the bow-legged Rivaldo and his show-off Catalonian mates.

5 APRIL, UEFA CUP SEMI-FINAL FIRST LEG:
BARCELONA 0, LIVERPOOL 0

Jimmy Burns's great book on FC Barcelona, *Barca – A People's Passion* and Phil Ball's recent wonderful account of Spanish Football, *Morbo*, tells you all you need to know about why it should be both a thrill and an honour to pit yourselves against FC Barcelona. Sport and politics seldom mix with the sort of passion and intrigue which runs through the history of this proud club and some of its closest Spanish rivals.

It would be nice, of course, to see this great Catalan club as an uncomplicated historical and cultural buffer to the fascism of the Franco regime, to *his* club, Real, and to the political right more generally in Spain, but inevitably the Barca story is more muddied. Barca has also housed Franco apologists as administrators and the club stands, above all, for a *nationalist* cause rather than anything which is, politically, necessarily more complex or attractive. Nevertheless the voting *socios* the club members, of Barca do offer the sort of basic democratisation which is so obviously absent from the major sports clubs in Britain. And Barca's role as a *polideportivo* (multi-sport) institution, and its progressive cosmopolitanism and *internationalism* also stands as a marker to set against some of its more parochial, if historically important, political concerns.

Finally, any sports club which not only sponsors a prestigious art competition – and then has Salvador Dali as an entrant – but can boast the Pope himself as a *socio*, and also houses a museum which is the most visited of all those a city like Barcelona has to offer, is some very special place. And this *is* indeed a very special club.

A visit to the Barca sports museum, with its amazing modernist posters and sculptures and its beautifully crafted display cabinets and knowingly low-tech settings, a *homage* to Barca heroes such as legendary goalkeeper Ricardo Zamora, *el devino*, and the 1950s Hungarian magician, Ladislao Kubala, gives a real clue about the importance of history, art and aesthetics to the current footballing sensibilities in the city. Here, it seems, football and the other arts can, and do, comfortably co-exist.

Unlike the more collectivist football traditions at a club such as Liverpool, Barca's great teams have tended to be built around an effervescent and expressive style of play and memorable stars – Kubala in the 1950s, Cruyff in the 1970s, Maradona in the 1980s, Schuster in the early 1990s, and Rivaldo today. The Dutchman Van Gaal was sacked recently for trying to produce a team of robots at Barca: worse, they were Dutch robots.

And yet the two cities, Barcelona and Liverpool, are also indisputably linked via their football history. The Witty brothers, British merchants and ex-public schoolboys from the Merchant Taylors school in Crosby, North Liverpool, actually helped found the great FC Barcelona with the Swiss Hans (later Joan) Gamper during the period of the English dissemination of football around Europe in the late nineteenth century. The distinctive maroon and blue Barca colours of today are actually the Merchant Taylors' own sports colours transferred in 1899 by the Wittys from the gentleman's playing fields of Crosby to the sporting heartlands of Catalonia. Barcelona's early football roots actually lie, properly, on Merseyside.

So with all of this art, history and symbolism to play with, and given the contrast in styles between the two teams, some of us had expected an expansive, even memorable encounter in the first meeting between these proud rivals since 1976, when a John Toshack goal at the Nou Camp eventually decided a tight UEFA Cup semi-final. Houllier has even told the press this time that he could not see the game ending scoreless – a 5–5 draw was a more likely result, he twinkled. But by now we know something about Houllier. In the Frenchman's head something craftier and much less attractive is already brewing: French pragmatism is about to meet Catalonian flair full on. I warn you, it will not be a pretty sight.

Tickets. Liverpool have been allocated just 3,500 in a stadium which is said to hold just under 100,000 (mysteriously, no one seems to know the exact capacity of the Nou Camp). At least twice that number of Reds fans are expected. Local touts have had plenty of recent practice at dealing with eager English guests from cities like Manchester and Leeds, so the usual ritual dance, the ticket auction, is now taking place at the Nou Camp early on Thursday morning. The early asking price is 25,000 ptas, about £100. By grabbing his own throat between thumb and forefinger one Catalan tout demonstrates to us why the prices are high: his neck is on the line. We sympathise, naturally. Another has to take refuge in a passing cab as a couple of brawny scousers take violent exception to the morning asking price. All this goes on in full view of the ticket office and the police. Scalping is obviously part of the local scene here. We could have a philosophical discussion now about touts and UEFA policy, of course, but this is not the time or place: we need tickets. This could be a long and anxious day.

We meet a near-mythical footballing figure, the 'Good Tout'. He's little less street-worn than some of the others here, a Barca fan, and he takes me away for a long, private, broken-English chat about how he holds a lot of season-ticket cards in good seats here and how he has fixed up Man United and Leeds fans already this season. For just 15,000 ptas, payable *inside* the ground, he will do the same for my friends. But no Liverpool colours, please, and nobody speaks until they make the seats. This sounds kosher; after all, he wants to deal with us because we look unlikely to get wrecked or to kick his head in, and he only gets paid if our crew actually gets inside. So we arrange to meet him later and, relieved, head off into town.

We have travelled to Barcelona independently – it's cheaper and better than the club offers, of course – but we have already been to one of the stylish four-star city centre hotels which house some of the Reds fans who are here on the longer official trips. The dreadful fun here is seeing the faces of concerned Spanish hotel staff – who are more used to hosting affluent foreign tourists – as Reds stumble around completely hapless and bladdered. Incapable. On Las Ramblas as the afternoon wears on, hundreds of Reds fans begin to take ownership of the central area around the Liceu metro stop, and they soon start moving through the 'We are English football supporters and are noisily boisterous' phase to the 'Now we're here in numbers and some of us are starting to get so pissed we may look obnoxious and scary' stage.

Despite unlikely warnings about the allegedly dangerous *bloisin noirs* Barca *culos*, there are no signs of any locals who might invite this increasingly chaotic city scene to move into something rather more focused and dangerous. Instead, bemused passers-by begin to keep their distance and simply look on in increasingly troubled astonishment as the *cervesa* flows – rivers of it. Most of the bevvying here is harmless and celebratory, no problem. But things can move quickly in these situations from a laugh, to excess and then embarrassment – or worse. Locally, of course, it's seen as a lack of respect, this blind bevvying: for yourself, and for your hosts. No wonder the local bizzies get nervous. But for us, the battling English, it's just another foreign trip. The afternoon is moving on. We head back out to the Nou Camp.

Jimmy Burns reported that the Barca *culos* he talked to had sneered at the new Old Trafford because of its alleged lack of real presence and grandeur. But let me tell you, for all its size and its cultural and symbolic resonance, the Nou Camp itself is no architechural treat: from the outside it looks like a super-large multi-storey car park, marked with concrete venetian blinds. The frontage is understated, too, though a huge, modernist statue of a footballer is stunning, and simply beyond the imagination of the keepers of the English game. Earnest figurative stuff – usually paid for by a greedy sponsor – is about the closest you ever get to design, vision or aesthetics near an English football ground. This says something, of course, about who we are.

Someone in the Flattie later tells us that it was 182 steps to reach our spec tonight; it felt like more, before we finally arrive at a spot which is like being pinned high up on a seated cliff-edge. As usual in Europe, no one goes to their real seats; late arrivals – and there are plenty of these tonight – are simply squeezed in anywhere, as this Liverpool end swells. Two rows in front of us Stephane Henchoz's parents and girlfriend are soon giving it the full continental 'Allez Liverpooool', his mum wearing a real SH shirt. In the far distance we can see other Reds fans jumping and waving – but we can't hear them. In fact, we can't hear anything coming from inside the ground at all, save the echo of the bass drum of the tiny number of Barca *culos* who are sited behind the goal miles below us. Now, this is like being both inside and outside the stadium; football watching from the moon. 'Get stuck in, whoever yer are,' says someone behind us, as a tiny white figure (our surprise new kit tonight) chases for the Liverpool cause. You kind of know what he means.

We hear, later, that while we are still peering for signs of friends in the seats behind, hanging grimly on to this sheer face and waiting for the teams to emerge, our cerebral manager, Houllier, has actually gone off for a quiet *read* inside the Nou Camp. When Rick Parry goes in search of the manager he finds Houllier in the bowels of the stadium minutes before kick-off poring over *Passing Rhythms* – our own new book on the new Liverpool FC. Maybe it is this text which bends our manager's mind because this distant eyrie turns out to be no bad place from which to observe the rather sorry football tale which is about to unfold below.

You see, Liverpool, shamelessly, barely leave their own penalty area for the entire 90 minutes tonight. This much we *can* see. But Sander also hardly has a save to make, as Barca looked completely bamboozled by the depths to which we are willing to defend, and the aimlessness with which we hack the ball clear from our own box. Rivaldo (I think it's him) shows nothing. Babbel sees off Overmars, Carragher bravely blocks two goal-bound shots from Luis Enrique. Kluivert looks confused. There is some complaint in our section at the sheer scale of our self-imposed impotence – 'Have a fuckin' go, Liverpool!' – but it is also tempered by the knowledge that 0–0 is actually a fantastic result here. Barca, truth be told, have no one, not even the graceful Guardiola, to 'invent' the game from midfield tonight. And so it eventually ends virtually football-free and goal-less – a terrible match, a vital scoreline – to howls of protests from the few Barca fans who remain at the bitter end. The beautiful game has been brutally beaten and finally subdued tonight. *We* have been responsible.

As we get ready to leave the Barca ground a little later, the Spanish riot police and a couple of our own 'warriors' play at mutual provocation, a prickly, tetchy honour contest. And it's no fun being trapped in a crowded stairwell abroad as the local police are pushed towards maybe losing it, because panic can easily set in and then heads get broken, possibly even limbs trampled. They are armed but massively outnumbered, these edgy young policemen, so we can also smell their fear. Our guys don't even see the weapons, just the hemmed-in jumpy young men behind the perspex masks; these gobshite foreigners. An older officer now pleads for calm and, thankfully, it stops just short of a full-on assault from either side, this stand-off, and the tension and macho expectancy subsides.

We are finally released late into the Barcelona night, and fortunately, as this is not Rome, there is no threat to life and limb here. We find a discarded Barca flag on the walk back to a bar and then our hotel. It says in faded red on white: 'Liverpool, kiss my ass.' We may yet have some unpleasant oral work before this tie is over, but at least it will now be performed back in the familiar environs of Liverpool 4. And who knows how we will try to play there?

CUP AND LEAGUE

Woody Allen says that half of the secret of life is just turning up. So Wycombe Wanderers expect to have a chance in an FA Cup semi-final, which is the sort of gruelling non-event we had feared, especially given GH's public concern to show true respect to our lower-league opponents. As well as red sombreros in the rain, courtesy of our recent Iberian jaunt, there are also vast gaps in the Red areas of Villa Park today, supporter priorities clearly stated. It *feels* nothing like a semi-final for us. Gerrard and Heskey start on the bench, for example, and Wycombe defend gamely, hoping to snatch something from a set-piece. We fearfully half-expect manager Lawrie Sanchez himself to come on for anything delivered from their left. It doesn't happen. We should be ahead at half-time, but Michael has already missed a couple.

Eventually, our substitute tyros are introduced to the action and they change the game immediately with their power and speed. With 12 minutes left Steven Gerrard finally delivers with pace into the box and Emile pumps his near-post header high and beyond Taylor. Within four minutes Robbie does the Wycombe keeper in the same spot with a left-foot free kick, won by Heskey. Robbie then celebrates, typically, by diving on top of a comical invading fan/steward sandwich in front of the Doug Ellis Stand. There is still time for Ryan to score a streaky one for Wycombe, so we can all run through our 'Didn't they battle hard?' definitely *not* patronising assessment of our brave and lowly opponents. A scrubby 2–1 to Liverpool then, and Sanchez is aiming for a move upwards: he looks like he may be the real deal. We'll now meet

Arsenal in Cardiff in May, a Welsh/French festival for sure – but the *round* ball will be in play, not the oval one.

At Ipswich Town in the league a mere two days later, Vignal is in and Heskey plays alone up front as we try to flood the middle and bore our nice agricultural hosts into submission. Ziege (remember him?) misses a first-half sitter and Heskey even squeezes us ahead right after half-time, but some sloppy defending lets in Armstrong for a late equaliser. We deserve no more than a point, and this is a decent result in the circumstances. As long, that is, as we can deal with dangerous Leeds at home on Friday. They are coming on strong, heading again for a top-three finish themselves, so this is no gimme, no way.

13 APRIL: LIVERPOOL 1, LEEDS UNITED 2

Before Leeds United at Anfield on Good Friday morning the Flattie is already chocca behind closed doors and curtains at 10 a.m. The Bluenose landlord has to think fast when the bizzies come knocking: 'It's last orders, boss – I couldn't get their glasses from them last night.' We drink on. The Kop, this morning, collectively sports more Barca scarves and baseball hats than a Catalonian wine festival. Maybe we are officially twinned, or someone is knocking them out in the club shop – or on Walton Breck Road? It could easily be the late 1970s again.

The Liverpool crowd is still reasonably chipper, if a little distracted, for this hour: my new mate, Barcelona Bob, one of the Fellahs in Front I met out at the Nou Camp, even brings me the Spanish holiday snaps to consider. But our team looks mentally exhausted. Robbie and Michael play up front again – not a great option – and fit-again and fresh Smicer is only on the bench with Heskey. Steven Gerrard plays wide against Kewell, and Murphy starts in the middle of midfield but is bypassed from the start by the speed and aggression of Dacourt. Berger is also having trouble on the left coping with the spritely Bowyer. Robbie is simply sloppy. But the early first goal we concede really gives it away; Rio Ferdinand, unmarked at the far post from a corner, a defensive howler, a desperate mental lapse. Bowyer, crucially, nicks another before the break, slipping Berger, and we look poor, simply not in gear.

With Smicer and McAllister on for our first-half midfield dunces, we threaten at last after the interval, and Gerrard forces home Michael's cross from the left. But then hapless referee Wiley sends off Stevie G. (two yellows), following a timid foul on Batty. So a prospective rousing last 20 minutes, with Leeds pressed back and Liverpool straining, becomes instead a ragged mess with the Kop howling at the idiotic Wiley. My mate, Steve, needs intensive care here as he leads the Kop in full official-abuse mode.

Overall, Leeds have deserved their win, and look strong and able to mix it (Batty, Mills, Smith, Harte, Dacourt) but also full of good movement and pace (Kewell, Smith, Bowyer). We, on the other hand, look as if we need time to recharge. But there is none. Instead, it's off to a neighbourly Goodison Park on Easter Monday for the Bluenoses' own 'top match', with a chastened and no doubt determined Barca soon to follow. Leeds and Ipswich are now ahead of Liverpool in the race for third spot. Like unseated jockeys in the recent epic Grand National, we may soon have to remount in this sapping and endless campaign, just to get to The Elbow.

AND THE WINNER IS . . .

With five matches still to go, and a full month of the 2000–01 season left, the Corporation now claim another championship, their seventh in nine years, an extraordinary record. And they're good. Any Premier League Select XI today would probably include Stam, Scholes, Keane, Beckham and Giggs. Perhaps Sheringham and Barthez too. On current form, we could offer Hyypia, Babbel, Gerrard and Heskey, possibly Robbie and Michael. Of course, the chasing pack are no longer really 'chasers' these days, one obvious effect of the new Champions League targets. Wenger and Houllier, disgracefully, settled for a top-three finish months ago, and off United floated. Our crippling schedule and sometimes our lack of ambition away from home means we will now struggle, once again, even to finish third. We are currently sixth. Arsenal's away form has also been atrocious, so maybe it is a French thing, this allergy to travel.

Before the knock-out fixtures came piling in we were already giving up vital league points away – at Southampton, Tottenham, Middlesbrough, Manchester City and Newcastle, for example – *thirteen* points lost just here. And at every one of these venues we were clearly the superior side. Costly, costly misjudgements. More courage *then* might have spared us the need to go to places like a hostile Goodison now – and *have* to win. A scouser, a Red I'm sure, rings up Littlejohn's 606 tonight calling for Houllier's head because of our league struggles. Outrageous – isn't it?

16 APRIL: EVERTON 2, LIVERPOOL 3

> Everton was a magical name. It conjured up . . . the Toffee Shop in the village . . . skaters on the frozen St Domingo's pit. Sledges racing down snowy Mere Lane. Everton players taking the field in salmon and blue. These uplifting images contrasted sharply with the stark realities of nineteenth-century life . . .'
>
> John Wilson, *The Original Blue Boys*

If I may quote the bearded lady from Crosby: Walter [Smith, Everton manager] you are the weakest link. Fuck off.

Message on *When Skies are Grey*, Everton fanzine chatline

Sporting commercialisation and globalisation and the arrival of the bloated Champions League is supposed to have done away with the significance of matches like this mild Merseyside tiff. I had a radio debate this week with the writer Chris Horrie about the state of the English game on the tenth anniversary of the Premier League, and this issue came up. He got the easy part – arguing that since the Sky/Premier League marriage everything in football is now simply TV fodder, commercialised and bland, and lacks meaning and a local rootedness (he is a United fan, Horrie, so maybe he has a point). I said he was arguing too strong and too far, and that despite the endemic greed and the business focus (ring any bells?), the game still grips people and touches them outside the confines of the market.

And here, this evening, is some of the gritty proof: an abused minute's silence; two comebacks; 12 bookings, including one sending-off; two penalties (one missed); bench aggro; five goals; and an incredible last-minute winner scored by a 36-year-old slaphead starting his first Merseyside derby. And all of this played out against an atmosphere that would positively singe your hair. Forget Barcelona and all the rest for a minute: this still matters, boy.

This 'friendly' football derby has been getting much less so for some years now as Liverpool has become a more obviously national club and the Blues have struggled down in the basement, a state of affairs which encourages their fans to invest all on beating Liverpool in the twice-a - season Everton 'Cup final'. Moreover, we haven't won here since 1990, frequently getting blown away in the last decade by the sheer venom and commitment of the Goodison faithful. The signs tonight are that, once again, this will be a tense, possibly poisonous, atmosphere.

A 6 p.m. Easter Monday kick-off for TV has added all-day boozing to this already combustible equation, so that outside the Carisbrooke, a noted Blue watering-hole off County Road, an ugly mob has already gathered behind a large street banner. It says: 'Anfield closed due to 39 murder inquiries.' Nice one. This reference to Heysel is partly a 'reply' to an earlier, less emotive Anfield banner this season which had Goodison Park closed because of the national foot and mouth outbreak. But it is also still about Liverpool's shame, which meant a Europe ban on Everton's talented Champions of 1985. There is also drunken racist chanting here about Liverpool's Heskey, as well as a witty song about the Italian dead in Brussels. So, this is our neighbourly welcome.

Our fellahs are not angels in all of this, of course. The favoured Liverpool song tonight is another psychotherapist's delight, with also an appreciative nod to Charles and Camilla. It has Everton striker, Duncan Ferguson, as an unlikely *tampon* because (due to injuries) he is 'In for a week and out for a month'. Get it? This is gynaecologically, as well as comically, suspect but it is apparently satisfying enough for some of ours tonight. The Liverpool women fans here – and there are some – just grimace. Outside the Bullens Road away area, meanwhile, Evertonians brush through the queues for the Liverpool end, whispering 'murderers' to their guests as they go.

A disgracefully disrupted (from the home Park End) and therefore foreshortened minute's silence for the dead at Hillsborough, and at this week's latest football tragedy in Johannesburg, improves nobody's temper ('What about Heysel?' comes from the Blues on our left). As a result, we loudly call their homeboys 'Scum,' while the Everton brain surgeons in the Park End leer back, delighted that this ugly disrespect has really hurt us. A ball has not yet been kicked in anger, but now this *feels* as if something more is at stake than three important points and local pride.

We watch tonight from the Archibald Leitch-designed and wooden-floored Bullens Road upper tier, a mere £27 for a piece of cramped and impaired-viewing football history. Goodison, historically one of the great English grounds, is creaky and ill-placed now, hence the desperate Blues' scramble for the new Kings Dock site. Liverpool rest Gerrard and Owen tonight. Biscan starts wide right, with Smicer on the left and Hamann and McAllister in the centre. Hamann's recent good form has meant he has virtually joined the ranks of 'those who cannot be rotated'. He deserves it. Robbie and Emile play up front. Ferguson and Campbell play twin strikers for Everton, so we await the inevitable aerial bombardment.

But Liverpool strike first – and early. As an Everton attack breaks down, the alert Hamann plays a cute forward ball to Heskey through a hole the size of Unsworth's formidable arse in the centre of the Blues' defence, and Emile scores. This five-minute lead gives the Reds an unexpected chance to settle and we seem comfortable as Everton look disjointed and slow. Hyypia is standing up well to the lumbering Ferguson, but the Blues keep lumping it into the box, hoping for a break. And just before half-time they get one. Ferguson, for once, wins a header to Campbell, who is squeezed out by Carragher and Henchoz, but the ball breaks out of the tackle again to Ferguson who scores. So, it is 1–1 at half-time, tight and tense, as we knew it would be. We spend the interval picking up the taped-together two-pence pieces which have winged in from the Park End during the first half.

Rather than lifting Everton, this equaliser actually seems to spur Liverpool on, and we attack at the start of the second period. On the hour Hamann, again, sets Robbie away wide on Everton's left and our ex-Bluenose urchin looks for Smicer in the Everton box, but the ball breaks instead to the following-up Babbel who finishes expertly low ('Like Gerd Muller' writes one hack later), for 2–1. When referee Winter kindly adjudges the elderly Gough to have fouled Robbie in the Everton box minutes later, it already looks all over. In the Bullens Road upper we are wildly celebrating. Prematurely. Because Fowler, no Jari he, fucks around with the kick – no real run-up, a stop-start approach – and hits Gerrard's left-hand post.

A penalty missed is worse than one not given, much worse. Because Everton gain heart from this let-off. And now it really gets lively, bookings flying around, little feuds sprouting up all over. Old times. Biscan, who has looked forlorn on the Liverpool right, jumps in on Unsworth and is dismissed by Winter on a second yellow. Can we hang on with ten again? Not if this ref can help it, because Sami is pulled up in the box soon after for slapping an arm over the backing-on Bird Man of Barlinnie, drunken Duncan. Penalty (says Winter). The fleshy Unsworth scores and the home crowd stirs, smelling another Everton derby triumph. So, I'm ashamed to say, do we.

But in these last dozen or so minutes Liverpool really show some balls. 'Little Vignal', as Houllier will later call him, comes on for Robbie and is lively and brave on the Liverpool left as we continue, very un-Houllier-like, to press forward despite being a man down once more. Inside the Everton box, first Smicer and then Vignal himself have plausible penalty appeals turned down before, in injury time, the young Frenchman is hauled over once more by Alexandersson, left of centre but more than 40 yards from the Everton goal. McAllister lines up the kick and ushers our big men diagonally forward to the left of goalkeeper Gerrard. Our last chance.

Minutes before this kick Hyypia has won a header in just this area and Gerrard had been forced to save, diving to his right at full stretch. So now the Everton keeper is eyeing Hyypia again, thinking he might claim the high cross which is bound to come this way. As referee Winter paces back Everton's cursory wall, McAllister slyly moves the ball forward. Sky TV measures the final distance later at 44 yards. Within minutes of what is about to happen, believe me, Liverpool fans will be working in pubs on new derby-day songs for *next* season which have the words 'forty-four yards' in every cruel and meaningful verse.

As Everton's Gerrard edges slowly, slowly to his left, towards the waiting Hyypia and Babbel, and as the upper Bullens Road collectively wills at least a decent cross and a last Liverpool header on target, the crazy, alien-headed McAllister – who is actually still looking at Hyypia – outrageously strikes a swerving ball low towards the *right*-hand corner of Gerrard's goal. The physics, the geometry of this looks all wrong. Obviously, he can't score from here, so this is wasted – worthless. Hyypia is visibly crestfallen. Except that, like a deadly bouncing bomb, this distant, improbable shot seems somehow to gather pace off the pitch and Gerrard, scurrying desperately to his right now, suddenly sees he has just too much ground to cover. A beat, and the Everton net is billowing behind him. From 44 yards.

'YEEEARRGH!!!' the primeval, gargling sound which now fills every aural cubic inch of the Red upper Bullens Road. Through the indescribable din, and between the trellis of flailing arms and bodies which is now churning over seats around me and the criss-cross of the Bullens' roof superstructure above, I can just about see Blues keeper Gerrard, alone and still hunched in a despairing, sub-foetal position on the Everton goal-line. McAllister, a man suddenly with ecstatic Red friends – and many Blue enemies – is under a scrum at the Liverpool bench. The Park End is already cramming into the exits, devastated. Deliriously, 'Ten men, we only had ten men' swells from the Bullens Road, from Reds fans positively wild-eyed and drunk with victory as the final whistle goes. It's pandemonium, I swear, sheer emotional excess.

Outside, and in the pubs and streets in this city later tonight, much more of this will be played out, much more. Some of it will spill over into real violence, sure. But most of it will be Blues cursing, staring glumly into beer glasses, and Reds with uncontrollable, 44-yard, grins. And, like it or not, most of the latter will also tell anyone who cares to listen tonight that: '*This* is why I watch. I don't care about all the business stuff, or where the players come from; and give Michael fucking Owen his sixty grand a week, if that's what he's worth. Just give me ten willing Red shirts, some skill and heart and more, *much* more, of this.' More, they mean, of course, of Everton 2, Last-Minute-44-Yard Liverpool 3.

MUNICH PRANKS – AND THANKS
A well-known Manchester blagger and United fan, Karl Power – Fat Neck to his buddies – manages not only to get pitchside at the Bayern v United vital Champions League tie in Munich but, in full kit, actually *onto* the official United team photo just before the off. Andy Cole looks at this new squad member as if he can't quite place the face but he's sure he must have seen him somewhere before, perhaps deep in the United defence. Power just leers. Squad rotation breeds unfamiliarity, clearly.

Top stuff this – and it gets better. Because at half-time Sir Alex tells

Power to warm up, as it's already Bayern 2 United 0, with the runaway English champions sliding out of Europe and captain Roy Keane already rehearsing his 'No one in this team is now good enough for me' speech for the morning papers. Ferguson cannot now equal Bob Paisley's unique record of three European Cup wins, and it looks like time might also be running out for 'shagger' Yorke, Sheringham, Butt and perhaps even the perpetually serious Giggs for next season. A sad night all round, then, and another United season when they will just have to 'settle' for the league title.

19 APRIL, UEFA CUP SEMI-FINAL, SECOND LEG: LIVERPOOL 1, BARCELONA 0 (AGG: 1–0)

Merseyside awaits, while GH is angry, fuming. The Spanish press have called his Liverpool's performance at the Nou Camp a fortnight ago a 'betrayal' of the game. A mild charge I'd say. He faces them now, his inquisitors, in Anfield's press room before the second leg and is defiant, unrepentant. 'We need to score goals, we know that. This is a final to qualify for a final and my team will not let me down,' he says. That's clear then. Meanwhile, Barca midfielder Guardiola, who last gave the ball away sometime in the mid-'90s, is rumoured to be looking for a way out from the Nou Camp, possibly to England, and Houllier is interested. 'Include us in that rumour,' he says mysteriously. Also a mystery is what, exactly, might tempt the Spaniard from Catalonia to Anfield: apart, of course, from the snow-white beaches on the Wirral, the exotic Albert Dock, and the incredible Liverpool fans. More likely is the fact that footballers in England pay 39 per cent of gross income in tax, compared to 45 per cent in Italy, 46 per cent in Spain, 50 per cent in Germany and 57 per cent in France. When you earn what these guys make, these are big numbers, believe me. So we have hopes.

Reds fans singing in the Flattie before the match is a signal of the palpitating feelings around here for tonight's encounter. We have really missed these, the European heavyweight contests, watching enviously on TV as United down the M62 have routinely hosted the high and European-football mighty. Barcelona are a real test – all right, not in the main event yet – but a top side, and now we have the stage once again and are in sight of our first major final in Europe since Heysel in 1985. So, if we win this, the Liverpool fans will also have a chance to show the world we are not the 'beasts' and 'savages' the international press labelled us back in those awful times. And all that stands tonight between Liverpool and a May 16 massive bevvy and shakedown with little Alavés in Dortmund is this lot: Rivaldo, Kluivert, Luis Enrique, Guardiola, Overmars, Petit, Cocu and De Boer. Easy.

Flags in all areas of Anfield: 'Unparalleled history, glorious future' says the best of them, even the spelling immaculate – well, what would you expect? The noise and the singing is wonderful too, tear-jerking or inspirational, perhaps both, as the players take the field. We are, arms stretched upwards like some divine cult, with hundreds of others underneath a massive, moving flag on the Kop as 'Walk Alone' thunders around the ground, an ethereal moment.

For Liverpool, Smicer will play just behind Heskey and Owen, at the top of our midfield diamond, and a signal to Houllier's Iberian critics of his attacking intent tonight. McAllister, presumably on some new super stimulant, plays *again* in Liverpool's midfield, where Gerrard is back to patrol the right side. You know the rest of the Reds' line-up by now. The team huddles in the centre circle, Sander late for the friendly Liverpool scrum. On the Kop we mentally huddle too, and stand and wait, our hearts almost audibly thumping.

And as we had hoped, tonight's high-tempo Liverpool try to get at Barcelona from the beginning, with Smicer, especially, bouncing around like the skilful, combative workaholic Houllier has insisted he becomes. Heskey also muscles around impressively, but half-chances for Owen and Smicer come to nothing. Suddenly Rivaldo swerves a 40-yard shot at Wester, which needs some serious aid over the top. A wake-up call.

So the pattern is set: they will pass, pass, pass at pace and try to release Luis Enrique and Rivaldo, or perhaps Overmars on the left, and we will hustle, through Hamann and Gerrard, pump it up to Heskey and get men forward when we can. At least we know now. On half an hour the only real clear chance of the match comes: Overmars burns Babbel on the left and pulls back perfectly for Luis Enrique, who squirts the opening wide, in front of the Kop. We look skywards with thanks for this escape, eyes rolling, cheeks sucked in, giving our neighbours that 'How did that not go in?' look. And then a goal.

Kluivert has thus far offered one of those 'definitely maybe' displays which seem to sum him up: plenty of talent and promise, but just not enough end product. Now, back in the Barca box on half-time and defending a Liverpool corner, he inexplicably handles high, above all-comers. The competent Swiss referee Meier does some impressive origami moves with his hands before we realise that what he is actually trying, correctly, to say is: 'Penalty – for Liverpool'. McAllister scores past Reina with little fuss – Robbie and Michael take note – and somehow we lead 1–0 at the half. For 15 minutes we can all calm down.

The second-half soon becomes a story of Barca's frightening attack against Liverpool's quite magnificent defence. Steven Gerrard almost steals a second goal for us, but mostly it is the home guard repelling all-comers. Wester has a kicking nightmare, for once, showing us an impressive air shot which Kluivert doesn't quite read, thank God. We survive. And it is really *fantastic*, this Liverpool spirit and resilience. As someone will say later in the Flattie, 'We may not be as good as these yet, but at least we have a team now, players you can really get behind.' And this is quite true. Out of this unlikely mix of the monied foreign legion, willing local boys and veteran recruits, Houllier and his coaches have managed to forge an amazing sense of togetherness and bloody-minded resistance when the chips are really down. And we see it all now.

Tired as these red-shirted fellahs really are, they just dig in for the last 20 minutes, Henchoz and Hyypia unpassable, Hamann ubiquitous and simply irresistible in the tackle, young Carragher defiant. And when the final whistle blows, to tumultuous cheering and baying in the Liverpool crowd, all of us as relieved, exhausted and drained as the men who stand to receive our thanks, Houllier and his coaches in a corner somewhere will smile quietly to each other and say: 'Two games against this Barca team – and no goals conceded. This is a sign that we are really progressing.'

In the bubbling Flattie later, people already have maps of Germany at hand. And out of the more reflective post-match talk comes the truth that, in the cold light of day, Roma and Barca have both been better than us in this competition – we're not fucking daft. But for all their superior quality, they haven't been able to overcome this Liverpool team, a team which has struggled at places like Maine Road and the Riverside this season, but has simply refused to be beaten in the hot spots of the Nou Camp and the Stadio Olympico, and has also stood up at home. Critics will say we have simply battled our way here – that it is perspiration, not inspiration, which has brought us this far. This is probably true, too. But for all that, we also deserve to be in Dortmund, more than either Roma or Barcelona, for all their stars and millions. We have earned this place in the sun – and believe me, we *will* enjoy it.

DANCING IN THE SIX-YARD BOX

A wonderful tale: Scottish choreographer, Andy Howitt, has created a new *dance*, copying Archie Gemmill's World Cup goal for the Scots against Holland in the finals in 1978. It's designed to get more young lads interested in dance, a Billy Elliot incentive, and he'll perform it at a 'dance the goal' event at Hampden as part of a celebration of the game (I'm not making this up). And it gets spooky because Howitt, then 13, was watching the Gemmill goal with his grandad on TV and the old man passed away with a heart attack due to the excitement of seeing wee Archie weave through the Orange. He missed nothing: the Scots still went out.

Gemmill, gnarled old lag that he is, says it's a 'compliment' that someone's written a dance around his goal. Yeah, and Kenny Burns was a Christian Socialist. Anyway, Howitt plans next to write something around Michael Owen's goal against Argentina – he'll need a long dance-floor for that. Which got me thinking about other Liverpool goals fit to set to dance. Macca's against Celtic at Celtic Park, obviously. John Barnes versus QPR. Robbie's second against Newcastle in the first 4–3, a sweeping move down the right flank from a throw from Jameo. Any Billy Liddell (according to Sheila Spiers). The 5–0 against Forest, a complete ballet. There's *loads* of material.

22 APRIL: LIVERPOOL 3, TOTTENHAM 1

Season-ticket voucher No. 35: keep hold of it, it might be FA Cup final gold dust for the situation we are in. There are gloomy season-ticket Reds in the Flattie today who have followed Liverpool for years and to the darkest parts of Europe this season, as well as to the Southamptons and Sunderlands, who now have no Cup final ticket. Some will still go to Wales looking for tickets in pubs and bars at almost any price. But not everyone can afford this, not some of the grafters with young families, or the doleys, certainly. Some will go to Cardiff just to watch it in a pub on TV – to at least be *part* of the event. This new stress – as well as ticket and travel uncertainty for Dortmund – is subject number one in our dinner-time debate today. It's a deflating prospect for the unlucky ones.

Today, Tottenham bring a very young side to Anfield to contest a match which Houllier describes as more important to us than the Barcelona UEFA Cup semi. With the Kop struggling to summon up real enthusiasm in the rain today after the epic events of Thursday night, after six minutes Berger, suddenly popping up on the right, plays Heskey through a Mersey Tunnel-like hole in the Spurs back line and Emile finishes well, no longer troubled it seems by facing a keeper alone: now he just takes the shot confidently and early. But rather than buckle, this young Spurs team, led by the veteran Sherwood, starts to force the pace after this setback. Heskey, injured, is soon replaced by Robbie. When Hyypia then misses a tackle on Leonhardsen, our ex-Norge picks out Korsten in the box and he scores easily at the Kop end. Level at half-time, we are noticeably beginning to labour to keep on top.

We huff and puff towards the Kop goal after the interval, but only when Hamann comes on do we begin to get some real order in midfield. Vignal comes on too, for the spent Carragher, and is soon clattered: 'Stick some fuckin' garlic up his nose,' says one of the Fellahs in Front, helpfully, as our French Gregory fails, initially, to respond to treatment. On a greasy pitch like we have today, claims for defender handball are always a useful prospect to dig yourself out of a hole. We have three in front of the Kop, none of them really convincing, but referee Knight decides otherwise and offers McAllister just one opportunity from the spot to make it a perfect personal week. Which he naturally and nervelessly takes, for 2–1.

This is hard on Spurs (Hoddle later blames us, in the Kop, for winning this vital kick. I hope he's right). And to make it even harder, with three minutes left Babbel floats a perfect diagonal cross towards Robbie who is moving between Thelwell and Gardner towards the six-yard box. We have seen this all before: we know how brave and talented Robbie is in the air, how he plays way above his height. From here he's lethal, we can reel off the goals. Sullivan's decision to rest on his line means curtains for Tottenham and the ball ends in the only place it could, bottom left-hand corner of the rooted keeper's net.

A WORD FROM OUR SPONSORS
From the *Reebok Annual Report 2000* on the new Liverpoolfc.tv official club website:

> In 2000 Reebok re-signed Liverpool FC, one of the world's best-known soccer teams, and has a major sponsorship agreement with the Argentina Football Association, a two-time World Cup winner. In addition, Reebok has a sponsorship arrangement with the Colombian national team, and sponsors other club teams, including Sporting Lisbon . . .
>
> Net sales for the year ended 31 December were $2.865 billion . . . International sales of the Reebok Division were $1.176 billion in 2000, a decrease of 1.7 per cent from sales in 1999. Net sales in Europe decreased 9.2 per cent and net sales in the Asia Pacific region increased 14.3 per cent in the year. The company's overall gross margin was 37.9 per cent of sales for 2000 . . .
>
> Reebok has dedicated its corporate resources to protect human rights across all national geographic and ethnic boundaries. On 10 December 1948 the General Assembly of the United Nations adopted and proclaimed the Universal Declaration of Human Rights, the full text of which appears in the following pages . . .
>
> ARTICLE 23: Everyone has the right to work, and the right to favourable conditions of work without discrimination. Everyone who works has the right to just and favourable remuneration. Everyone has the right to form and join trade unions for the protection of his interests . . .
>
> As of 31 December 2000, Reebok has approximately 6,000 employees in all operating units. None of these employees is represented by a labour union. Reebok has never suffered a

material disruption of business caused by labour disputes with employees. Management considers employee relations to be good.

A model partner, obviously.

PAIN OR GLORY?

In a nervous and uncertain performance, Liverpool beat Coventry City away 2–0, Hyppia and McAllister both scoring in the last seven minutes. Michael, all wound-up, fidgety pace and direct-running, comes on for the last 20 minutes and suddenly makes the home back four look what it really is, fragile and slow. He also makes any long ball from the back – our stock-in-trade – look strategic and dangerous. Owen now looks sharp, ready for the season's finale.

Gary Mac, an ex-Coventry man, might have condemned the Sky Blues to the drop by scoring another free kick. Kirkland leans to the right at the vital moment to cover a possible curling shot *over* the wall, as McAllister unerringly attacks the side of the goal which is covered by the keeper. Except not all of it *is* covered, and it this unguarded sliver that Mac finds, high to Kirkland's left. 'He is not overwhelmed with joy,' GH tells the press later, while the hacks seek Mac out, as they might quiz a parent who has won the lottery and lost a child. Coventry are not yet down – but they are on another brink. Gordon Strachan's reddening face tells you that much. Meanwhile, we have our priceless three points, won without honour. Three points closer.

So this April spell has brought eight games in three competitions, including two against Barcelona, and we have won five, drawn two (both away) and suffered only one vital loss at home to Leeds. Although we have reached two further cup finals this month, Houllier will still claim we have lost our most important fixture in this period, because Leeds now look a real Champions League threat again for third place. We are currently fifth, behind United, Arsenal, Leeds and Ipswich for the Champions League slots, three points out of third place but with a game in hand and a superior goal difference to our main rivals.

Which means, of course, that if we can win *all* of our last six matches – four in the league and two cup finals – we can still reach our goal. This looks a tough prospect, of course. Our away form has been poor all season, so picking up maximum league points even at relegated Bradford and at Charlton will not be easy, not for us. And Houllier knows that his long-term plans – to catch United, to sign top players, and to keep the ones he has – probably depends more on Liverpool playing next season in the Champions League than it does on offering us cup glory now. So he would trade both these finals for third place in the league; this is what he tells us, ever the hardened professional.

But really, Houllier also wants it all: why else would we have strived so hard in Italy and Spain, battled so vigorously at Tranmere and at Leeds? You go back now and look at Houllier's face after we stole that FA Cup tie at Leeds. Just look at GH, after Emile scores our second goal and tell me is this the face of a miserable man? And how much did this early FA Cup success also spur us on in the Worthington and UEFA Cups and in the tough league games which followed? Swings and roundabouts.

The Reds players from the 1970s and 1980s said you only feel tired, only notice how many games you're playing, if you are losing. The Liverpool supporters, like all fans, worry about the league, but they also talk of the great cup finals, the days out, the prospects of glory. Sure, you have to build for the future, but the game is about more than the cash and the long term. It is also about *now*. If we have to live with another season out of the Champions League – if that's what it costs for glory now – it might be a price worth paying. I would take it. I'll take the cups, every time, because I don't want to travel to Cardiff and Germany now to lose. What – for *third* place in the league, and a mile and more behind United? But I'm also like Houllier, and like every spoilt fan here: I really want it all. And who is to tell me, exactly, that I can't yet have it?

12. GATHERING CUPS IN MAY

1 MAY: BRADFORD CITY 0, LIVERPOOL 2

Bradford City have come a long way quickly, the signs of architectural bends in the home ground here tells you as much. The quaint little double-decker 'Symphony' goal-end stand to our left, for example, looks like it needs only a water-wheel behind to go merrily sailing down the Mississippi, while the corner tea-bar and three-lamp Subbuteo floodlights at the Pulse Stadium are right out of the Nationwide Conference. Meanwhile, across the park a colossal new seating structure is edging its incongruous way up into the sky and around the pitchside, its completion only slowing as the pound signs sink to follow the Bantams' slide back into the Football League. So from our perch opposite in the romantic Ciba (chemicals) Stand, and with warm Tetleys already despatched, we can still peek across the pitch-green into the streets outside and gorge on the Victorian sandstone splendour of old Bradford in this early evening May sunshine. Bliss.

It all ended for us here last season: Bradford won to stay up, we flunked and let Leeds into the Champions League, and tomorrow Leeds, not us, play Valencia for a place in the 2001 European Cup final. All that happened here. Tonight, relegated Bradford have nothing to play for – or to lose – and we have come on a winning run, needing all three points to go third. There are no real surprises now in Houllier's teams, with rotation becoming much less of an unpredictable feature of his thinking as the matches get harder and bigger. Steven Gerrard is back to play on the right, Murphy moving to the left. McAllister plays again, scorer of four in four, Owen and Heskey forward.

We have no width and not much real invention in this formation but, bar the question of who plays left midfield, I think this is Houllier's favoured selection now, tight and hard-working, with the real goal threat coming from set-pieces and Michael's pace. No Robbie. Bradford field both Carbone and Blake up front, good, clever footballers, but overall the locals also look lightweight, lacking in real pace and power. The first half is an interesting clash of styles, the home team playing neat, considered football – as we want Liverpool to – and the visitors bustling to get the ball forward early, trying to free the lively Owen. And it's even at the break, no goals and little between the sides.

But we also *know* that Michael is going to have chances in the second half, that Myers will get the wrong side at least once, thus opening up Walsh's goal to the Boy Wonder. And as scousers are still tumbling up the stairs, carrying hot pies and coffee, Owen strikes. Put through by McAllister down the left channel, the home goalkeeper Walsh conveniently lies down so that even *left*-footed Michael finds it hard to miss. Which means it is shit or bust for Bradford, now forced to push forward and vulnerable on the break.

Soon after, Owen wins a free kick of his own on the Bradford right on the edge of the home box. Walsh chooses to guard the same left corner that Kirkland did so badly at covering at Coventry, but his mind is now racing: 'I mustn't move too soon to my right, or this cute cunt [Gary Mac] will beat me on the left.' This small hesitation, and McAllister gently beats him high on the right: easily. A goal scored in Bradford and made in Coventry, and enough to wrap this up. Eventually, we convey our condolences and say our goodbyes – and this time there are no City fans kissing the turf and cartwheeling with delight. Not for 0–2, and relegation out of the big time.

SURVIVAL STRATEGIES

According to the Football League National Fan Survey, Crewe Alexandra supporters favour closer financial and other links between larger FA Premier League and smaller Football League clubs. Crewe, of course, once had a 'special relationship' with Liverpool FC. When I asked Rick Parry about this recently he confessed he had no idea exactly what went on between the two clubs. The best we could come up with is that Liverpool offered coaching support, and maybe some resources, got first option on promising Crewe players (like Rob Jones and Danny Murphy), and that we had also sent young players to try out Gresty Road – such as Stephen Wright and Jon Newby – on loan, to learn their football trade. Everyone wins.

Maybe more smaller clubs would benefit from this sort of loose tie-up, which seems to offer no threat or loss of independence. But now a new proposition: QPR and Wimbledon are talking of merging. The former are relegated and in debt, the latter have no ground – or fans –

but an impressive young manager and players good enough, possibly, to challenge for promotion to the top level next season. So the 'logic' of the merger is that, combined, these clubs solve their different problems and have a realistic stab at getting to the big Premiership money in 2002. Why else exist at all, they seem to say?

QPR's backers originally got on board because they thought they could smell the big time in one quick promotion to the top flight – instead they'll be playing at Bury and Cardiff City next term. It was always going to be a struggle for Wimbledon to climb straight back into the higher level – even with foreign investors in charge. But a new London hybrid –*Wimbledon Rangers* – offers a potential quick-fix and a cash return, when otherwise only pain and debt lies ahead. But supporters don't mind a bit of pain, would prefer it in fact, to future pleasure from a creature stitched together by surgeon-accountants, a club which nobody loves and to which no one feels attached. So, for the moment, at least, QPR will continue to haemorrhage cash and Wimbledon will still sleep out. But it won't always be like this.

5 MAY: LIVERPOOL 3, NEWCASTLE UNITED 0

Newcastle United, teased by Keegan, bored rigid by Kenny and almost wrecked by Gullit, are now one of those clubs which seem to symbolise some of the worst aspects of the new global game and the constant ebb and flow of players and managers who shape the future of football clubs at the highest levels in Europe. Their player profile reads like a collection of nearly-men from all points distant – Marcelino, Acuna, Bassedas, Cordone, Solano, LuaLua, Dabizas. Who? Only the grizzly Shearer is a resident Geordie now, and he cost £15 million to repatriate. Not that the bellied black-and-whites who pour into the Flattie today seem too concerned about this. Seventy-four years without a league title. They deserve better – *we* would not show their patience.

Rogan Taylor is back in his Kop seat again, returned once more from Brazil with reports on the sorry state of the Brazilian national team (1–1 latest, with Peru), which is now in real danger of failing to make it to the 2002 World Cup finals. 'What if Brazil doesn't qualify?' he asked an official in Rio. 'The Government will fall,' is the matter-of-fact reply. FIFA might also be pressed to reconsider the rules of World Cup qualification if the world's most famous football brand fails to reach the required mark. No doubt TV contracts demand Brazil are involved in Japan and Korea. This is Rogan's last Liverpool match of the season, he tells us: tomorrow he flies to China for more international football negotiations. The world is now Rogan's football.

The domestic Footballer of the Year awards have just been announced, with Steven Gerrard winning the Young Player award. The

Premiership select team, chosen by players, actually includes only one Liverpool regular, Gerrard. Which means that there must be *two* centre-backs in the FA Premier League who have been better this season than Sami Hyypia. I don't think so. Hyypia leads Liverpool again today in match No. 59 because Robbie is benched once more. We start with no left-footed players, and three – Fowler, Berger and Ziege – in the dug-out. Smicer and Gerrard get the wide midfield berths, flanking Didi and Mac. Even this one change, Smicer rather than Murphy, alters the whole shape and balance of our team: it signals more attacking intent, more flow and invention than we saw at either Coventry or Bradford.

And so it proves, because we get at Newcastle in the first half, give them a torrid time, and the artful Smicer is at the heart of it, probing, running with the ball, tackling back. Michael also looks lively again, showing good touch and movement, and so when the Newcastle centre-backs switch off for an instant – 'Dabizas fell asleep,' says a sad-eyed Robson later – Markus and Michael spot it right away, the German playing in Owen through a wide fissure to finish low to Given's right. This setback obviously unnerves the visiting keeper because he soon gives the ball to unmarked Gary Mac – who freezes and just chips it back into the hands of the embarrassed and relieved Given.

So we should score more before the half, and good passing and pressurising by Newcastle at the start of the second half suggests we might yet regret not building a bigger lead. With grit – and a little luck – we survive this spell of pressure and begin to climb back on top. GH weighs in at this point with critical substitutions: Murphy for Gerrard, Berger for a tiring Smicer, and eventually Robbie for Heskey. After dancing out of a number of early tasty tackles – 'Fucking get in, Patrik!' from us, ever the cerebral critics – Berger meanders across midfield before putting Michael in again down the middle and this time our little torturer flicks an ungainly shot over Given, which for 95 per cent of its short life looks like it is sure to squirt wide of the Kop's right-hand post – before going in. The Fellahs in Front turn smugly to chide us about getting on Berger's back. We try to look ashamed.

Can Michael get three? Have you been listening at all? With ten minutes left, Robbie floats a gorgeous 30-yard pass from left midfield towards the right corner flag and over the Newcastle defence, and Owen is hungrily on to it, controlling and finishing convincingly this time, low to Given's right. Owen is back alright. The black and whites of Anfield Road now start to drift away, another wasted journey to L4. 'I feel stronger and faster again,' says Owen later. 'Trying to get back after a long injury is always hard, but now I'm using my pace to break through and score more often.' All right, it's not Camus – or even Ron Atkinson – but it says all you need to know about Owen's confidence and positive mental state at the moment. Jamie Carragher reveals that one of Owen's dressing-room nicknames is 'golden bollocks'. He's in the sort of form to justify it. Which means that you-know-who, the scourge of Arsenal and also our beloved scouse captain, is likely to be collecting the tracksuit tops in Cardiff. Interesting.

CHAMPIONS LEAGUE CALLING

Results elsewhere mean a win at home to poor travellers Chelsea on Tuesday night will make us favourites for a Champions League slot next season, getting close to what Houllier set out as our main goal for 2001. Qualification will also mean more leverage for Liverpool in the transfer market – GH has told the LFC board we will need two or three new signings simply to keep up next season. Our cup runs this season will earn £9 million. Similar success in Europe could bring £30 million. Football mathematics.

And this is how the football world divides these days. A few months ago we were not that much better placed even than Coventry City and we have had a worse away league record for most of the season than Manchester City. Now these two relegated clubs will be checking out the home colours of Rotherham in the First Division next season, while we will be hoping to have a crack at the fat cats, the Juventuses and Real Madrids. Next season we hope fixture congestion will be a given, of course, but because this is Liverpool, and because we have made progress this term, Houllier knows that, above all else, we will want the league title in 2002. The pressure never stops.

8 MAY: LIVERPOOL 2, CHELSEA 2

Oliver Kay in *The Times* gets it just about cruelly right following this classy affair: 'Sixty matches into their marathon season, Liverpool are none the wiser as to whether they can call it a success.' GH, charmingly, describes the match later as 'very smashing'. But it is not a result we want, and almost for the first time this season there are real signs of fatigue in our ranks. Crucially, goalkeeping doubts also return at this critical phase.

Having lectured us and scolded sceptics on the merits of rotation, there is now a view in the Advanced Coaching School in the Flat Iron public house, L4, that this is perhaps not the time for Houllier to persist with soldiers who have been in the front line for pretty much the whole of the last few months of this extended campaign. Others argue we should now play our best team for *all* these remaining games – fuck rotation. Such is the all-consuming intensity of this debate that Paul Hyland asks: 'What did we used to talk about here before we had rotation?' It's hard to remember: the latest Stan Collymore tale, perhaps? Stig Bjornebye's abject crosses? Tonight, Hamann and even McAllister look like they may have flat batteries, and even the mighty Hyypia has that air of a man playing just a game too far.

Though this is to diminish Chelsea, who arrive here with just three crappy away wins all term and then proceed to pass and move with real style and confidence throughout. Left side for Liverpool? Berger, in for Smicer. But by playing five in midfield, and with Zola pretty much untouchable, it is our guests who have no trouble keeping the ball for long spells in the first half. But Michael, in a really hot vein now, still scores early on, cutting through on Chelsea's right, dummied in by McAllister, and flicking past Cudicini.

If we can hold this lead, even for twenty minutes, a team with Chelsea's lousy away record and full of different languages may fold (I'm giving you clues, now). Westerveld has looked calm and solid for so long we might have forgotton his early-season lapses: until Hasselbaink strikes low from over 30 yards, Kop end, and our gloved Dutchman, stuck flatfooted on his goal-line and ill-prepared for action, allows this pacy, bouncing, *speculative* shot to sneak in.

This contest has real quality and bite; we are made to play, to raise our game, by Chelsea's superior technique and their imagination. So GH and Thommo alter the pattern at the break, pushing up our full-backs, raising the tempo and cutting down on the time we have allowed Morris and Zola on the ball. Steven Gerrard also steps up, now bossing the game higher up the field, spraying passes and following the ball, driving hard into the Chelsea box. Both sides make chances and both goalkeepers make good saves before, on the hour, Owen (who else?) emerges from an ugly scrum in the Chelsea box to hook his shot high into the night – and Chelsea's net.

Again, if Liverpool can just hold on to this lead for a spell, increase Chelsea's anxiety and make them lose their shape at the back, we have the resolve to win this. But hesitation between Hyypia and Hamann (am I dreaming this?) soon allows the ball to run to Hasselbaink, who shrugs off Carragher down the Liverpool left before he positively blasts a low shot past Sander in the Anfield Road goal. There is still time for Heskey and Owen to go close and for Zola to be subbed to an appreciative ovation from the coaching heads in the Liverpool Main Stand Paddock. As he leaves, a voice behind us in the Kemlyn tells nearby Dennis Wise: 'You're the only fuckin' glove puppet left now, Wise.' But Dennis knows the score: when Smicer comes on to replace Berger, the little Chelsea man has a harsh word in Vladdy's ear and then slyly kicks him off the ball while awaiting a throw-in. The Czech pretty much packed it in, there and then. Two-all, very smashing, and no fucking use to us. Charlton (A) 19 May matters once more. We might have guessed.

'HURRY UP, 'ARRY: YOU'RE SACKED'

Harry Redknapp, used-car salesman, wheeler-dealer London spiv, football manager of his time, is unceremoniously dismissed from his East End kingdom. West Ham have flattered to deceive this season, but the bigger truth is that Harry is also out of his time. We have unwittingly played a part here, selling both Titi and Songey to our cockney friend, and they have wasted his cash, not performed at all. This has put him in the dock. But the new technocrats are also now taking over, replacing the intuitive, rough-edged style of Harry and his family staff with their diets, videos and science. Joe Royle is also soon kicked out at Manchester City, this time against a background of press comment about the drinkers in his squad, while disciplinarians, such as Houllier and others, keep their own playing staff on an ever tighter leash. It's the new times in football, the time of the technocrats. Two new leaders will soon be at it in a Cup final in Wales: besuited, Perrier Frenchmen.

12 MAY: FA CUP FINAL, MILLENNIUM STADIUM, CARDIFF: ARSENAL 1, LIVERPOOL 2

'This is an important message. If anyone has a spare ticket for the match, can they come to the guards' van immediately.' A smart-arse on a packed Swansea to Cardiff train, standing room only, on the morning of the 2001 FA Cup final, the first ever played outside England. The Reds of Arsenal and Liverpool have been stirred in West Wales, accents from Islington and Merseyside chiming alongside singalong Swansea tunes. But local enmities have been stilled, not dissipated. Sitting to my right, a young Swansea City supporter now charts our progress towards Cardiff with increasing disgust and a violently twitching nose: 'Can you start to smell it now? The smell of scum?' On passing the crumbling Ninian Park on our right, it's: 'Burn the fuckin' thing down, man.' Welcome to Wales.

But actually local spats are largely out the window today. This is, instead, a meeting of two English footballing heavyweights, both trying to hold on to the coat-tails of the Corporation, and both managed by rival French football *professeurs*.The press have been full of this Houllier v Wenger battle of wits all week, as well as the Steven Gerrard v Vieira showdown, but there are other, more important, things in play today. One is the issue of Houllier's preferred team, and especially whether Robbie has a place in it. The sharks on the back pages are already lining him up with new clubs – including Arsenal, of course.

There has also been more talk this week – too much – about the sliding place of the FA Cup in the domestic football firmament. Also, some critics argue that this present Cup final stint away from Wembley – until at least 2005, and then, who knows – will detach the tournament from some more of its vital, life-giving history and prestige. But I doubt whether you would find many travellers from Liverpool – or even Highbury – wishing we were now in darkest Brent. In sunny Cardiff, the bars and pubs are soon bursting with impromptu ale-and-butty picnics and football matches springing into life. This feels like a European final and it also feels like a million welcome miles from the north circular and the concrete jungle around the flaking twin towers. With decent transport links sorted out here, you can keep Wembley for me: for good.

The National Museum of Wales is acting as the impressive 'main stand' to one of these fans' matches and is, itself, hosting an exhibition about Paul Robeson, prospective US grid-iron great, incomparable singer, actor, socialist and anti-fascist, and remarkable friend and supporter of both the South Wales miners and the International Brigades. A teacher from Somerville College in the US memorably commended Robeson for his scholastic ability and humanity in the 1920s before admitting that he could never forget, however, that Robeson was still a negro.

A trickle of visiting football supporters have stopped by Robeson today, some to add their thoughts to the walls of space allocated to visitors' comments. The walls are full. 'Paul Robeson would have been a Liverpool fan,' says one message. Not so fanciful, this: a Liverpool banner spotted later in the Millennium Stadium reads: 'What we achieve in life echoes in eternity.' It might have been written by Robeson himself, rather than by some vainglorious *Gladiator* screenwriter, but it is typically more lyrical than anything offered today from the North London ranks, with their tired 'Gunners' banners and impressive Senegalese flags.

In a pub before the match we watch Sky TV focus in ugly, forensic detail on Robbie Fowler's arrival in Cardiff. He's not playing, that's for sure. Robbie's pissed off – who wouldn't be? But he doesn't deserve this sort of intrusive public exposure, as if members of his family had tragically died. Later, inside the Millennium Stadium as we await the announcement of the teams, we can see Little Vignal has been noticeably geeing up the Reds' starting eleven in the warm-up – which does not include Fowler or Gary McAllister. Houllier has been both cute and possibly reckless here. McAllister has almost certainly been sacrificed to help Robbie swallow the bitter pill of his own exclusion. 'The boss watches how you react,' says model professional Macca later, rationalising his own omission. GH is actually saying to Robbie in this piece of self-denial: 'Look, I'm also leaving out our best, our most experienced performer. You are not alone. Watch how *he* responds and learn.' This is a cheap and risky trick which could easily be punished.

And all this hokus pokus means that Murphy is the surprise beneficiary. His recent form has been unimpressive, but he now starts on the right, Smicer on the left. If Vieira gets on top of Gerrard, much will depend on Vladdy v 37-year-old Dixon in this formation. But Wenger is also defensive, preferring the dull Grimandi in midfield to both Bergkamp and Parlour. Wiltord starts up front with Henry, with the wily Kanu in reserve. The sun lights up the red and white check which is splashed in the seats all around the stadium today, a pattern interrupted only by the uncommitted blue and white shirtsleeves in the exposed royal box. The high-ups are in for some Welsh sunstroke, for once.

Meanwhile, in the pre-match darkness of the Liverpool dressing-room below, Michael Owen is flexing and stretching his new kangaroo-skin Umbro boots; part of his astronomic sponsorship deal is to wear these new lightweight shoes in today's final before they hit the sports shop shelves next week at a cool £120 a shot. He gets stick from the rest of the squad for his new kit, of course. A passing Houllier eyes the shoes and asks Michael whether he is certain he wants to start a Cup final in a *new* pair of boots: surely Michael's current 'lucky' scoring pair is a better bet on a hot day which is made for blisters? Owen concedes and slips on his trusted old pair. After all, there are goals in these boots.

Liverpool actually start brightly, with Gerrard and Murphy doing well early on, but Arsenal soon begin to grind their way back into the match, eventually freeing Henry on the Liverpool left and around the stranded Westerveld. A key moment this, because Henchoz, on the goal-line, keeps out Henry's near-post shot with a raised elbow, which is clearly seen by Henry but by no one else on the field. The range of potential options for a sharp-eyed official here stretch from red card/penalty, a penalty or a corner. Naturally, referee Steve Dunn decides on a goal kick.

But Henry is now leading Henchoz a merry dance, even if Arsenal's midfielders sit deep and Wiltord is anonymous. Which means plenty of Arsenal ball into Liverpool's penalty area but little real danger. Smicer has had little decent ball at all – nor shows much interest – while Heskey is dominated by Adams and Keown. Apparently, Owen is playing – somewhere. Houllier steps out of the dug-out, urging the Liverpool central midfield to be more positive. Nil-nil at the half: we haven't played, not at all.

It gets worse after half-time, because Arsenal, more confident now, become more ambitious and Vieira begins to stride forward and *through* Gerrard and Hamann. Hyypia now seems to have taken permanent and necessary residence on the Reds' goal-line, clearing away shots and headers from the rampant Londoners. Anxiety in the Liverpool crowd is matched by frustration in the Arsenal ranks. Later, Henry will regret the fact that Arsenal lack a 'poaching fox' to snap up some of these chances (who can he mean?). Maybe Arsenal are destined not to score today; that *our* cautious name is actually on the FA Cup, as it has seemed all season since Nick Barmby scored at Leeds?

And then it happens – with 18 minutes left, an Arsenal goal. Sander collects a misplaced Arsenal pass and plays a crude ball wide to Babbel, who returns it. Westerveld's next clearance is even worse, a weak grass-cutter, and Pires puts Ljungberg in on the Liverpool right as a result, and into the space left by Markus. The Swede easily rounds Wester and shoots high towards goal and this time neither Hyypia nor Carragher on the line can perform the required heroics.

Okay, let's get real; this is now officially over. We have shown little, and deserve less, and we have yet to come back from a goal down in the whole of the 2000–01 league campaign, let alone against these accomplished and experienced misers in a major final. Arsenal have yet to lose this season from a goal in front. So this begins to feel like the emptiness of the 1996 'spice boys' Liverpool FA Cup final loss against United, another major occasion when we simply failed to turn up. Before Berger and Fowler come on for Smicer and Murphy, our 99th and 100th substitutes this season, respectively – and both too late – Hyypia clears away another goal-bound Henry poke, as if to strengthen the point.

Despite all this, McAllister has actually given us a much better shape and more purpose since his arrival and Arsenal are at least *not* trying to close the match down – a policy which almost lets in the previously sleeping Owen (remember him?) but Keown gets back to clear. With just seven minutes left, Carragher wins a last-chance free kick right in front of us and wide on Arsenal's right. McAllister steps up to take it and delivers to the top of Keown's straining head. Michael has come near-post but now follows the arc of this mis-header back towards the far post where Babbel fights Adams in the air to squeeze the ball down and into Owen's curving path. And his reaction to this bouncing ball is gloriously instant, the Boy Wonder, old 'golden bollocks' himself: body twisting sharply sideways, Michael's lucky right boot instantly hooking the gently rising ball low around Keown and past the watching Seaman, deep into the right corner of Arsenal's goal. The Liverpool end erupts.

'As soon as Michael scored it was a different game,' said Houllier. 'Their defence was superb, but when we scored they lost that authority.' This is all gloriously true, because as the disbelieving, goal-induced carnage in our seats slowly dies away, the mighty Arsenal are suddenly visibly wilting, broken. Fowler starts to taunt them now. Two minutes left, and Berger aims a sweeping ball up the left touch-line. Owen, again, wriggles and pushes his way in front of and against the gasping Dixon, like a small, sleepless child angrily entering a parent's bed at night. Adams honestly lumbers across and pushes Michael wider onto his left side, confident his job is now done. Except – and we are right behind this, see it all the way – Owen, all right side and hopelessly positioned, suddenly starts an early low, threaded left-foot shot initially just *outside* Seaman's far post, which somehow dips below the startled keeper's left-hand dive and hits the *inside* of the goal-netting, about a foot within the post.

Norman Whiteside's precise winning goal for ten-man United against Everton in the 1985 final or Gary Lineker's wonderful threaded World Cup strike against the Germans in the semi-final in Turin in 1990 perhaps have something in common. I watched 'that' Michael goal against Argentina in France '98 with members of the FIFA Executive in the Hotel Bristol in Paris, the World Cup itself sitting in a glass case just a few feet behind where we danced in semi-drunken delight. But for precocious skill and timing, audacity and sheer star quality, *this* is simply unmatched.

Michael, in this one moment, has climbed above all our early season uncertainties and anxieties about his form and fitness, and even his wilful right-sided limits, to single-handedly win the 2001 FA Cup for Liverpool. We have positively *stolen* this final, destroyed Arsenal's resolve, and in the Sunday newspapers, caught soon after this stunning first goal, St Michael looks more like Christ Himself: arms stretched wide, beatific sunlit smile, and with his young 'disciples' Gerrard, Fowler and Heskey in rapt and adoring attendance. We are not worthy.

Houllier will point again later to the effects of his substitutes and to the character of this Liverpool team in never accepting defeat, a sign of a club at one with itself, full of trust and belief, he says. But the other truth here is more that Owen's nerveless, big-match unwillingness to accept the inevitable has seen us through. Two shots, two goals – and two cups already won. Michael is voted undisputed Man of the Match – for *seven minutes'* work. He does little else. New football, for sure.

Back on the late-night train to Swansea, and by now considerably the worse for countless gleeful hugs and troughs of Welsh ale, we are cornered by other Liverpool fans who identify me as 'the fellah on the telly' the ' football professor'. So now the serious footy questions come in a flood, and they are good these boys, steeped in Liverpool's extraordinary history. We offer up a few of our own impressive queries and the answers unerringly come back, flat-vowelled and true. The only question which defeats us all on this deliciously sweet night, which is now slipping mistily into drink, is how it is that it is *Liverpool* who leave this city with the FA Cup? And do we really care, at all, that no one in this carriage can answer?

BRAZILIAN DIDI AND GARY MAC, BLOOD BROTHERS

Our FA Cup larceny sits a little uneasily with the reported death this weekend of the legendary Brazilian winger, Didi, the 'Ethiopian Prince'. He was a thrilling star of the 1958 and 1962 Brazilian World Cup-winning teams and played briefly in Europe in the late 1950s before eventually returning to South America to later manage Peru to the quarter-finals of the World Cup in Mexico, where they fell to the incomparable 1970 Brazilians.

Like our own Gary Mac, Didi was a free-kick specialist, known as *folha seca* ('dry leaves') for his ability to dip the ball abruptly, as if like a leaf falling from a tree. He was also reputed to sleep with a football under his bed so that he could touch it at night. 'I always had affection for the ball,' he once said, 'because if you do not treat it with affection it will not obey you. I treat it with as much affection as my wife.' Gary Mac actually dedicates his recent fantastic form and autumnal footballing successes at Liverpool to his own wife, a brave battler this season against breast cancer. Didi was a gentle genius from a different culture, of course, and from a very different time. But it is clearly not all lost today, this sense that there is more to the game, and to life, than the next big deal.

16 MAY, UEFA CUP FINAL, DORTMUND: LIVERPOOL 5, DEPORTIVO ALAVÉS 4

We have no time to properly savour the FA Cup win because within days, and like a second sickly cream cake from a too-long-hidden dessert plate, we have another treat to face, our first European final for 16 years. And let's be honest, Deportivo Alavés from Vitoria in north-east Spain is not one of the great names of European football – this is the Basque club's first major final. So we are most people's favourites. Alavés are known in Spain for their 'second chance' team of club rejects, and for their muscular counter-attacking style epitomised by Javi Moreno, a chunky and combative centre-forward and leading goal-scorer in Spain this season, and also by the rehabilitated Jordi Cruyff. We hear much, too, about their Romanian wing-back Contra, a real flyer and a likely Barcelona transfer target. 'They are tireless,' says John Toshack, Spanish and scouser football guru, 'Liverpool should be frightened of them.' I *am* frightened, Tosh, more than you know.

The Basque club is also known as *Los Babazorros*, apparently literally in Basque 'people too keen on broad beans', a reference to earlier times of want following a nineteenth-century potato famine. A bastardised version, in fact, would have our opponents, bizarrely, as the 'potato aphids', a variation perhaps on our own 'sheep-shaggers' or 'tractor boys'. Ipswich Town might be a good comparision here: Alavés, after all, have thrashed Kaiserslautern 9–2 in the UEFA semis, so no lambs-to-the-slaughter, country bumpkins are these boys. They deserve respect, though they offer Liverpool little in return. Centre-back Tellez describes the Reds as an 'unsophisticated' side which gives up possession and is in love with the long ball. He has clearly been watching us.

Some experts have this match down as a stand-off defensive stalemate. But we can also see that Houllier has been badly stung by criticism in Spain following the No mas Barcelona affair, and in England after our dramatic, defensive scraping past Arsenal in Cardiff. Johan Cryuff publicly described our no-show in Spain as 'horrible'. But Houllier has an ego, too – a considerable one – and he may well want to show the football world that his Liverpool can also play. Outrageous, and utterly out of character, I know. So bet, instead, on another grating struggle and extra time.

Dortmund is hardly a lip-smacking venue for this final, but this *is* serious football country, deep in the Ruhr heartlands and with Hitzfeld's Borussia Dortmund recent worthy winners of the European Cup. The local club also has a Reds link, having sold us Riedle (a classy pup) and Berger in recent years, so we might reasonably expect some 'home' support tonight. What we don't expect is the lashing rain which swamps the Alt Markt, the central square, which is already filling with Liverpudlians and their lager cans from early morning.

Locals might wonder at the obtuse English test set them by their surprisingly literate visitors from the British north-west, whose voluminous flags now stretch around the central area and are positively packed with phrases and aphorisms culled from the Bard, Hollywood and the Glenbuck poet, Shankly himself. It is as if the city of Liverpool has been waiting, mute, for 16 long years after Heysel for this international football moment in order to speak, without shame, once more. This will not clear our Belgian debt, this meeting tonight, but it will, please God, be at least a start.

Our Basque rivals – some wearing funny paper signs warning about wrongly calling them Spaniards – are charming enthusiasts of both sexes and all ages, pitched up as they are with their brass bands, exaggerated Basque berets, traditional leather drinking pouches full of paztaran, a potent purple hooch, and the now famous Alavés shirt, which has the names of the club's fans woven into its colours. Scousers are soon eagerly swapping corporate Carlsberg red for the inclusive Basque blue and yellow.

Compared to our equivalents from Spain, we look like worn, crop-headed, sports-shop invaders, who have been sternly instructed that any Liverpudlian access to the ground tonight depends on us drinking the local supermarkets and bars tinderbox dry. So we make a strong start. The authorities in Alavés have thoughtfully provided their own followers and the locals here with tourist agency tents and free paella and ice-cream in the central area. *We* get murky street bars and our own music stage churning out endless renditions of 'YNWA'. Fair enough.

When the rain clears and the organisers finally drag a stage-struck (and pissed) Dr Fun out from the limelight, and after Liverpool FC's own Brian Hall has 'entertained' the crowd from the stage, the real festival begins. John Power (from Liverpool band, Cast) and the irrepressible Pete Wylie briefly convert this corner of Germany into a delirious musical tribute to Liverpool and Liverpudlians everywhere. As the red and white crowd surges to the stage Wylie, looking daily more and more like a ravaged Elvis impersonator, also offers a necessary Hillsborough-style warning: 'There's people at the front 'ere gettin' fuckin' crushed. Remember the 96: we don't want none of that at a fuckin' gig, for fuck's sake. Look after each other out there.' Amen to that.

As late afternoon drifts into evening, most Liverpool fans now start catching the local trams up to the nearby Westfalenstadion. We hear later of the intolerable crowding and delays on the system. Some fans get off the trams and walk up the line to the ground. Instead, we catch a car ride to the venue with Moenchengladbach Berndt, who has turned up with Paul Hyland. Berndt insists on playing us CDs of intolerable German punk and local football songs, so it is a relief when we eventually park in the stadium gardens near an impressive concert hall, where the painfully middle-class German audience for Riverdance is now arriving, agog at the red flood which is drunkenly engulfing them.

Outside the stadium now it is virtually *all* red; inside, except for a large corner of noisy blue Basques to our left, Liverpool has also seeped into all areas. So, this is Rome 1977 all over again; 25,000 Merseyside hearts and voices, flags and banners proudly aloft. Behind us is the gently self-mocking and Europhile 'If Houllier had been at Waterloo we would all be speaking French', next to a large red banner for inebriated inmates at the 'Betty Ford Clinic'. As well as the images of Shankly and Paisley and the legions of Fowler and Owen flags, we also have the usual pub signs from Kirkby, Huyton, Bootle, Birkenhead and the rest. Classical singers boom out their anthems from the pitch, the pre-match entertainment here. We respond with 'YNWA', real singing for real football.

We watch these preliminary affairs from seats low down and just to the right of the Liverpool dug-out, so we are well placed to see from the darkness in his face during the warm-up that Robbie Fowler will not start again tonight. No one in the Liverpool squad smiles or speaks to him, or is even able to look him in the eye. McAllister looks happier, enthusiastic, busy: he's playing. All the squad looks nervous, as the setting sun now bathes the filling stands in a warm and congealing, post-rain orange glow. The ground is buzzing, humming with Merseyside anticipation: we have not come this far to lose.

Actually, after Cardiff I had convinced myself that winning here was no longer quite so important. Now I'm not so sure. Nerves are taking over. Houllier wants this one more than the FA Cup: a European title always means more, he says. As kick-off approaches I find I really want it now, too. It is hard not to think of all those other fellahs and women from the Kop who are now watching this on telly back home and are saying to their mates: 'I'll be there, next time.' I want us to win tonight for them. And for my dad, who saw us retain the European Cup against Bruges at Wembley in 1978. And also for all those who shed so many bitter tears back in 1985 and in 1989. Winning in Europe now, though it can't repair any of what has gone before, somehow seems strangely vital again.

McAllister, for Smicer, is the only Liverpool change from Cardiff, with Steven Gerrard moving to the right. This tinkering seems to do the trick because within 16 minutes Liverpool are two goals up. Firstly, Babbel easily heads home from a McAllister free kick and then Hamann and Owen put Gerrard through, unopposed, on the Alavés left and Steven beats Herrera comfortably. A win without stress is thus in the offing.

A manager in England on the end of this kind of dreadful start would probably regroup and hold on now, and maybe try to sneak a goal before the half. Instead, after just 22 minutes, Alavés manager, Jose Esnal, boldly replaces centre-back Eggen with Alonso, a clever Uruguayan forward. It pays. Suddenly the elusive Contra beats Murphy and crosses deep to the far post where Alonso gets up much earlier than Babbel to loop a decisive header over the stranded Westerveld. Sander simply glares, pointing at Murphy and Carragher, relocating the blame as usual. Put the Euro-cigars away: game on.

Alavés are now confident, and Cruyff, Moreno and Contra are starting to cause Liverpool real problems. Which is what Alavés need to do, because Karmona and his own mates at the back are struggling to hold Michael. Just before the half, Hamann finds another large hole on the Alavés left and Michael is into it and round the advancing Herrera, until the goalkeeper sweeps Owen's legs from under him. Penalty, no doubts. McAllister scores from the spot, and we go in a healthy, if wobbly, 3–1 to the good, the Liverpool stands bubbling once again. The half-time bratwurst tastes good.

But it doesn't last, this lead. Right after the interval, Contra twists and turns Carragher once more, before delivering to the lurking Moreno who beats Gerrard to the header. Within minutes Moreno scuffs a free kick *under* a jumping Liverpool wall to make it a catastrophic 3–3. This time Sander simply walks slowly away, hands clasped behind his back, as if compiling a damning closing statement for the prosecution of the Liverpool defence. Houllier chips in, as hanging judge, by taking off Henchoz (for Smicer), who has been shredded by Moreno. Magno then dives in the Liverpool box and is rightly booked by referee Veissiere. Sami waves his Nobel Peace Prize finger at Magno, who shrugs his own professional's 'by any means necessary' message back.

The Alavés fans are now doing that bouncy continental jig, which makes it look as if all their 8,000 fans are roped together in noisy, choreographed joy. They sense back-from-the-dead glory, the best kind in football. Then, two substitutions on 64 minutes show what an inexact and mistake-ridden science football coaching really is. First, the dangerous Moreno, two goals already scored, is *withdrawn* by Esnal. Okay, Moreno has only recently returned from injury, but this is still a stunning miscalculation, and a huge bonus for Liverpool. The portly striker slumps with undisguised disgust into the Alavés dug-out, mystified at his demotion. His team-mates' shoulders visibly drop. At the same time, Fowler replaces the impotent Heskey and he immediately begins to find space inside Contra, down the Alavés right.

Even Robbie's touch-line warm-up routine now signals an outpouring of expectation and unreflective love from most Liverpool supporters. It is no different here. And the great footballing *Book of Irony*, hundreds of pages long and stuffed with similar tales, also dictates that Robbie, miserable and unloved at Wembley and only minutes ago in a black dog depression on the Liverpool bench in Dortmund, will now score the winner here and, with two-fingers up to GH, claim first hands on the 2001 UEFA Cup. So no one in red is really surprised when, with Hamann and McAllister taking control, Mac puts Fowler away on the Alavés right for a mazy run across the box which ends with Robbie sliding a right-foot shot through the legs of Tellez and beyond Herrera, who watches the ball into the net on his frozen haunches.

After the pandemonium has died away, the exhausted feeling where we are sitting is 'Great match, brave Alavés: let's have a rousing chorus of "YNWA", present the cup and we'll all try to find a bar'. Houllier must feel the same way because he now takes off Michael – which means he thinks we will need no more goals in this match. So we wait respectfully for the end. What else can happen? Goal for Alavés, that's what: two minutes to go, an unchallenged near-post header from a corner, Jordi Cruyff. 'Fuck off, Westerveld!' from behind us, pinpointing the cause. *Three* headed goals conceded by Liverpool, and 4–4 in a match which was supposed to be a tight, defensive affair.

Either they will score now, or they will be fresher and wear us down in extra time. Get used to it, we are going to lose, I say to myself, and I actually imagine how the ridiculous 'Liverpool 4, Alavés 5' scoreline will look on the huge scoreboard which faces us in the corner of the Westfalenstadion. But fate takes a large extra-time hand. The cheating Magno now foolishly catches Babbel late and is sent off, for two yellows. Manager Esnal and his staff are distraught, fuming at the fourth official for this 'injustice'.

Ten-man Alavés now look as if they are happy with the idea of penalties and we are struggling, unsurprisingly, for the necessary energy to score a winning goal. So the contest drifts towards the shoot-out, except with just four minutes left Smicer is wrestled down by Karmona, wide on the Liverpool left: which means another Alavés dismissal, and a free kick. Thompson and Houllier are up off the bench, gesticulating wildly now, rearranging our formation. How will we play for these final few minutes against just nine tired opponents? Penalties, of course, would make the inequality in numbers irrelevant, so we *must* press forward hard in what time is left. McAllister, meanwhile, lines up the free kick.

We learn later that only supporters like us, in the Main Stands, have actually *heard* the earlier PA message about the use of the 'golden goal' tonight. So when McAllister's free kick skims Geli's blond head and clears the flying Herrera's fists to nestle in the Alavés goal, many Reds fans initially interpret the Basques' ground-beating despair as a normal response to a crushing – but not a terminal – late goal in extra time. Only when there are no signs of players returning to their formations for a restart does it slowly dawn on everyone here that this cruel and stupid way of resolving an epic contest has actually handed the trophy to Liverpool. That after dragging themselves back from the brink, nine-man Alavés can hurt us no more.

Apart from the hugging and the dancing, the presentations and the TV interviews which go on right in front of us, two things are really memorable about what follows next. First, the collective, tear-jerking singing of 'YNWA' with the entire Liverpool staff, arms linked, facing the red hordes in the Westfalenstadion. Even English journalists say later that they stopped dictating their match accounts to fully take in this moment, and it brings welling tears to me again now as I type this. Robbie and GH, together, face a huge red banner, centre-stage, during this ecstatic moment which says: 'All those who have a red heart can rejoice, for they have seen GOD.' They mean, of course, the urchin genius, Fowler. We watch this incomparable moment, by the way, with a delirious Elvis Costello sporting a daft pillbox hat, and his wife Caitlin, who have now appeared in the seats in front of us.

The second truly memorable thing is the magnificent Alavés fans who wait and wait in the stadium to a man and woman, even in their bitter disappointment, to applaud not only their own players but also the shattered Liverpool team. No English fans would have shown such patience and grace, would have handled their sadness with such dignity. Later, Mike Lee, of UEFA, will rightly congratulate Liverpool fans on our sportsmanship for chanting for brave Alavés at the presentations, suggesting even a special award might be merited for this. I say our Basque rivals – the losers tonight, a much harder role – deserve at least as much.

This turbulent, roller-coaster of a match is described in later British press reports, with typical hyperbole, as possibly the greatest European final ever. Jeff Powell, in the *Daily Mail* goes as far to suggest that it might even restore lost faith in football itself for its revival of the 'Olympian ideal'. This has been an enthralling contest, of course, but it has also lacked the highest quality to be a truly great football match. Atrocious defending, questionable management, some inspired midfield and forward play, and magnificent, magnificent support have all added to an unmissable occasion. But not a truly great match. We are not a top team yet, not by any stretch. But Don Bradman's dry comment about there being 'Plenty of batsmen who are better then me – it's just that they keep getting out' also strangely fits this gutsy Liverpool side. As Houllier himself says, we are still some way behind Roma, Barcelona, United, Arsenal and others: but somehow we can also manage to beat such teams when it really matters. We have done it this season.

Back in our hotel in Hagen, just outside Dortmund, we talk late into the night about our club and our fans with other Reds supporters, oil-rig workers who have travelled in from Norway and Aberdeen for the game: 'The match was great, but so were the supporters: there were just six arrests, that's all. And the police said the fans behaved fantastically.' The Aberdeen guy had asked the German police about this, because it mattered to him. It matters to me, too. We agree that this is also something to be proud of, perhaps as much as anything else: that we are also decent people, real football fans. The ghosts of 1985 have grown a little dimmer as a result. And it means an unprecedented three cups won by Liverpool in 2001, and just one more test now remains, the last of Houllier's 'finals'. We reconvene at The Valley, Greenwich: at stake, a Champions League place.

THEY THINK IT'S ALL OVER (IT IS)

Liverpool v Arsenal at Anfield was the first match covered in washed-out black and white by BBC 2's *Match of the Day* on 22 August 1964. 'As you can see, we're in Beatleville,' said a very hip Kenneth Wolstenhome in his kinky intro. King Roger (Hunt) scored the first-ever goal on the highlights show, as we wiped out the Arse 3–2. Liverpool also featured in the first colour coverage for *MOTD* in November 1969, at home against West Ham. We were there, too, for the first Sky live TV match v Forest in the new FA Premier League in

August 1992. Now we will also star against Charlton in the *MOTD* funeral show, because next season ITV has bought the FA Premier League highlights rights and is already talking about an early Saturday evening slot for football, probably at 7 p.m.

Not that the Premier League has thought hard about the relative quality of coverage on the Beeb compared to ITV, or about supporter preferences for the placing or timing of highlights coverage. Nor is there any loyalty shown here by the game towards a valued media partner after 37 long years together. Instead, it is simply 'How deep are your pockets?'. It's the way too much of the modern game (and the modern world) works. Maybe the commercial boys will do a decent job of replacing Lineker and Hansen, but somehow I doubt it. Rumour has it the 7 p.m. ITV start is mainly because Des doesn't fancy the late 10.30 slot anymore. Should we be surprised?

19 MAY: CHARLTON ATHLETIC 0, LIVERPOOL 4

Last rites. Leeds are at home to struggling Leicester, Ipswich away to uncertain Middlesbrough. Liverpool need to win in Greenwich not to have to rely on unlikely results elsewhere for their coveted Champions League place. The bad news? The Addicks have lost just two home games all season, a record which is up there with the best. The good? Charlton manager Curbishley has not altogether ruled out a move to fill in for Harry Redknapp at West Ham, so there is a chance of some uncertainty and disillusionment in the home camp. There is definitely some of the same among Charlton fans in the Royal Oak pub, Charlton Lane, before kick-off: they seem convinced their manager will leave, and they say as much. How will the home players respond today to all of this? This is all we care about, naturally.

The scramble for away tickets for today means I'm in the Charlton Main Stand with Ben Tegg, *Kick It Out* anti-racism campaign stalwart and deep Charlton man, so I can quickly feel the worries for the future among the locally committed. We are applauded onto the pitch by the home crowd, a standing ovation, and some local diva even sings 'YNWA', a nice touch. But that's when the hospitality ends. In fact, in the first half here I have to suffer the ever-present prospect of celebrations all around me for a home goal. It's gritty hell, naturally. For Liverpool, Fowler replaces Heskey and 'Little Vignal' comes in for Henchoz. Babbel continues at centre-back, with Carragher moving to the right. Hamann is missing, not even making the bench, so Berger starts.

At least I think Berger starts, because like the entire Liverpool midfield, for the first 45 minutes our flaxon-haired Czech is anonymous. Instead, after a slow opening, Charlton begin to bombard our goal, only Westerveld and the valiant Hyypia – and slabs of luck – keeping them at bay. Carragher gets away with a clear penalty handball, Vignal is under siege, and the goalpost also intervenes when we need it most. Jensen, Kinsella and Stuart are murdering Liverpool, showing Curbishley exactly why he should stay. So 0–0 at half-time is a brilliant score for us, brilliant. And totally undeserved.

Which all means that when *we* score early in the second half I have to hold up my hands to people nearby – this is a weird game, isn't it? Houllier says: 'We had a little talk at half-time, but I won't tell you what I said.' I'd really like to know – as if *this* changed the pattern. It's Robbie who scores, hooking a half-cleared Liverpool corner back over his head and high into the home net. Most strikers would have tried a simple overhead kick from here, opting for power, risking losing control. Not Fowler: he has completely shaped this gently looped reverse shot, knowing exactly where the space is behind him, a classy finish.

And now it is as if the Charlton team collectively gives up the ghost, is simply aghast and demoralised at the gross injustice of it all. Berger and Gerrard are imperiously in charge in midfield, Owen is suddenly running the Charlton back line ragged. Danny Murphy is on only for a few minutes before Michael feeds him on the edge of the box for Murphy to finish, low down to Illic's left, for 2–0. Charlton's defence is now in a sad, disorganised heap.

This score now fully opens the Charlton minds to the fact that this doesn't *really* matter to them, a psychological black hole; their competitive edge is gone. Gerrard and Owen eagerly break up home possession for Michael to slip the ball wide left to Fowler who hits an unstoppable, low left-foot cross-shot past Illic. Michael deservedly gets his goal, our fourth, when he robs Fish to score. 'If we have to dig in, we dig in. If we have to play, then we play,' says Houllier later. A 4–0 travesty for Liverpool and a Champions League passport is finally won.

CLOSING TIMES

Half a million people turn out in Liverpool on Sunday to see the cups brought triumphantly home. Our terrible away form and the frustrations and defeats of November and December now seem like another place. Houllier says the turning point was McAllister's crazy late free kick at Everton: from there he believed we could win the lot. The press are making their own assessments, of course, and some have Liverpool already challenging next season for United's league title. Houllier has certainly instilled a discipline and a belief in this squad and a willingness to work and battle when matches are coming thick and fast. 'If you look at our games this season,' he says, 'we have won a lot of them in the last 20 to 25 minutes. I hope that's the hallmark of future champions.' It is one of them, but more, much more, will also be needed to catch up with this United.

Okay, we have had luck this season when we have needed it: to beat both Barcelona and Roma, to overcome Leeds and Arsenal in the FA Cup, even to get the better of Birmingham City at the Millennium Stadium, and certainly to win our final, crucial league match at Charlton. Our outstanding younger players have grown up during the campaign: Gerrard to overcome his injury and his 'growing' problems; Owen to put his own fears behind him; Carragher to become a defensive rock on the left; and Murphy to contend seriously in the squad. Signing a foreign legion has never meant losing the local core. 'I think there should be a kind of Liverpool heart that would prevent me from doing that,' Houllier says after Alavés. 'I'm too keen and too happy to have four or five lads who are Liverpool-born.' Good.

Hyypia, nevertheless, has become, arguably, the top defender in England, with Henchoz and Babbel as his dogged aides. These three have been crucial. Hamann, after a slow start, has been a massive defensive presence in midfield, especially in the big matches, and McAllister is easily the season's top transfer. Westerveld has made important saves – and crucial blunders. Add to this Heskey's obvious strengths and Fowler's guile and goals, Barmby's enthusiasm, and the sheer pace and ability of Berger, Smicer and, briefly, Litmanen and the reasons for our success are clear. We have scored goals from all around the team, averaging two a game, and after a wobbly start the defence has tightened up at the critical moments. Managing all these resources – and adding cleverly to them – will be another crucial future test for Houllier and his staff.

Houllier has stressed that this Liverpool is still a very young team, it still has much to learn. He needs more time. At the Champions League final, he commented, approvingly, on the strong defensive base of both Bayern Munich and Valencia, but a top football coach these days also needs to have the courage and perception to know when to attack hard, and with guile. In the bathing glow of general media praise for Liverpool after the Charlton victory , James Lawton of *The Independent* wrote, instead – and perceptively – about the flaws which remain in the current Anfield set-up and of the 'passive' approach of Liverpool teams to some crucial matches this season. And of Houllier he said:

> The worry is that for all his virtues, and his engaging nature, the coach has a meddlesome theoretical streak which at times appears to have overridden a gut instinct for going for the other team's jugular. This at times compounds the problems caused by a lack of fluency from the back which was for so long the trademark of Liverpool, and which Arsène Wenger, while using the same

personnel as his predecessors, quickly introduced at Highbury . . .
The question is simple enough: having provided a new set of
values which have swept away the old Spice Boys image, a depth
of playing strength that is only second to Manchester United's and
a competitive character of thrice-proven force, when does Houllier
hand down a clear playing philosophy, a tactical conviction that
was the hallmark of the great Liverpool teams?

This is both harsh and true: we have shored up our problems, battled
brilliantly, but now we also need to assert ourselves. And there it is again,
of course, Liverpool's damned glorious recent past, which Houllier also
sees looming in every TV debate and match analysis involving the army
of the club's ex-players who are now television pundits. 'It is thanks to
the achievements of previous generations of famous players that
Liverpool's name is revered across Europe,' he says. 'There are something
like 20 of them commenting on our games every week for television,
radio and newspapers, and I sometimes think they could be a little more
indulgent in their view of how we are trying to take Liverpool back to the
top.' He has a point. This is only a beginning.

It is true that having returned the resilience, spirit, professional pride
and discipline – and silverware – to Anfield, Houllier will now be
expected to reveal the 'big idea' behind his new Reds, the new direction
which will get us up there on a par with the European giants. Soon after
the UEFA final in Dortmund, Phil Thompson, Houllier's assistant,
recalled hearing some scouse kids in the city calling the Frenchman the
new Bill Shankly. Thompson thought that they may be right; but
nothing could, really, be further from the truth, could it? *Houllier's* new
Liverpool: now *that* could be something worth watching in years to
come. In Kop block 207 we wait to be amazed.

In 2001–02 this new Liverpool will try swimming with the really big
European fish again, glorious memories of Paisley and Fagan strongly to
the fore, our hopes for the future ablaze. And what could possibly replace
what we have experienced in these past ten months: the traumas and the
triumphs; the thrills and the low points; the camaraderie and the defeated
loneliness? Football is dead? Not yet, at least not where we come from.
The new LFC stadium talk is still strong and the newspaper summer
transfer gossip has been addictive reading. Will Robbie stay? Can Michael
keep his marvellous form? Will Gerrard stay fit? Will Westerveld survive?
And what do we order in the Flattie to toast these incredible, incredible
past few months, as well as our possible new arrivals? *Trebles* all round,
naturally. What a season!

13. WE CAN MANAGE: SEASON 2001-02

SUMMER 2001: GONE, BUT NOT FORGOTTEN

In the close season of 2001, as trebled-up Liverpool supporters, worldwide, awaited another campaign with renewed hope of possible championship – perhaps even European Cup – success, Liverpool FC lost three of its former title winners.

Billy Liddell, a teetotaller, wartime bomber command pilot officer and once record-appearance holder for Liverpool, was a peerless left-winger of the post-war era, who could also play on the right and in defence and who eventually ended up at centre-forward. Liddell, a committed Christian and a man who would briefly retire to the toilets before games to pray for the well-being of *all* the afternoon's combatants, scored 216 goals for the club in 495 appearances and starred in the 1946–47 Reds' championship team. His retirement, in 1961, probably signalled the end of a football era. Television, celebrity culture, new spectator traditions and the end of the maximum wage and the 'part-time' football player, were all just around the corner. Billy became a Justice of the Peace and remained a modest season-ticket holder at Anfield for many years after his retirement until Alzheimer's gradually and cruelly stole away his life too early. He died at 79 years old.

Tom Saunders, ex-school teacher and a member of the inner-circle boot room elite through his role in selecting youth players for the club and later in scouting virtually all prospective new signings, also sadly died after many years of largely unsung service for Liverpool Football Club. Saunders, officially the club's 'youth development officer' lacked some of the rougher edges of the working-class football backgrounds of the other club staff, and he used his educational expertise to deal with cautions, official requests and writing speeches, especially for Bob Paisley in the Liverpool backroom. 'Tom was very much the man who made a lot of the decisions about the recruitment of new players,' Peter Robinson recalled later. 'Tom's word would be accepted by all of them.' Saunders' loss was deeply felt by all those who really know this football club.

The great Joe Fagan also died in the summer of 2001, at 80 years old.

Though a Liverpudlian to his marrow, Joe spent much of his playing career as a no-nonsense, never-miss-a-match centre-half at Manchester City, before ending up as a trainer under Harry Catterick at Rochdale in 1953. He joined Liverpool in 1958, and for the next 27 years Fagan's astute and reassuring presence underpinned the greatest extended period of English football club success in the history of the sport.

At Anfield Fagan played a cheery, rubbery-faced 'soft cop' and player confidant to the rather harsher tones of Shankly, Paisley, Reuben Bennett and later the volcanic Ronnie Moran. He also helped keep the famous Melwood training diaries, the putative football science of its day, and the precursor to the modern methods later approved by Gérard Houllier. At 62 years old, the 'treble' season of 1983–84 was Joe's managerial triumph – due reward for his exceptional club service: Heysel was, undoubtedly, the low point. Joe continued to visit Melwood after 1985, passing on his experience and knowledge to the younger players. Those who favour the Red side of Merseyside owe him much more than we know.

OPENING ACCOUNTS

After the heavy spending of previous close seasons, Gérard Houllier – and the Anfield accountants – decided that the Liverpool Cup treble squad of 2000–01 needed little reinforcement for the new challenges ahead. With the raw Traore sent on a season's loan to Lens, Fulham did all the difficult recruitment work here, agreeing terms with Monaco's 21-year-old Norwegian international left-back John Arne Riise before Houllier – hard professional that he is – stepped in to chat up Riise's mum, who is also his agent. Four million pounds later and the red-head had his 'dream move', not to west London with Tigana, but to Anfield to join another Frenchman.

Riise seemed built for the English game – a stamina machine. In the months before he signed for Monaco he did 24 training sessions a week to build up his strength and fitness: 'Even if I had to wake up at 6 a.m. to train before school, I loved it.' Robbie Fowler might take note. He was versatile, could shoot and, as an ex-volleyball player, Riise could also *throw* a football prodigious distances. How useful could this be? With the Champions League in the offing this season, we would definitely need more strength in depth.

Elsewhere, Alex Ferguson, in what he announced to be his last season at Manchester United, seemed to be building a team designed to win the Champions League more than the Premiership. United coach, Steve McClaren, left for Boro, and Jaap Stam was sent packing after criticising he-who-must-be-obeyed, to be replaced by a noticeably slowing Laurent Blanc. Ruud van Nistelrooy finally arrived to step in for the Spurs-bound Sheringham – and the Dutchman looked choc-full of goals. But the pick of the new faces was, clearly, the £28 million Juan Sebastian Veron from SS Lazio: the British press fair vomited up praise for this South American thoroughbred. United, as always, looked hugely competitive.

Arsenal were also stronger, bringing in Spurs turncoat Sol Campbell, Richard Wright from Ipswich Town, Giovanni van Bronckhorst in left midfield from Rangers, and Francis Jeffers from Everton. If the young Bluenose could stay fit he would score goals in north London. *If*. But Bergkamp seemed to be waning at Highbury, so who would now 'invent' the game for Arsenal? Leeds United looked menacing, too, but they had spent no close-season cash and were still dogged by the Woodgate/Bowyer affair. The alarming David O'Leary also looked flaky under pressure. Could they really stay focused? Finally, Chelsea had the players – and possibly the manager – to make a stab at a top four slot. But the title? It looked like a four-horse race, with Fergie's longing for a Glasgow Euro final send-off our best hope of United taking their eye off the ball at home. We also had our own Glasgow ambitions, of course.

The pre-season warm-ups were followed by a Michael Owen-inspired Liverpool qualifying-round Euro rout of little FC Haka, and then by a Charity Shield victory over United. We were starting to get used to beating these East Lancs. Road fakers. Michael looked sharp again in Cardiff and so, too, did the veteran McAllister and new boy Riise. The 2–1 felt comfortable, but not for Robbie Fowler. After a training-ground spat with Phil Thompson he never even made the squad.

27 AUGUST: SANDER CASTLED

A tough first home League win against West Ham is followed by some Euro Super-Cup-winning nonsense against Bayern Munich in Monaco (*five* trophies, the wags said, this Houllier team had now won), before the early season wheels soon started to come off. Bolton Wanderers were first on everyone's list for 2002 Premiership relegation – before, that is, they clattered Leicester 5–0 at Filbert Street on the opening day. Liverpool dominated possession on their Reebok visit, but looked lifeless, Fowler and Babbel (disturbingly) substituted. Emile, on for Fowler and scoring, looked as if he has rescued at least a point, but then, already, a defining moment. Daft Dean Holdsworth, on a rare, late excursion into Liverpool territory, tries a hopeful long-range dip, nothing more – which somehow squirms under Sander, and in. The result? Bolton – who else – top of the Premiership: Fowler pissed off; Westerveld sacked; and Markus Babbel possibly facing a wheelchair.

At the press conference later Houllier dutifully stresses the number of times Sander had previously saved us (when, exactly?) but he also immediately issues the dreaded P45 by going out and buying not one but *two* new goalkeepers: Chris Kirkland from Coventry City, a young prospect, and Jerzy Dudek, an established Polish international, from Feyenoord. Even by Houllier's considerable standards, this is £11 million worth of ruthless work. He had told Westerveld in the summer that the keeper had to work harder on his game. The Dutchman would now be doing this elsewhere – ideally as soon as possible.

Markus Babbel's life has also suddenly changed. He has looked listless and tired in the early games and no wonder – he is soon diagnosed as having the energy-sapping Guillain Barre Syndrome, which threatens not just this season, but his whole career, and even his daily life. The right-back spot, previously nailed on for Babbel, is now a problem. And maybe this awful illness is contagious because a limp Reds' home loss follows to Aston Villa, Dudek conceding three on his Liverpool debut. A young Birmingham kid, Darius Vassell, torments the home defence and Dion Dublin does his usual solid stuff. Steven Gerrard does his – by nearly slicing through the annoying Boateng for a deserved red card.

Three games, two losses and 15th place: Fowler's in a strop; we have already lost a goalkeeper and a right-back; and our best midfielder still has serious excess testosterone trouble. Barmby is nowhere, and Berger and Smicer, our Czech mates, are also out injured. We do not look early title material, not even close. And we are now faced with *seven* vital games in September.

ROBBIE, MICHAEL AND 9/11

Liverpool draw Boavista, the Portuguese champions, Borussia Dortmund the tough Germans and Lobanovsky's Dynamo Kiev in the first Champions League group phase. But count Robbie Fowler out for a while: he is still digging in his heels in the Thommo affair, trying to save face. Houllier is playing the boss card, reining Robbie back in. Potential buyers watch on, sensing a crucial moment is approaching. Meanwhile, Houllier is already building for Fowler's departure: two top French youth players, Le Tallec and Sinama Pongolle, have been signed from Le Havre. Sir Lloyd Webber himself will have to work on the Kop chants for these two. The future is already here.

Working, and then driving to Anfield for the Boavista game on the evening of September 11, I have seen nothing of the aircraft assaults on the World Trade Centre, but the TVs in the Flattie before the game carry little else. So, it is hard to get too worked up for this, our first Champions League encounter, as the WTC pile simmers and the rest of the globe cowers. UEFA reckoned it was too short notice to postpone the match, so the evening is entirely flat, ending in an honours-shared 1–1 draw. It is not what we had waited 16 years for, but Michael has now scored almost all Liverpool's important early goals.

Houllier wonders aloud whether the weekend fixtures – including the first derby game at Goodison – should be postponed out of respect for the WTC dead. But we go ahead, with a minute's silence: football survives all. Vignal and Riise make a young, and potentially exciting, partnership on the Liverpool left, but Campbell suckers Sami, of all people, into allowing him penalty-area space for an early Blues' goal. Steven Gerrard now takes over, thumping a huge cross shot past his Everton goalkeeping namesake, and then celebrating by tongue wagging in front of the raging Bullens Road like a scouse Jim Carey in *Mask*. A penalty from Michael (who else) is followed, early in the second half, by a box-to-box classic from new man Riise, for 3–1. We are moving again.

Borussia Dortmund away is a soaking bore: we travel aiming not to concede; they play not to be beaten. More ambition might have brought goals, but instead we settle, as is Houllier's way, for a numbing 0–0. Two European points lost. Much worse is to follow. Spurs play impressively in L4, beaten only by substitute Litmanen's ambitious second-half strike, but Fowler, temporarily back in the first-team fold, is substituted and leaves with a gob like thunder. Michael is mysteriously brought on by Houllier for a 20-minute spurt (Why, the game is already won?). One serious, lengthy sprint and stretch later, and Owen is already signalling to the Liverpool bench. As he moves past Houllier, and off the pitch, Michael mouths just one word to the furrowed *Le Boss*: 'Hamstring'. You can hear the Main Stand Paddock gasp.

In Michael's absence, Litmanen starts and scores again, to see off a cerebral Kiev at Anfield, while at St James' Park there are more goalscoring heroics from Riise, fast becoming an L4 crowd favourite. He soon has his own thunderous song. Newcastle United are positively flying, having already seen off the Manx. But Fowler and Murphy (another goal) step up here – even Biscan gets a workmanlike start – while Jamie Carragher plays aggressive English collie to Laurent Robert's frightened French lamb. Bobby Robson talks later of the impassable 'four bloody trees' at the back for Liverpool. There are no away substitutions – a sure and unusual vote from the manager on a job well done. Dudek already looks formidable, his fourth straight clean sheet. It is embarrassingly easy, for 2–0. The Geordies, as usual, are crestfallen.

A COAL MINER'S GOALKEEPER

Jerzy Dudek is surprisingly slight for a modern goalkeeper; he is brave, athletic and assured, and comes for crosses Sander would have waved away. He is described by the wily Dutch coach Beenhakker as the best goalkeeper he has seen in 30 years in the game. Born in the mining town of Knurow, Dudek was already enrolled in mining school when he was offered his first semi-pro contract with local club Concordia. His roots – and his affection for Liverpool – are already crystal clear. 'I like it here,' he said soon after his arrival: 'There is no arrogance, no one walking around with their nose in the air. I come from a hard-working area of Poland, and I couldn't be arrogant. Liverpool is a working-class city and I feel comfortable here. I have played all my career in similar places.' This 'Big Pole in our Goal' suits us, no danger.

Vlad (The Impaler) Smicer, starts his own injury-hampered season at home to Grimsby Town, in a limp 'defence' of the Worthington Cup won by Liverpool just last February. Goalkeeper Kirkland also has his first taste of a real Anfield match night. Last season we put eight past the Stokies, but with no Fowler, Owen or Heskey to start, goals might be harder to come by tonight, even against these lowly fisher-folk. So it proves. McAllister eventually obliges for Liverpool in extra time, but there is still scope for the visitors to score two for a dogged win, wildly celebrated at the Anfield Road end. Kirkland's record for Liverpool: played one, lost one. An authentic upset.

13 OCTOBER: TOTAL ECLIPSE OF THE HEART

Leeds United at home – a testing League fixture by any measure and one which found us out last season. Another noon kick-off, sees Robbie and Emile starting up front, with Steven Gerrard restored with McAllister to midfield and Riise at the back following an injury to Vignal. Carragher is still at right-back for Babbel. We look solid but hardly packed with goals – unless Robbie and Emile can add to their *one* each for the season so far. Leeds work hard and press the Kop goal, eventually coaxing a mistake from McAllister, a weak penalty-box header, which falls invitingly to the sullen Kewell. He makes no mistake in the early afternoon sunshine: 0-1.

More troubles. At the start of the second half, a rumour is already circulating the Kop, via the vital – and reliable – Anfield stewards' network, that Gérard Houllier has been taken off to hospital with stomach or chest pains. We strain to try to catch sight of him on the bench or on the touchline. And see nothing. This could be anything, of course: a touch of angina, or even food poisoning. But football managers seldom vacate the dugout, mid-match, do they? Does a film director hand over the script? Does a politician easily leave the House, his speech only half-delivered? Houllier could be in the Main Stand, of course, checking the moaning decibel levels. Or else, he could already be on a cold operating slab in Broadgreen, his body summarily sliced apart. A terrible thought.

The Liverpool players know nothing about the seriousness of this. Locked inside the FA Premier League bubble, they are inured to the darkness of the real world outside. So when the teams come out for the second half it is the home Reds who have a spring in their step – unlike us on the Kop. Even the Fellahs in Front have a fearful foreboding about the manager. It is Fowler who eventually draws Liverpool level. Danny Murphy scores, but it is Robbie's turn and delicious chip onto Nigel Martin's bar that invites Danny boy to head the rebound into the empty Kop goal. Without Fowler there is no goal at all – a message to Thompson and even to the stricken manager. So we share the spoils with Leeds before rushing to the Flattie for more post-match Houllier news. Which is all bad.

Eleven hours of heart work in an operating theatre, your body violated and gaping, is no preparation for the stresses of football management, no preparation at all. Just be glad you are alive. So when the club tells us later that *of course* Houllier will be back before the season ends and that Phil Thompson will carry on as manager in the meantime, we wonder exactly who is fooling who here? We know that Houllier is crucial to our cause; he is our strategist and figurehead. All right, we don't always agree with his tactics and style, but he has got us this far – rising up the League, beating the Manx, looking for Champions League success. *Five* trophies. We chant his name, produce Kop-size mosaics in his honour, defend his cautious selections. We even generally accept his harsh words for Robbie Fowler and others. He has our respect, and more. The loyal Thommo is a jobbing touchline ranter by comparison. Could Prescott replace Blair? Even the dogs in the street know the answer to this stupid question.

Later, Houllier concedes that he had been working too hard in August and September while his damaged aorta was probably already leaking, draining his lifeblood away. Exhaustion, more than stress, is the cause of his problems – *and* a football man's unwillingness to own up to his own vulnerability: 'I felt something was wrong, but I did not show that to my players. If you show you are weak your team will be weak.' So he soldiered on. But now we *are* weak, worryingly adrift with no Owen or Houllier, and heading for Kiev's fortress lair for crucial Champions League action.

16 OCTOBER: THOMMO IN CHARGE

In situations such as these, football players will either succumb to their own doubts or else draw on reserves of belief and emotion in simply playing 'for' the boss. This is crude but effective psychology, and the rookie Thompson uses it well. We see more than a bit of the respect for GH, and the collective balls and talent of these players tonight – and at a venue where no British club has ever won.

Houllier would have enjoyed this battle with the great Valery Lobanovsky, coach at Kiev for all but five years since 1971. Like Houllier, Lobanovsky has built his approach to the sport around the scientific evaluation of players and football systems, but he did so long before the technocratic revolution drifted up onto British shores. The sumptuous youth academy at Dynamo still hosts thousands of wide-eyed kids, as the coaches at Kiev patiently sift and measure, drumming the art of passing and moving into the very pores of their young hopefuls.

Houllier's Liverpool often win in an ugly fashion, but at Kiev Lobanovsky's genius manages, in the words of *The Guardian*'s Richard Williams, 'to use a laboratory to produce poetry'. His teams are beautiful to watch, if sometimes lacking the killer instinct. Alas, this is the last time we will ever see him slumped in the opposing dugout: he would die later in the season, at 63, carried from the touchline after a brain haemorrhage. He is a man born to football – and fated to die there.

Nor is this a vintage Kiev, no longer drawing on Soviet strength and lacking a Blokhin or a Shevchenko. So Liverpool, with Heskey a willing, lone workhorse up front and Dudek and his centre-backs looking resolute, are well able to contend, with Steven Gerrard looking close to his best once more. It is his clipped cross to Murphy which produces a calm side-footed finish just before the break. On the hour, Ghioane equalises for Kiev, inexplicably unmarked at Dudek's far post. But Gerrard soon replies with a deflected cross shot that squirms past Reva. And we hang on.

So Thommo has his first historic win, the post-match press conference awash with rich scouse allusions to the 'magnificent', 'tremendous' and occasionally the 'fantastic' show by the men in red. Though one scouser is noticeably missing from the deserved celebrations: Robbie Fowler plays no part once more. 'Me and Robbie get on great,' Thommo tells an inquiring press. 'There is no problem.' Right.

Robbie *is* back for Leicester City away, our last ever visit to Filbert Street because a new City stadium is flowering nearby, all flashy white struts and blue tiling. Leicester are still floundering, rooted to the bottom – doomed. City striker Akinbiyi is a near national laughing stock for his inept penalty-area work. So as Fowler bags *three*, the home man misses from all parts and we take a 4–1 away win, which could have been 4–4. Thommo's Liverpool, while not always convincing, are now up to a season's best 4th.

24–30 OCTOBER: CHAMPIONS LEAGUE PROGRESS

Days later, in the Champions League, we can't better a fortunate Boavista away – which means we need to beat Dortmund at home to keep alive our European hopes. Hyypia is also injured in Portugal, but Danny Murphy scores again, doing what Nick Barmby managed last season – scoring early season, crucial goals. Later GH, exploring the surreal, will say Murphy has something of the Platini about him. Mmmm. Michael, seven games out, finally returns at Charlton Athletic and scores, after Redknapp (who?) has done the same. A 2–0 half-time Greenwich stroll becomes a scruffy second half battle, with Stephen Wright sent off. 'Caviar and cabbage,' Sgt. Major Thompson tells the press later, not shirking.

The Dortmund decider is an Anfield banker, Smicer and a near-mental Wright scoring the killer goals. In the absence of Hyypia and perennial substitute Fowler, Carragher captains from the back, his puffed-up scouse heart enough on its own to see off the dangerous beanpole Czech, Koller. A convalescing GH is soon on the mobile to Thommo, all proud and emotional. 'I'm just baby-sitting,' the smiling Kirkby man tells the press. His Anfield message for other clubs in the second phase in Europe? 'Just be aware of Liverpool FC.' We may have no manager, but we *are* back.

TOTALLY DEVOTED

In goal celebration, Stephen Wright's new song: 'He's big. He's scouse. He'll never rob yer house. Ste-phen Wright, Ste-phen Wright.' It's ironic.

4 NOVEMBER: OUR FRIENDS FROM THE NORTH WEST

So all this drama is the backcloth to the first League square-up with United, set for a gently autumnal Saturday morning in L4. Villa are the surprise early Premiership leaders, followed by Leeds and Arsenal, with United only 5th and winning only five of their first ten games. Trying to accommodate the strolling Veron and playing only van Nistelrooy up front in Europe seems to have confused rather than improved OT matters. Scholes, of all people, is glumly warming the bench today. I could cry.

And United do look invitingly weak on paper. No Keane or Blanc, with Fortune in midfield, Brown and Neville at the back and a leisurely Veron – who is set upon by Murphy and Gerrard right from the off. So when Michael picks up Heskey's pass on the half-hour behind young Brown's right shoulder, and then opens up his body to bend his shot over Barthez we are happy, sure – but not surprised. And when Riise thunders a free kick past Barthez just before the break, the Fellahs in Front try to stay cool, but they already know we will win this.

Even Beckham's second-half goal, from Riise's blunder, receives its instant reply from Michael who actually *outjumps* Silvestre to score after Barthez flaps at Riise's volleyball-long throw. Owen will also score a header next week to win a desultory point at Blackburn, mystifying the rooted Berg in the process. It is Houllier, of course, who has insisted the tiny striker is capable in the air: it is the Frenchman who is owed these goals.

Which all means that United are in trouble. And we are top. Not even a Champions League 'group of death' draw involving old friends Barcelona and Roma and the fierce Galatasary will dampen our spirits. Not yet. And for an hour against Barca at Anfield we even back ourselves to win. But at 1–1 Michael (he's human, after all) misses a six-yard box gimme, and then for 20 minutes these Catalans actually break our spirit with slick passing and two craftsmen's goals. Without our defensive destroyer, Hamman, we can only watch and applaud in the unique Kop fashion. 'Sorry, mate,' Thommo tells the heart guy later on the mobile. He means it.

25 NOVEMBER: EMILE HESKEY SCORES!

Hamman is back for Sunderland (H) – but just for 43 minutes. The Makem gobshite, Haas, makes a meal of it, but Didi's tackle is a two-footed assault and he has to go. So does Robbie, it seems: substituted at half-time in the Liverpool re-arrangement. Heskey manfully battles to protect the lead he has given the ten men – his first goal since Bolton. The players love Emile, and applaud him into the dressing-room after this brave win today.

Thommo, for one, is always singing Heskey's praises – perhaps too much. But the big man also really misses Houllier: GH is his football father. The fans are much more divided. Emile gives us shape up front, he always tries and occasionally he really powers past defenders. But he invites the long ball and two League goals so far is a miserly return for a striker – this failure only increases the pressure on Michael. Not that you would notice: another winning Owen goal at Derby, made so by Jerzy's late penalty save. Another scrambled win.

FOWLER – FOR *LEEDS*?
Being taken off like this is no way for any player to leave any club, but it is the last straw for Robbie Fowler. And he is not just *any* player. No way. 171 goals in 329 matches for Liverpool hides Robbie's recent familiarity with the bench. He is a truly *great* striker. But Houllier's way – and Thompson's law – is no longer Fowler's, so he probably has to leave. Houllier's new mate, O'Leary, steps in. But why push Robbie out now? And to Leeds, one of our strongest rivals? And for a paltry £12 million? You buy average midfielders for less these days. Selling top players to rivals is not the Liverpool way.

In the Flattie, Robbie has divided the football heads for years, but even his staunchest supporters knew this day must come. He no longer fits. This really hurts, for sure – but we will have to deal with it. We also have to reassure ourselves (ridiculous, isn't it?) that, for Fowler, Leeds is just another job. Watch Robbie, we say, even when he scores in his crappy new white shirt. Is he *truly* happy?

12–23 DECEMBER: THREE KEY GAMES – NO WINS
A battling and very necessary 0–0 at Roma – the Champions League is now on hold until February – deflects from the pleasant fact that we are suddenly away from the Premiership pack, which is led by Arsenal, and are an astonishing game-in-hand 11 points clear of a stuttering United. Liverpool's next three games – Fulham (H), Chelsea (A), Arsenal (H) – are now key pre-Christmas League tests. Okay, we have not always been pretty, but Thommo and the staff have also been positive and resolute in GH's absence. Three decent results here and we can even approach the turn with realistic title ambitions – Houllier, or no Houllier.

So a home 0–0, first off, is not what we'd hoped for. We miss chances but also lack ideas: Fulham are pretty, but toothless. Chelsea, by contrast, are razor-sharp – and have loads of luck. So a weekend 4–0 west London drubbing is down to more than just our Stamford Bridge hoodoo, a missed McAllister penalty, and not having the run of the ball. After five straight clean sheets this is a big blow to our defensive morale. LFC should take no tickets for Chelsea next year – or else the club should fund our trip for this annual torture.

Which leaves Arsenal at home. My mate Chris's kid, Barnes, a nine-year-old season-ticket holder – and named after JB of course – can already tell you all you need to know about this Liverpool squad: their appearances; goal-scoring records; weaknesses. He's scary. So he knows all about the 4–0 here last season, a massive result. Wenger will say later that this latest Anfield performance really lifted Arsenal; it convinced them that *they* could win the title. It badly hurts us, perhaps fatally.

Wenger also moans (really?) about van Bronckhorst's early dismissal for diving, but we can see it clearly from the Kop; the guy is *waiting* to fall, testing out the officials. But being a ten just raises the visitors' 'fuck you' quotient. Today you can really spot their key players: Campbell, all fist-pumping, last-man defiance; Ljungberg, a lung-busting midfield goal-scorer whose runs into the box produce two here; and the conductor, the unlikely buccaneer, Pires.

Last season Pires was just a foreign luxury, a rabbit, another mediocre import. Now he *runs* this Arsenal side, overwhelming Gerrard today with his pace and skill. And as we no longer have Fowler to damage these, his favourite, visitors, it ends up 2–1 for ten-man Arsenal. On the Kop, as we wait to drift away for consoling beer, we fear we can already hear the north London dressing-room title whoops.

WE'VE SIGNED *WHO*?

So, how do we lift ourselves after this cruel setback? Who do we sign on loan to replace Robbie, already scoring goals at Leeds? It is a man who once refused to board a team bus because he was convinced his team-mates hated him (they did). A man who moaned his way out of north London and then sulked at Real Madrid and PSG. A man for whom the notion of the team ethic, so patiently nurtured by GH and Thompson at Melwood, seems utterly alien. A man whose advisors and agents seem little short of wealthy extortionists, planning only for their client's next big transfer. A modern football mercenary, for sure. And *we* sign him.

After starting on the bench at Aston Villa on Boxing Day – where the Reds hold on for a jittery 2–1 – Nicolas Anelka gets his first Liverpool start at West Ham on 29 December, and looks rusty and slow. He'll need to improve – a lot. Michael comes on to score his 100th Liverpool goal, another rescuing equaliser. We are now 4th again, our once huge lead suddenly evaporated, and behind Leeds, Manchester United (oh, shit) and Arsenal. We have had our slump.

HALFWAY HOME

How do we look at the turn of 2001? We are solid – if unspectacular – away, but rather more suspect at home. We have struggled to score at Anfield and we just don't *excite*. Smicer can't last the pace, Heskey can't score, McAllister's legs are starting to creak, and our other potential spark, Litmanen, is suspect. The fans plead for him, but he is not trusted by the coaches in our rigid 4–4–2. We can't blame Thommo, the shop minder, for being ultra conservative, but we did seem to get even more afraid when topping the league: afraid to win.

Owen excepted, all our heroes so far are, tellingly, at the back. Steven

Gerrard has struggled, at times, with both injuries and form. We will need much more from him in 2002. But because the other challengers are also vulnerable, we are still well in touch at the top. And, despite the hard lesson from Barca, the Champions League isn't over for us yet – we do have our one precious point, after all. With more belief – and with Houllier back – we can still win something. *This* is my Christmas message.

BLACK JANUARY, 2002

Which looks a stupid message now. So can we not talk about this start to 2002? Can't we just move on? Okay, at the month's end we manage to beat United (again) at Old Trafford, raising our belief and multiplying their confusion and misery. (Ferguson will now stay at OT, he says, to sort it all out. A nation rejoices.) We even steal a League draw at Arsenal. Great results, obviously. But at Anfield it is purgatory: we can't beat Bolton or Southampton in L4 and only just scrape past the now detached Leicester City. When we slump at home 1–1 against the Saints, the Main Stand actually starts *booing*, exciting plenty of local debate about whether this response is really 'the Liverpool way'. And it gets no better.

At the re-match at the new St Mary's Stadium – an impressive piece of neo-Soviet supremacist architecture, by the way – we positively capitulate to Strachan's men. Our lowest ebb. Even the usually serene Hyypia looks panicky and lost, giving away a penalty, while our season's darling, Riise, manages to deflect one beyond Dudek for a crazy – and clinching – second-half o.g. Anelka outshines European Footballer of the Year, Owen: but both are piss poor. Smicer is worse, embarrassing. Which means we have gifted the relegation-threatened Saints and the Reebok Wanderers together 10 points this season. How can we even pretend to be title hopefuls with this grotesque record?

25 JANUARY: NINE BEATS TEN TO CARDIFF

We are also, too soon, back in the rear of the Clock End, north London, this time for unfinished Arsenal FA Cup business. From here, mercifully, we have only a letter-box-thin view of the wet, fourth-round, misery which is about to unfold. Van Bronkhorst and Henry soon undo the defend-by-numbers Stephen Wright down the Liverpool right and Bergkamp glances in the cross for 1–0 at the break. Liverpool, as usual, are creating too little. Behind us, giggling scallies are soon dividing up the half-time coke. Not to be sniffed at under these difficult circumstances.

In the second period – just showing off, now – Arsenal have *two* men dismissed in three minutes: Keown for routine defenders' black arts stuff on Owen, and Bergkamp, a violent saint, for stamping. But we don't get to play 11 against the home 9 because, even as Dennis is leaving, Carragher follows him – for chucking coins back into the home crowd. Referee Riley's notebook bulges. The press goes mental about this alleged 'return of fan hooliganism', but outside the ground there's nothing going on. *Nothing*. Inside, we just can't get back into this match: we don't even really look like we know how. Arsenal will soon insist on kicking off all games at least one man light if this carries on. It ends 1–0, our 2002 Wales' plans binned. Arsenal, meanwhile, still have Cardiff hopes.

3–9 FEBRUARY: A MEETING WITH ROBBIE – AND 'WHO LET THE GOALS OUT?'

The press are full of 'Fowler's revenge' crap when we travel, still bruised and unsure, to Elland Road in early February. But Robbie's having none of it, refusing to criticise Liverpool or any of their staff. There are also rumours that Houllier, now returned from convalescence in France, has been around Melwood this week, offering pep talks to our key men. They need it, especially the goal-shy Heskey – 14 consecutive dry appearances. Anelka has managed just one goal in 10. Though Leeds have recently slipped down the table, Fowler has been banging them in, including a hat-trick at Bolton, our nemesis. So the 'I told you so' Robbie cheerleaders have already been out in force on Merseyside.

But the great man doesn't look keen today. He's not *relishing* playing against us at all, that's clear. Whereas Heskey looks full of beans after his managerial chat, feeding off Steven Gerrard's renewed vim in midfield and even helping himself to two second-half goals, in what ends up as a happy rout. Kewell looks uninterested, perhaps unfit. Leeds look a mess, Robbie the sorry best of them. A 4–0 landslide to Liverpool. 'Not bad for a boring team,' Thommo smugly tells the press later. Fine, and we'll all have a good celebratory bevvy later. But this is still only one, sweet swallow . . .

Let me eat my words right now, because eight-wins-in-nine *Ipswich 0, Liverpool 6* is how we all want these Reds to play away. White-bearded Bluenose, Abel Xavier, has been dragged across Stanley Park to cover at right back in L4 and, presumably, to double up as a politically correct Santa Claus at the LFC Christmas party. Xavier says it's great playing for Liverpool because, 'You don't have to call for the ball.' What sort of rules do they use over at Goodison? He even scores in a pretty level first half, which Heskey's late goal, our second, tips rather more in our favour than we deserve.

Our usual *modus operandi* now is to huddle up, with defensive autism, in front of Jerzy's goal. But, instead, we flow forward in the Suffolk sunshine, playing without fear and scoring almost at will. Reds' fans, eternally hopeful travellers, are now, quite literally, falling about in the seats around us with the sheer joy of it all. Out of this gleeful scrum, an obvious question emerges: WHY CAN'T IT ALWAYS BE LIKE THIS? Thommo says later that we have, simply, taken our chances today – as if this is the big difference. We say: Bring on the men from Galatasary! Which is a mistake, naturally.

TWO TURKISH POINTS

Columbian, Mondragon sounds, I know, like it should be converted into powder-driven profit, but for Liverpool in the Champions League it simply means: 'No way through'. We pummel the Turks at Anfield, but the visiting South American keeper – who *we* almost signed – just refuses to be passed. In Istanbul a week later we do enough to win again, but have to settle for 1–1 with Galatasary, this time in front of the cheeky travelling 'If you think this is hell' Grafton Rooms banner.

The real message here, though, is that the prospect of Champions League progress for Liverpool is now looking bleak – and we can't complain. We have *no* second phase wins, and a brave 0–0 in Barcelona – the Catalan public are not bursting to see this Liverpool team much more, I can tell you – means we will need to defeat Italian Champions and Serie A leaders, Roma, by two clear goals at Anfield to qualify. Porkers might, more reliably, seek guidance from air-traffic control.

23 FEBRUARY–16 MARCH: ANELKA'S LITTLE SPELL

Nic Anelka, ineligible for all this dull Champions League stuff, now decides to show what he can really do in the League. Goals against Everton and Fulham are just the start. Away at Middlesbrough he also shines in a typical patchy, ground out, post-Champions League Reds' win. But for 35 minutes at home to League challengers Newcastle United in a mid-week in early March, he positively lights up Anfield, after a pre-match power failure has the Kop wondering if shady characters in the Far East are already picking up their winnings. Later, *The Echo* gushes about the new boy's show: 'world class'; 'back to his best'; 'balance and poise'. We *must* sign him.

Anelka *is* playing for a contract now that Houllier is getting back on the scene at Melwood. But will he always show this kind of motivation and commitment to the cause? And will he score enough goals? We wonder. Tonight, at least, his dazzling show makes space for goals for Murphy (two more), and even the shot-shy Hamann scores to close out Newcastle, 3–0. With eight games left we have forced our way back to the top once more, two points clear of United and Arsenal – but the dangerous Gunners still have two games in hand. The really bad news? Didi is suspended and Michael's newly 'tight' hamstring, received tonight, means we will have to face Capello's glossy Roma stars without both our defensive shield and our only reliable goalscorer. Great.

19 MARCH: *ALLEZ!* HOULLIER'S BIG NIGHT OUT

There is nothing beyond the touchline.

Jacques Derrida

Oh my God, I'm miraculously alive. It's wonderful to be here.

Gérard Houllier

Perhaps only great music, collectively experienced, gets anywhere close to the emotional buzz, the visceral high, of a really big football night. But even a top music gig is, in the end, usually just a hall full of strangers; a group of disconnected CD punters. They have no collective history; no binding membership drawn from ties of family or place; and no convincing claim for deep psychic investment in the season's journey. They don't *care* like we do, about each other and about our team – or, like all football supporters, anxiously emote about the outcome of a defining contest.

So, after losing our first Champions League match at home to Barca back in November, we would have settled then for needing to beat Roma on a draining and passionate L4 football night to qualify for the knock-out phase. But not by two goals – and not without Michael or Hamann and certainly not without the manager. Which is also why the rumours circulating the Flattie tonight, about Houllier's possible touchline return, give all of us *that* familiar shiver about this evening's events.

Truly great nights like these also help to see you through the darkest match days, the suppressed nightmares: a 5–1 capitulation at Coventry; humiliation at Peterborough in the League Cup under Souey; Paris in '96; the 'spice boys' FA Cup final; countless, spineless Liverpool losses at Chelsea. Only rage and despair live here. But beating Totti and Montella, and Samuel and Delvecchio and Batistuta – crushing all of these seasoned internationals tonight – will make all the earlier calamities somehow much easier to bear. And a hunching Houllier – thinner, more gaunt, *older* – is indeed back in the home dugout to direct our passage once more. He is welcomed by Capello's gracious, managers' union hug, and his presence tonight produces the wild waves of sound which come pounding out from all areas of this old ground. It is good to see him alive – and working once more.

Jari Litmanen, so often ignored here, is also our guru tonight, scoring an early penalty and, like Gerrard and our resolute, immovable defenders, he draws earned respect from the hardened Europeans and South Americans we must overcome to move on. Heskey also delivers, his muscular presence and a piercing second-half header finally killing off Roma's dreams – and giving life to our own. Perhaps Emile can indeed grow to become the dominant force GH believes is still hidden inside this gentle Leicester man.

A thrilling 2–0, this is Houllier's great Anfield European night, one to set alongside those of 1965 and 1977 and the rest; one to be endlessly retold and re-embroidered in years ahead in the Flattie, and in hundreds of pubs like it in the city. And even as the Centenary Stand drains of its still hyperventilating occupants tonight, it is already a part of this club's glorious European history – the night that Houllier came back to beat Roma. Which also means that, greedy as we must be, we already have to ask: is there still more to come?

TEN GAMES FROM GLORY?

Maybe GH is simply overcome by the vapours of the Roma triumph, or else he has developed a very different 'life' perspective following his illness (who wouldn't?). Because, after all the familiar, 'Each game as it comes' rhetoric of last season, suddenly Houllier is off on an unlikely, 'Ten games from glory' rant about this one. After drawing Bayer Leverkusen, Houllier thinks we can actually *win* the Champions League and is also convinced that if we win our remaining eight League games we will also take the League title, as Arsenal must stumble.

So outstaying a superior Chelsea and also beating Charlton at home, and then creeping past Leverkusen at Anfield, 1–0, seems only to strengthen the reborn Frenchman in his predictions. We are still often unconvincing but, just like last season, we keep on winning and concede virtually no goals. However, Arsenal also seem worryingly resolute, refusing to buckle at all, home or away. So it is strangely troubling, this new Liverpool breast-beating, about what is still a dangerous future. It could yet undo us.

9 APRIL: GERMANY CALLING – AND OUT

The unlikely place to find out is in the modest BayArena, half the size of Anfield and sited in pleasant parkland north of Cologne. Cologne seems easy-going, urbane, civilised – unlike some of our fellahs, who are uncontrollably pissed and fucking off the late-night staff in the central Ibis Hotel for no good reason other than this is football and we are English – and abroad.

In the ground later, the Leverkusen fans seem moderately keen on a home win – not much more. A bought-in-Germany match ticket means I'm seated in a home area, behind the goal, getting on fine with the locals, who seem faintly embarrassed about getting this far. They pretend to be a German Norwich City, against our established European football pedigree. They have come to watch our 'stars', they say. None of these are good signs, by the way.

We know that scoring here holds the key to our sure progress: after all, no one scores *three* against Hyypia and his two lines of four defensive props. So when Ballack fools Gerrard and Dudek and scores from long range early on, it is disturbing – but not fatal. In an open game, Xavier's headed equaliser just before the break is more significant – it deflates the locals, both fans and players. The official Liverpool fan group to my left now perks up, singing throughout the half-time interval. My new German mates simply shrug and happily concede to superior opponents.

Except their heroes have not yet given up, not by a long chalk. Nevertheless, Michael, restored once more, soon has two clear chances right in front of me – two sure semi-final clinchers, one-on-one Owen certainties. He misses both. And then Leverkusen surge. At 1–1 we are still two goals clear, but Houllier, incredibly, panics taking off Hamann and replacing him with Smicer. Okay, we *are* stuttering, no midfield grip, with Ballack, Basturk and Schneider supreme. The home full-back Placente is also getting at us down the Bayer left. But do you really think *Smicer* is going to stop that? And do you withdraw, at this crucial moment when defence is everything, the keystone of the team, the man the entire Liverpool away strategy has been built around? This change is a huge mistake. It costs us.

Ballack's second goal, a header, adds to our fears and within five minutes Berbatov has actually put Leverkusen ahead in the tie. Now the Germans near me are fast losing their earlier reserve: they can see – as I can – that *this* Liverpool team are actually vulnerable, weak. Litmanen momentarily demurs, slicing across the home penalty area and sliding in a shot beyond bodies and the home goalkeeper, Butt, directly in front of me. Twelve minutes left. A stomach-churning 2–3. In the crazy world of Football Europe, this puts us back in front.

The dominant emotion now from the visitors' areas – from *me* – is sheer relief. We have been close to the edge – and survived. Let these nice local people now go to their nice homes and we will march on. But it is still not over – not for Lucio, a loping Brazilian centre-back, a South American Hyypia, but someone with ambitions all over the field. He gets forward and behind the flagging Carragher with barely five minutes remaining, and scores from the left side of the penalty area, apparently *through* Dudek. I feel deflated: no, physically sick.

And so it finally begins to sink in for us: that after countless unbeaten trips and a run of 17 matches in Europe with only one defeat, we have now lost this crucial tie, beaten by a superior, more talented, team. At the end, I even tell this to my new pals and, through gritted teeth, I wish them luck. I don't mean it – any of it. Unless, of course, they *do* play United in the semis. Goodbye Glasgow. Find a Cologne bar. DRINK.

27 APRIL: THE BEGINNING OF THE END

We can still win the League. This is now our desperate mantra. Fucking Leverkusen have *never* even won the Bundesliga, so what do they know? Wins at Sunderland and at home to Derby (both courtesy of Michael) and a scrambled goal-glut victory over Blackburn at Anfield keep our sagging spirits high. But Arsenal – even without the injured Pires – also march on, and, like us, they win at United, where we had banked on them failing. So an insipid 1–0 loss at Tottenham, although officially the killer blow for Liverpool, feels less like the deciding moment than does an earlier, clear Kanoute goal for West Ham at Highbury – which is stupidly ruled out. Another Arsenal home win.

In fact, Arsenal win all their remaining games – and end up losing *no* away games all season. Staggering. Their resolution signals another north London League and Cup Double. Routing relegated Ipswich Town 5–0 at Anfield (and 11–0 for the season) at least signs us off above United and directly into the 2002–03 Champions League – in second place, with 80 points, and no trophies. Houllier later describes 2001–02 as a season of real Liverpool progress, calibrating our annual advance up the League table since he took charge. This is all true. Even without a manager for much of the campaign, we have learned much more about ourselves and about coping in Europe. We have come very close to glory.

DESTINATION SENEGAL?

We know we are a young, hard-working, well-organised and disciplined team which others fear to play. The new men, Dudek and Riise, have done well and Murphy has certainly progressed, Heskey less so. Carragher, Henchoz and Hamann have been reliable, as always, but Smicer and especially Barmby and Berger have had a season ruined by injury and doubt. They won't all stay. Owen, and Gerrard, have also had fitness and form doubts. But Michael has usually delivered. Anelka has intrigued – but not wholly convinced. Litmanen still seems underused and, like Fowler, is a victim of the Houllier system. It has also been just one campaign too far for the departing Gary Mac.

More worryingly, we still have no real authoritative style or clear vision when we have to match up against the very best players or teams. We can sometimes quell their talent, squeeze their resolve, as we did so magnificently against Roma. But we have trouble really imposing our own vision and attacking authority on matches we should win. Houllier's critics argue that he seems to want *all* team ethic and no individual flair – and that he always thinks first of defence. We have too few players, in short, who can run with the ball and commit opponents, especially in wide areas.

The press – and some opponents – have called this Liverpool a 'long ball' team, even a 'boring' side: Dudek, to Heskey, on to Owen. Some Red's fans do, too. So the post-season Houllier rejection of Anelka, and his interest, instead, in the African power and trickery of Senegalese midfielder Salif Diao and forward El Hadji Diouf might be a real indicator of change. After all, there is rather more than a championship still to win for GH and the loyal Thompson. Red heads – as well as hearts – will need to be engaged in 2002–03. Are we any closer to our ultimate goal? I think so. But ask me again in May 2003.